S0-AXB-570

1979-80 EDITION OF

Arthur Frommer's Guide to

NEW YORK

by
FAYE HAMMEL

Published by
THE FROMMER/PASMANTIER PUBLISHING CORPORATION
380 Madison Avenue
New York, New York 10017

Distributed by
SIMON & SCHUSTER
A GULF+WESTERN COMPANY
1230 Avenue of the Americas
New York, New York 10020
0-671-24914-2

Distributed outside the U.S. and Canada by
FLEETBOOKS
c/o Feffer and Simons, Inc.
100 Park Avenue
New York, New York 10017

Distributed in Canada by
P J PAPERBACKS LTD.
330 Steelcase Road East
Markham, Ontario L3R2M1

Motif drawings by Paul Berkow

NOTE: Although every effort was made to insure the accuracy of price information appearing in this book, it should be kept in mind that prices can and do fluctuate in the course of time.

Manufactured in the United States of America

CONTENTS

MAPS

Chapter I

WHYS AND WHEREFORES

IT ALWAYS HAPPENS. People from out of town who've become New Yorkers (like us) are invariably held up as Ultimate Authorities by the folks back home. When our friends come into the city, they are *sure* we can advise them on the best hotels, the newest "in" restaurants, and which plays on Broadway are really worth seeing. And even more important, they expect us to know where they can get the best values for their money, whether they're planning to spend $20 a day or $200. For in a city as complex, as varied—and as expensive—as New York, it's much too easy to waste time and money if you don't have inside information.

And that's what we intend to give you in the pages ahead: the inside dope, the special tips that can make all the difference between your feeling like a native or a newcomer. We'll tell you which hotels, in our opinion, offer the best value for your dollar, from the Waldorf to the "Y"; which restaurants are worth going into bankruptcy for, which will feed you well for pennies; how to get tickets for a top Broadway musical without paying scalper's rates or even having an uncle who works for the producer; how to enjoy the big and little sights of the city in the most efficient, relaxed manner possible; how to discover the shopping secrets of New York's smartest women in out-of-the-way bargain meccas where the Kimberleys and Calvin Kleins go for peanuts; how to find the coziest pub, the latest discotheque or the most total "total environment"; how to catch the most interesting entertainments, lectures, concerts with free or nominal admissions; and how to venture into New York's exotic world of swamis, astrologers, and Zen masters. As an added fillip, we'll tell you where to wander, when fancy strikes, off the well-trod road of the major sights and experiences and head off the beaten path for a world of surprises. We hope this catalogue of what we consider the best New York has to offer will be useful to you, whether it's your first trip to the city or your 110th. First, though, let us issue a warning to newcomers.

THE FIRST TIME IN NEW YORK: You should be advised that there is one dangerous aspect of coming to New York for the first time: not of getting lost, mobbed or caught in a blackout, but of falling so desperately in love with the city that you may not want to go home again. Or, if you do, it may be just to pack your bags. With most visitors to New York, it's usually love or hate at first sight. Either you are so enthralled by the dazzle, the tempo, the sense of adventure that only a great city can give, that you immediately make it your own. Or you may find the noise, the smog, the traffic, the seeming callousness of the natives just too much. But be warned: New York is still the magic town, the beckoning metropolis, the mighty citadel of power. And the younger you are, the more potent is its spell. *Caveat emptor.*

WHAT MAKES NEW YORK TICK: To describe New York fully would take volumes—and besides, it's indescribable. You might study New York history for a year, cram your head with statistics about population and industry and geography, become an expert on urban problems—and still not have the slightest feeling of what New York is about. New York simply must be experienced, in all its incredible variety, to be comprehended. It is really unlike any other city in America, and more like a small (or not-so-small) country of its own. New York is a lot more like London than it is like Chicago or Washington, D.C., but it is really an entity only to itself. It is noted for its size (with a population close to eight million, it is the world's third-largest city); its diversity (more different kinds of people do their thing here than just about anywhere else); and perhaps most important of all, the magnetism that attracts to it the brightest, most creative, most ambitious, most determined people from everywhere. For this is the central city, the megalopolis, the nerve center of the world's finance and trade, of advertising and publishing and fashion, of theater and ballet and music, and now, with the United Nations here, of world diplomacy as well. It is the vortex that pulls into its center a lot of the best (and worst) people and projects and theories and schemes from everywhere. New York is in the eye of the hurricane. This is what gives the city its special feeling of intensity, the high-powered vibration that is felt immediately by even the most casual visitor. It is what makes New York one of the most exciting places on the planet.

THE WEATHER AND WHEN TO COME TO NEW YORK: Expect hot summers and cold winters in New York, plus sometimes idyllic, 70-degree-ish springs and falls. The city is great to visit anytime you can. Both central heating and air conditioning are practically universal, so the weather is never a problem. The winter is the height of the theater and entertainment season, but if you come in the summer you're ahead of the game, since most residents will be out at the beach, and you have the city practically to yourself. It's much easier then to get into the charming little restaurants, to pick up tickets for Broadway plays at the last minute, and you don't have to fight off the mobs in the big stores.

NEW YORK: AVERAGE MONTHLY TEMPERATURES

Month	Temp	Month	Temp
January	32.3	July	76.8
February	33.4	August	75.1
March	40.5	September	68.5
April	51.4	October	58.3
May	62.4	November	47.0
June	71.4	December	35.9

HOW TO GET HERE: You can get to New York by a variety of means—by bike or bus, auto or train, ship or plane, and we've tried them all. We've driven down from the north at night and seen the George Washington Bridge, like a giant rope of pearls, span the Hudson; we've arrived from Europe at dawn via a great ocean liner and watched the sun rise over the sleeping city; most often, we've crossed the country by giant jet, arriving at dusk to circle Manhattan as a thousand lights winked on and the great city came alive below us. This was New York.

Chapter II

BIG CITY LOGISTICS

IF YOU COME TO NEW YORK by train or bus, you will arrive at either Pennsylvania Station (34th Street and Seventh Avenue), Grand Central Terminal (42nd Street and Park Avenue), or the Port of New York Authority Bus Terminal (41st Street and Eighth Avenue). All three are located in midtown, minutes from your hotel. If you come by plane, you will arrive at Kennedy, LaGuardia, or Newark International Airports. Carey Transportation buses can take you to the East Side Airlines Terminal, 38th Street and First Avenue, for $4 from Kennedy, $3 from LaGuardia. (An express bus-and-subway service also runs from Kennedy to 57th Street and Avenue of the Americas, at a cost of $3.50. For information, phone 858-7272).

Taxi fare averages $15 from Kennedy, $8 from LaGuardia to the midtown area. From Newark Airport, a bus will take you to the Port of New York Authority Terminal for $1.95. Taxi fare may be as low as $8 under the informal group-ride program now in use from that airport. You can also get to and from the airports via helicopter. New York Airways Helicopter operates over 150 flights daily between the World Trade Center/Battery Park City Heliport and the three airports. The fare ranges from zero, that's right, zero (depending on your connecting airline) to $34.50. For reservations, phone 212/661-5100 in New York, 201/623-2590 in New Jersey, toll-free information only: 800/221-0200.

GEOGRAPHY: Before you arrive at your hotel, though, you should know a little about the geography of the city and the best means of getting around town. You probably already know that New York City is divided into five boroughs: Manhattan, the most important; the Bronx, to the north; Brooklyn, to the south; Queens (where the airports are and the World's Fair was), to the east; and Richmond, or Staten Island, south and east of New

York harbor. Since you'll probably be spending most of your time in Manhattan, there's no need to concern yourself with the details of getting around the other boroughs. If you visit them, be sure to get specific directions and pick up some good maps in advance.

Manhattan is, of course, an island, and a rather small one at that (12 miles long, 2½ miles across at its widest point), and its varied neighborhoods are easy to get to. The center of things is **Midtown,** an area that runs, roughly, from the East River to the Hudson and from 34th Street to 59th Street. Within this neighborhood you'll find the United Nations, the Empire State Building, Rockefeller Center, the Broadway theaters, the great shipping piers, the major department stores, many business offices—and, of course, most of the hotels and restaurants that cater to visitors. This is the heart of the city.

The area around 34th Street and Broadway is **Herald Square,** where you'll find the two department-store colossi, Macy's and Gimbels—and Korvette's as well. To the east are the shops of 34th Street and Fifth Avenue; to the west and south, the new Madison Square Garden Center rising above Pennsylvania Station. Below that, the streets become crowded with trucks and throngs of people and men pushing minks on racks along the sidewalks: this is the home of the **Garment Center,** the **Fur District,** and the legendary characters of Seventh Avenue. Further below, in the West 20s is the **Flower Market** (if you get up early in the morning, you can pick and choose with the city's retail florists).

The next most important area starts at 14th Street, goes south, roughly to Houston, and is the heart of New York's Bohemia: **Greenwich Village.** It begins on the west at the Hudson River and, although Fifth Avenue was for years its eastern boundary, it now extends all the way across town, on to First Avenue to the **East Village,** one-time home of the hippies and the flower children.

To the south, the East Village reverts to its old name, the **Lower East Side,** where thousands of immigrants settled into the New World in the early 1900s—to struggle, to be engulfed, some to conquer. Most of the Jews and Irish and Italians have fled from the ghettoes uptown or to the suburbs, but little colonies still remain, although most of the population is now Puerto Rican. Around Grand and Orchard Streets there is still a Jewish neighborhood, known mostly for incredible Sunday bargain shopping; the heart of **Little Italy** is Mulberry Street, and, of course, there is a **Chinatown,** centering on Mott and Pell Streets. West of Chinatown, around West Broadway, Spring, and Greene Streets, is the **SoHo** (south of Houston area), the world's largest collection of cast-iron commercial architecture and the lively home of New York's most vital artists' colony.

Continuing south, we come to the **Brooklyn Bridge,** the **City Hall** and courthouse area, and finally to the financial district, the site of **Wall Street,** the stock exchange, the giant insurance companies. From here on, Manhattan narrows sharply, winds its way past ancient streets and alleys and old buildings that are being bulldozed to make way for giant office complexes, and slips into the sea.

Picking up again from the Midtown area, we find **Central Park** beginning at 59th Street, and this magnificent sweep of greensward is now the great divide between East and West. To the east is the **Upper East Side,** home to the Beautiful People, the would-be BP's, the fashionable schools and shops, the prestigious **Metropolitan Museum of Art.** On the West, at 65th Street and Broadway, is **Lincoln Center for the Performing Arts,** a veritable fortress of culture (the Metropolitan Opera House, Avery Fisher Hall, the New York State Theatre, the Vivian Beaumont Theatre, etc.), which leads up Broadway, the heart of the **Upper West Side.** This is mostly a residential district, with the lovely buildings of Central Park West on one boundary, of Riverside Drive on the other. At 112th Street and Broadway is the campus of Columbia University, and as you go up Riverside Drive, you will see the massive structure of Grant's Tomb and the great Gothic spires of Riverside Church. **Harlem** begins at 125th Street on the West Side, and around 110th Street on the East centers the sprawling Puerto Rican neighborhood of New York: **El Barrio.** Further north on the West Side is **Washington Heights,** a middle-class residential neighborhood and, near the tip of the island, **Fort Tryon Park** and the beautiful Cloisters of the Metropolitan Museum of Art, a serene vantage point from which to contemplate the incredible diversity of incredible New York.

NAVIGATING: If you can count and you know your east from your west, you can find your way around Manhattan. Navigating is, in fact, so simple that the average twelve-year-old can do it with aplomb (in fact, we often see twelve-year-olds directing their parents around town). All you have to remember is that the

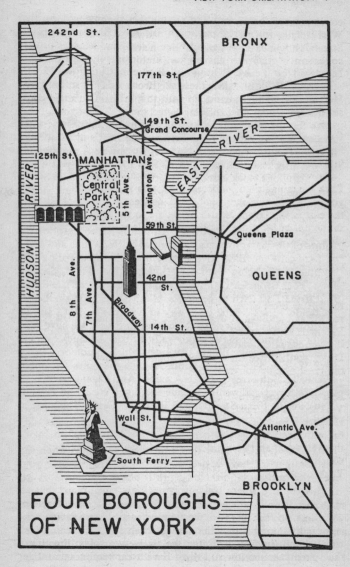

242nd St.

BRONX

177th St.

149th St.
Grand Concourse

RIVER

125th St.

MANHATTAN

Central
Park

RIVER

HUDSON

5th Ave.

Lexington Ave.

EAST

59th St.

Queens Plaza

42nd
St.

8th Ave.

7th Ave.

Broadway

QUEENS

14th St.

Wall St.

Atlantic Ave.

South Ferry

BROOKLYN

FOUR BOROUGHS
OF NEW YORK

streets run east and west and are numbered consecutively; that the avenues run north and south and most have numbers, although a few have names; and that streets and avenues usually bisect each other at right angles. (Unfortunately, this does not apply to Lower Manhattan—Wall Street, Chinatown, SoHo, Greenwich Village—since these neighborhoods just sort of grew, before the engineers came up with this brilliant scheme; you'd best have a map for exploring here.)

As for the East and West, the key to the mystery is **Fifth Avenue,** the big dividing line between the East and West Sides of town (below Washington Square, Broadway is the dividing line). So, for example, to get to 20 East 57th Street, you would walk about one block *east* of Fifth; to get to 20 West 57th Street, about one block *west.* To get *uptown* of a certain point, simply walk north of, or to a higher-numbered street than, where you are; *downtown* is south of (or to a lower-numbered street than) your current location. Got that? All that is left to learn are the names of the major avenues. Starting at Fifth Avenue and going east (toward the East River), they are: Madison, Park (Park Avenue South below 34th Street), Lexington, Third, Second, First, York (from East 60th Street to East 92nd Street), and East End (from East 79th Street to East 90th Street). On the Lower East Side, First Avenue gives way to Avenues A, B, C, and D. Starting again at Fifth Avenue and working west, we have Avenue of the Americas (everybody calls it Sixth Avenue), Seventh Avenue, Broadway, Eighth Avenue (which becomes Central Park West at 59th Street), Ninth Avenue (becomes Columbus Avenue at 59th Street), Tenth Avenue (Amsterdam Avenue after 59th Street), Eleventh Avenue (becomes West End Avenue from 59th to 107th Streets), and Riverside Drive, beginning at 72nd Street.

TRANSPORTATION: Now that you've got your navigation signals straight (or have a twelve-year-old in tow), choose your means of transportation. New York is one of the few cities left in this country where walking is not only encouraged, but altogether feasible, since everything is packed so close together. Walking, in fact, is often the quickest way to get somewhere, especially during the midday lunch crush and the evening rush hour (5 to 6), when surface traffic seems to move at the rate of two miles an hour. If you *must* have a car (recommended for trips outside the city), there are many reputable car-rental agencies listed in the phone book.

Taxis

The most convenient way to get around town, of course, is by cab. Since the recent fare hikes, they have become expensive. As soon as you step into the cab, the meter clicks to 75¢: the charge is then 10¢ for each additional one-seventh of a mile. You are, of course, expected to tip: on a $1 ride, at least 25¢. Incidentally, don't be surprised if the New York taxi drivers do not regale you with a discourse on the city's labor problems or a critique of the current administration; so much has been written on the cab driver's querulous opinions that the most talkative of them have either become shy or graduated to TV talk shows. Your ride is likely to be remarkably silent. Cabs can be hailed on almost any street: a light on top indicates that they are available.

Subways

Everyone should ride the New York subway at least once—just for the experience. If you manage to survive a rush-hour crush (8 to 9:30 in the morning, 5 to 6 in the evening on weekdays), you'll have something to tell the folks about back home. The rest of the time, the subway is relatively uncrowded, and will take you where you want to go quickly (no traffic!), efficiently, and relatively cheaply: tokens cost 50¢ (from 6 p.m. Saturday through 1 a.m. Monday, a return-fare "ticket" is available at no additional cost). The two lines that run through Manhattan are the IRT and the IND; the BMT runs mostly from lower Manhattan to Brooklyn and Queens. You can get a good map of the subway system at any token booth, but in general, keep in mind that the IRT runs trains north and south on both the East and West Sides of town. East Side trains run along Lexington Avenue; the line is popularly known as the "Lexington Avenue Subway." On the West Side, the trains go along Broadway and Seventh Avenue (the Broadway line goes north to Columbia University and Washington Heights; the Seventh Avenue line branches eastward north of 96th Street to Seventh Avenue and Harlem). The east and west branches of the IRT are connected by the Grand Central-to-Times Square Shuttle, and the 14th Street Canarsie Line. The Queensboro Line runs beneath the Shuttle from Times Square to Grand Central and then east into Queens. IND trains run along 6th and 8th Avenues, with major stops in Greenwich Village at West 4th Street and Sixth Avenue, at the Port of New York Authority Bus Terminal at 41st Street, and at Columbus Circle (59th Street).

Buses

Slower than subways but cheaper than the taxis, the buses solve a lot of transportation problems. Almost every major avenue has its own bus (they run either north or south: downtown on Fifth, uptown on Madison, downtown on Lexington, uptown on Third, etc.), and there are crosstown buses at strategic locations all around town: 8th Street, 14th, 23rd, 34th, 42nd, 50th (eastbound), 51st (westbound), 65th (eastbound), 66th (westbound), 79th, 86th, 96th, 116th, and 125th. Some of the buses, however, are erratic: the M104, for example, starts at the East River, then turns at Eighth Avenue and goes up Broadway. The buses of the Fifth Avenue line go up Madison or Sixth and follow various routes around the city. Check the maps on the bus signs, or ask the driver, to be sure. See details on Sunday's "Culture Bus" in Chapter VI, on the "Shopper's Special" in Chapter IX. Note that, since bus drivers are no longer allowed to make change, you must have your exact fare ready: 50¢ plus 25¢ for an Add-A-Ride (for transfer to an intersecting bus line). Subway tokens will be accepted. From 6 p.m. on Saturday through 1 a.m. on Monday, fares are reduced to 25¢ (10¢ for Add-A-Rides). The $1 Nightcoach ticket provides unlimited bus riding in Manhattan, Monday through Friday between 6 p.m. and 2 a.m. the following morning.

A Word About Money Changing

Foreign visitors often arrive in New York City without American currency believing that they can change it at any time. They can't: The foreign exchange companies maintain **only** Monday to Friday 9 to 5 hours: they are closed on weekends. Be sure, then, to change your money when you arrive in New York, at the airport. Canadian visitors should also be advised that their money is not freely negotiable here, as is ours in their country. They're the ones most often stuck with the wrong money and no place to exchange it.

SAFETY: Despite the fact that "crime in the streets of New York" seems to be about the favorite gag of every television comedian, we honestly feel that the subject has been grossly exaggerated. Let's look at the facts, first. True, New York does have a high incidence of crime, but so does every other major city in the United States; because it's in New York, it gets more publicity. (A recent survey, you may be pleased to learn, rated New York fairly far down in the scale of big-city crime.) Second, considering that some eight million people live in the city, that hundreds of thousands more come in and out every day, and that all go about their business freely, the out-of-towner's frequent impression that New York is a dangerous place just doesn't make sense. However, there are certain precautions that it's wise for a visitor to take—in any city—and there are certain areas of the city that we would avoid at night. It helps, first of all, if one does not obviously look like a tourist, flashing a big camera and a big wallet. Keep your camera inconspicuous, put your money in Travelers' Checks and leave your valuables in the hotel safe or at home. Third, there are certain areas much worse than others at night: one is the East Village, and the second is the area around Times Square, particularly between Seventh and Eighth Avenues, now lined with lurid pornographic theaters and bookstores. Though it may appeal to some, its appeal is most certainly limited, and nobody says you have to go there. Since there have been so many complaints, the city is now promising to clean the area up—and we're keeping our fingers crossed. The parks are tabu after sundown, unless you're going to a festival or theatrical performance in Central Park, in which case the access routes will be well lighted. And it's safer to take a cab home late at night than a subway. One final tip: on the cab ride from the airports to the city, foreign visitors should be wary of cab drivers demanding huge sums (several foreigners have recently been victimized badly); only take a metered cab, and only pay *exactly* what the meter reads, plus a tip and toll charges. Follow the rules, and a trip to New York should be no more dangerous than one to, say, your own hometown.

Chapter III

NEW YORK'S BEST HOTEL VALUES

NEW YORK CITY has more hotel rooms than some small countries have people. In a city where at least a handful of establishments can accommodate 2,000 guests, where a "small hotel" is considered one with fewer than 1,000 rooms, you won't spend your nights sleeping in Central Park. But—and it's a rather big but—getting exactly the kind of hotel room you want, in the location you want, at the price you want to pay is another cup of tea. If you haven't done your homework, you might not be too happy with where you stay. Sometimes it seems that choice hotel rooms in New York are as scarce as hot tickets to the top show on Broadway. But it needn't be that way, not if you understand some of the guidelines of the New York hotel scene.

First, of course, is the question of what you'll want to pay. So varied are the accommodations you can find in New York, that you might easily spend $250 a night in a sumptuous suite overlooking Central Park—or settle for a room with bath at $25 for a double. But you will, in general, be paying more for hotel accommodations in New York than in almost any other American city. Inflation is rampant at the moment and, what with real estate taxes and labor costs plus everything else constantly zooming up, the hotels are raising and raising and raising their rates. (In most cases, it's been necessary; in some, we suspect, it's taking advantage of what the traffic will bear.) In general, the price pricture breaks down like this. To stay in one of the top, elegant hotels of the city, you can expect to pay between $54 and $100 and up for a double room. To stay where most people stay, in one of the city's first-class, efficiently run, and comfortable hotels, expect to spend between $34 and $60 for a double; and to stay in a still-comfortable but more modest establishment, prepare to part with between $25 and $40. You can also, particularly if you're a student or a single person traveling alone, still find some respectable establishments where you can get a room for less than $25 a night. We have, therefore, divided our hotels into four categories and, allowing for some inevitable overlapping, they break down like this: (1) Elegant and Expensive; (2) First-Class; (3) Modest but Comfortable, and (4) For Budgeteers.

You will also note that we have described here some forty hotels—which, admittedly, is only a small segment of the huge number in the city. And we do not necessarily claim that they are the best in the city. They offer, however, in our opinion, excellent values in each price category, and they are representative of what you will find everywhere in New York.

Now, a few more preliminary remarks. All of the rates listed, unless otherwise stated, are for European Plan only, which means that no food is served, not even breakfast. The rates given are "transient rates": for those who stay in some hotels on a weekly or monthly basis, lower rates are usually available. Reservations in advance are *always* a good idea, especially during the busy summer months: from Easter to October is high season in New York. If you haven't planned in advance, you will almost always be able to get some sort of room, but perhaps not just the one you would like. And please note that although we have made every effort to be absolutely accurate about prices, the hotel business presents a highly competitive, changing situation, and prices may go up or down (usually up) a bit, depending on the season and the demand for rooms. Since new labor contracts are usually settled around the middle of the year, some of the hotels may raise their prices in June. But give or take a few dollars (and inflation notwithstanding), these rates will be in effect throughout most of 1979; and they will still represent excellent value for the dollar spent.

Finally, all rates are subject to an 8% New York City Room Tax, plus a $1-a-day occupancy tax.

FOR MOTORISTS ONLY: Here's a tip for those of you who are driving to New York. When you park your car in a New York hotel garage, it is assumed that you will keep it in more-or-less dead storage. There is really not much point in driving a car in Manhattan; everything is within easy bus or subway or cab distance, and besides, the parking situation is terrible. It will cost you more to pay for a garage than it will to take a cab. But if you will need your car, if you're driving out of the city or whatever, advise the hotel of this when you check in. That way, the car will be stored in an easy-to-reach part of the garage, and for an extra 50¢ or so tip per-use to the bellhop, you will have it handy. Also note that even when parking is free, as in most motor hotels, there is usually an in-and-out service charge of $1.50 or $2 each time the car is used.

One more word to the wise motorist: When checking out of a motor hotel, call for your car *two hours* before check-out time. It *is* conceivable that it will arrive earlier, but the worst that can happen is that you ask the bellhop to watch it while you're having your breakfast—and it's much better to have the car wait for you than the other way around.

And now, the details on finding the city's best hotel values. We'll begin in the pastures of plenty where the beautiful people play, where a room for the night goes, roughly, for from $54 to $100 . . . and up.

Elegant and Expensive: from $54 to $100, and Up

Synonymous with New York elegance, **The Plaza**, Fifth Avenue at 59th Street (tel. PL 9-3000), has been attracting the cognoscenti since early in the century. Built in 1907, it has officially been designated as a "landmark of New York." Frank Lloyd Wright called it his home-away-from-home; Eloise grew up there, and it is a favorite choice of visiting royalty. Looking incongruously like a European chateau on the New York skyline, the French Renaissance structure is full of splendid touches, inside and out. Rooms have 14-foot ceilings, copper window frames, ornamental plaster moldings, and thick mahogany doors, while parlors also have carved marble fireplaces and crystal chandeliers. All rooms have private baths, air conditioning, and color television. Twenty-four-hour room service is available. The Plaza's dining rooms include the romantic Palm Court (perfect for hand-holding), the Edwardian Room, and Trader Vic's for South Seas feasting. Single rooms go from $53 to $110, doubles and twins from $65 to $130, and suites from $135 to $350.

Ranking right up there with the Plaza, the **St. Regis-Sheraton**, Fifth Avenue and 55th Street (tel. PL 3-4500), is another longtime favorite with the social, diplomatic, and international set. Also built early in the century, it still has its European charm and grandeur, its large and graceful rooms with, of course, all the modern benefits of air conditioning, color television, and private baths. Sheraton Hotels took over the St. Regis a few years ago, and the result has been an unusually happy synthesis of old and new. Rates here go from $65 to $85 for a single; from $75 to $95, double and twin; and suites begin at $125 and run up to $200 (two-bedroom suites begin at $200). Down in the lobby, you can find just about the nicest shops: Gucci, Godiva, Mario Buccellati, all the names dear to the beautiful people. Elsewhere in the hotel, you can join the crowd for dinner and dancing in the King Cole Restaurant, perhaps for a drink at the St. Regis Bar.

Beautifully newer though it is, the **Park Lane,** 36 Central Park South (tel. 371-4000), still has all the elegance, good taste, and charm of the first two. There was a well-loved old hotel of this name, whose memories inspired the design and building of this tall, slim, 46-story tower rising gracefully over Central Park South. Because each floor is small, with only 16 rooms, there is a feeling of space, quiet, and privacy that is very appealing. The decor of the rooms and suites is varied, from contemporary to traditional, from bamboo summerhouse to elegant Victorian. Each has its own refrigerator, color TV with AM-FM radio, individual climate controls, and 10-foot-wide picture windows, from some of which the views of New York are the most spectacular anywhere. From the upper floors, especially, the panoramas are breathtaking, whether to the south, of Manhattan's skyline; to the west, of the Hudson River and New Jersey's Palisades; north, over the vast green expanses of Central Park; or east, over the fashionable areas of New York's East Side. For all this, the rates run from $60 to $100 for a single, $70 to $110 for double or twin rooms, $100 to $110 for king-size rooms. The suites offer a separate living room, with its own bar-refrigerator, a second bath, and a second color TV and radio: one-bedroom suites go from $180 to $250, two-bedroom suites from $250 to $335. The hotel offers fine food—and magnificent views—at the Park Room, a superbly elegant gold damask and red plush room, and good relaxing at the Park Lane Bar, beautifully dark, quiet, and understated. If you arrive by car, drive up to the special motor entrance, and an attendant will park it in the underground garage, about $12 per day.

One of New York's newest hotels, the **United Nations Plaza Hotel** at One United Nations Plaza (East 44th Street just west of First Avenue; tel. 355-3400), is a masterpiece of understated elegance, perfectly befitting the ambassadors, diplomats, and heads of state who choose it for the kind of serenity and security that few other New York hotels possess. Just across the street from the United Nations, and owned by it (although its rates are too steep for most U.N. personnel), the hotel was designed by Kevin Roche of Kevin Roche-John Dinkeloo and Associates, and his fine hand is seen in everything from the black-and-white marble floor in the lobby, to the pinpoint lighting over the reception desk, to the spacious, perfectly appointed rooms. The entrance and lobby have nothing to distinguish them from an East Side apartment house, but walk straight back to the Ambassador Grill and Lounge and you'll find yourself face to face with one of the most stunning rooms anywhere; the ceiling of mirrored glass, reflecting and refracting the light in a series of prisms within prisms within prisms makes the 14-foot ceiling seem cathedral-high. Sleeping rooms begin on the 28th floor, so there's scarcely a whisper of traffic noise, and all have beautiful views, subtly modern decor (fur throws as winter bedspreads, for example), TVs and radios, air conditioning, and all the amenities. Rooms and halls are decorated with beautiful ethnic art from U.N. member countries. Guests may swim in the glorious glass-enclosed swimming pool in the sky; use the facilities of the Turtle Bay Health Club, play tennis any time of day or night at a reduced fee. The Ambassador Grill serves breakfast (averaging $3.50 to $5), lunch ($4 to $8) and dinner ($6 to $12 for à la carte entrees); there's music in the adjoining Ambassador Lounge. Room service is available until midnight. The United Nations Plaza Hotel is a small place, with only 288 rooms, so its staff is able to give its guests all sorts of personal services. Between them, the desk staff alone speaks 27 languages; and no one is employed by the hotel who does not speak at least two.

The rates begin at $39 for a single studio and standard twins are $67 to $77; deluxe queens, from $78 to $88. King corner rooms are $89 to $99, and a bed-sitting room is $100 to $110. There is perhaps no grander place for entertaining in any New York hotel than in the U.N. Plaza's two two-story duplex, two-bedroom suites, each a fully equipped apartment, with thick, white shag carpeting and even a grand piano! These suites run from $300 to $350 per night. Two-story duplex one-bedroom suites are $195; hospitality suites are $150; and a one-bedroom suite, sans stairway, a mere $140.

The most reasonable rates of all are reserved for weekenders. Arrive on a Friday, Saturday, or Sunday night, and you can take advantage of a Big Apple Weekend package, which includes breakfast each morning, free use of the health club and pool, and runs $55 (single or double) for one night, $100 for two, $140 for three, in superior rooms. Discounts are also available on suites. The weekend package must be booked two weeks in advance and prepaid one week in advance. All sorts of imaginative extras, from a lunch and language lesson to a helicopter trip to the races, are available—at a price.

The United Nations Plaza Hotel is a Hyatt International Hotel, and reservations can be made by phoning 800/288-9000, toll free.

Could there be anyone who has heard of New York who has not also heard of **The Waldorf-Astoria?** As much a part of the New York scene as the Empire State Building (the site of the original Waldorf-Astoria), this grande dame of New York's luxury hotels holds forth at Park Avenue and 50th Street (tel. 355-3000). We often think that its lushly carpeted and beautifully furnished lobby, with its meandering arcades and quiet little corners, is one of the true hotel lobbies left in the city. Waldorf guests have always included the world famous: you might run into anyone here from Bob Hope to Princess Beatrix of the Netherlands. Not content to rest on its laurels, however, the Waldorf, under the Hilton banner, has refurnished and redecorated all of its rooms, and equipped them, of course, with all the necessaries: individual air conditioning, color TV (with first-run cinema service), private baths (many with boudoir), direct-dial telephones, and old-world amenities like nightly turn-down service. Special arrangements have been made for families (children occupying the same room as their parents are free); for honeymooners (flowers, champagne, honeymoon breakfasts, at extra rates), and even for guests in wheelchairs (ramps, extra-wide doors). Rates, for all this old-fashioned largesse, run from $54 to $72 for a single; from $69 to $87 for a double; from $120 to $210 for a suite. An extra person in the room is charged $15 a night. Oscar's, the famous coffee house at the Waldorf, has been redecorated to create a horticultural haven; Sir Harry's Cocktail Lounge serves intriguing juices of the jungle against an African safari background; and Shah Abbas, a new Iranian restaurant offers exotic dining. And, of course, there's still Peacock Alley which has always been, to our minds, one of the nicest *intime* spots in town.

Turning from the grandeur of the past to the up-to-the-minute pace of the present is no trouble at all for the Hilton people, and their **New York Hilton at Rockefeller Center,** Avenue of the

Americas between 53rd and 54th Streets (tel. JU 6-7000), is an outstanding example of the newer hotels of New York. The soaring, glass-sided column is one of the pioneers of the recent, modernistic architecture of the city and especially of the Avenue of the Americas–Rockefeller Center area. The largest hotel in town (2,131 rooms), the Hilton boasts convention halls big enough for small armies to parade in, and guests' rooms full of little luxurious surprises like a radiant-heated bathroom floor (delicious after stepping out of the tub), individually controlled heating and air conditioning, direct-dial phones, TV, and an electronic message and wake-up system. There are ice machines on most floors. The tab here runs from $49 to $69 in a single; from $63 to $83 in a double; from $145 to $160 for parlor and one-bedroom suites; from $185 to $200 for parlor and two-bedroom suites. There is no charge for children sharing their parent's room. A discotheque, steak house, continental restaurant, coffeeshop, a handsome and exciting lobby are, naturally, all downstairs. The International Promenade is great fun for people-watching. The Hilton's staff, by the way, is multilingual, and guest information, signs, and menus are in several languages.

Just about a block west of the Hilton, at Seventh Avenue between 52nd and 53rd Streets, is another of the newer giants on the New York hotel scene. This is, of course, the impressively modern **Sheraton-Centre Hotel** (tel. 581-1000). Soaring upward some 50 stories, it has enough convention halls, meeting rooms, shops, restaurants, supper clubs, and, oh yes, rooms—about 2,000 at last count—to outfit a small city. The guest rooms all have TV, radio, individually controlled heat and air conditioning, of course. For motorists, there's valet parking right in the hotel. The gold-ceilinged lobby fairly throbs with excitement, and while you're heading out or in, you might bump into writers from *Esquire* magazine or some members of the Puppet Guild of America, all holding their meetings at the Americana. Room rates range from $49 to $69 in a single, from $54 to $74 in a double or twin. One-bedroom suites go from $125 to $225; two-bedroom suites are $180 to $240, for four people. A third person in the room is charged $5 a day.

The luxurious new Kona Tiki Restaurant at the Americana is a fun place for Polynesian dining, entertainment in the Kona Lounge, and nightly dancing.

One of the most convenient, comfortable locations in town is enjoyed by the **New York Sheraton** at Seventh Avenue and 56th Street (tel. 247-8000) which, without being at all ostentatious, has just about everything one needs in a hotel. Diagonally across the street from Carnegie Hall, the Sheraton caters mostly to business people during the week; on weekends, it offers very attractive package rates to family visitors. The rooms, all beautifully furnished and decorated, complete with color TV, colonial-style beds, and all the amenities, rent from $46 to $60 for singles, from $56 to $70 for twins. Suites come in various combinations: some with one small bedroom or one large bedroom, with two small bedrooms or two large bedrooms, and run from $90 to $250. There is no charge for up to two children under 17 years of age in a regular double; either two double beds or rollaways will be provided. Two-room family units are also available. In-house movies are available in all rooms; there are some special facilities for handicapped people; and the multilingual clerks at the desk speak everything from Arabic on down the alphabet.

Don't worry about going hungry at the Sheraton: there's the Pavillion Coffee Shop for light meals, the Falstaff Room for deluxe dining at lunch and dinner; and Sally's Disco Bar, a swinging night spot which turns into Sally's Schnitzelhaus during weekday lunchtimes, serving a lavish Bavarian Buffet und Bierfest (three hot selections, plus dessert, beer and beverage, for $5.95).

Make reservations via Sheraton's toll-free number: 800/325-3535.

There's such a quiet, gracious air about **Loew's Warwick** that it's hard to realize that it's in the midst of one of New York's most vital locations, at 54th Street and Avenue of the Americas (tel. 247-2700). From the moment you enter the graceful lobby, filled with velvet upholstered sofas and chairs, you know you're in a special place. Accommodations in this 500-room hotel, choicely located close to Carnegie Hall, Lincoln Center, and the New York Coliseum, are special, too: rooms are large, graciously furnished, with spacious closets, decorator bathrooms, air conditioning, color TV. They run from $44 to $64 in a single; from $54 to $74, in a double or twin. The junior suites are particularly nice: the sitting area has a small refrigerator and a bar, and is partially separated from the sleeping area by a curtain. These run $65 for a single, $75 for a double. And the parlor and one-bedroom suites (from $75 to $150) and the parlor and two-bedroom suites (from $120 to $210) are truly lovely—perfect for business or social entertaining. There is no charge for children under 14 in the same room with their parents. A third person is charged $11 extra. The Warwick Bar is a great place to have a drink and perhaps rub elbows with the entertainment and communications VIPs who drop in here, and Sir Walter's Dining Room (with Sir Walter depicted in a wall mural) is a handsome spot for fine seafood and steaks.

Inquire about the Warwick's very special weekend packages, from $40 per person.

Heading south a bit, in the heart of the busy area in the low 30s that encompasses the Madison Square Garden Center, the Garment District, Pennsylvania Station, and of course, Macy's, one of the most satisfying places to stay is undoubtedly the **Statler Hilton,** 401 Seventh Avenue at 33rd Street (tel. 736-5000), just across the street from Madison Square Garden. It's a huge (1,592 rooms), bustling well-run hotel, with excellent services and facilities. The old Statler was long one of the city's favorite hotels, and the Hilton people have spent many millions in modernizing and bringing it up to date. The hotel is constantly being refurbished, and now, all the rooms have individually controlled air conditioning and heating, private baths, and color TV; decor is handsome, varying on each floor from traditional to modern. The corridors on each floor have those handy canteens for ice and soft drinks. Singles here go from $46 to $61; doubles and twins from $60 to $65; one-bedroom suites from $125 to $150; two-bedroom suites from $200 to $225. Executive singles (a room with a sitting area and possibly a bar) run $71 to $91; and executive doubles and twins are $85 to $105. And there's a free Family Plan for children who sleep in the same room with their parents.

Right at hand for eating and drinking is The Haymarket, serving all three meals; the Penn Bar Restaurant, a cozy, pub-style place for lunch and dinner, open until 1 a.m.; and the Lobby Bar, a great gathering place.

Over on the fashionable East Side is **Loew's Drake,** and it's oh-such-a-lovely place to spend a holiday. The Drake is right on Park Avenue, at 56th Street (tel. HA 1-0900), close to all the boutiques and galleries and theaters. And right at home is Shepheard's, that madly swinging disco straight out of Cairo where silent sphinxes watch the beautiful people dance the nights away. In the lobby, the mood is all European elegance, with French Empire antiques, Oriental carpet, crystal chandelier. We seldom wax enthusiastic about elevators, but here even the elevators are works of art: Chinese lacquer-screen paintings panel the interiors. The rooms are as nice as you would imagine, large and comfortable with every expected amenity plus one that you wouldn't expect: a refrigerator. There's color TV, of course, and the bedrooms of the suites even have an extra black-and-white set. Closets are enormous. Singles go from $57 to $77: doubles or twins, from $67 to $87, and the suites (some done in French Provincial, some with one-of-a-kind pieces of furniture) go from $90 to $150 for the parlor and one-bedroom suites; from $140 to $200 for the parlor and two-bedroom suites. There is no charge for one child under 14 in the same room with parents; no charge for a crib; a third person is $12 a day. If you're going to be in town for a weekend only, the Weekend Wonder Package—which includes two days and one night's stay (Friday or Saturday arrivals) plus dinner and show in Shepheard's plus a full breakfast—is a good buy at $49.95 per person. Besides Shepheards, Loew's Drake also boasts the lovely Drake Room for quiet, elegant breakfasts, lunches, and dinners.

First Class: from $34 to $60, Double

MIDTOWN: WEST SIDE: If you've come to New York to go to the theater, to see the sights, to conduct business, or just to be in the heart of everything, you can't pick a more convenient location than the midtown West Side area. Choose a hotel in this area, bounded on the north by Rockefeller Center in the 50s, passing through the Broadway theater district in the 40s, and bordered on the south by Madison Square Garden Center, and, chances are, you'll be within walking distance of just about everywhere you want to be.

It's in this area, too, that there are three hotels offering something that is not as easy to come by as one might think: a chance to take a swim before (or even after) a hard day's sightseeing. Hotel pools are, of course, *de rigueur* in Waikiki or Miami Beach, but not until fairly recently have they been introduced into the New York scene. Most of the pools are in motor inns, and not only do these establishments offer free parking for your car (in itself a saving of $6 to $8 a day), but usually the use of the pool and all the pleasant extras that go with it. One of our favorites in this category is the **Americana City Squire Motor Inn,** on Broadway between 51st and 52nd Streets (tel. 581-3300). The lobby is modern, not elegant, but comfortable in a stylish way, and all rooms, smartly furnished, have picture windows. Some have private terraces and striking views as well. But best of all is the view from the glass-enclosed swimming pool, open year round. It's great fun to swim or lie back in a comfortable chair and gaze at the crazy, mixed-up beach—the skyscrapers of New York surrounding you. Air conditioning, TV, private bath are all included in the room rates (and so is parking, with a $2 service charge each time you use your car), and the prices are as follows: singles go from $48 to $56; doubles or twins, from $49 to $61: suites from $95 (one-bedroom) to $135 (two-bedrooms). An extra person is charged $4 a night. Children may stay in their parents' room free. Also nice for kids is the Red Coach Grill, a popular family place that offers special menus and surprises for kids at lunch and dinner.

Another favorite swim-before-supper motel is the **Ramada Inn**, on Eighth Avenue, between 48th and 49th Streets (tel. 581-7000). The 366 rooms are nicely furnished, with picture windows, air conditioning, color TV, good-sized closets. It's a good place to stay with children, since there's no fancy hotel formality; they can stay in their parents' room free (under 18), and they'll love the open-air pool up on the roof with its cozy cabana deck and snackbar for poolside lounging. There's also a Wienerwald Restaurant for inexpensive German-Viennese food. Single rooms go from $34 to $46; twin- and double-bedded rooms, from $42 to $54; family rooms with two double beds, from $46 to $58. Parking is free, but there is a $2 charge for each additional in-and-out service.

A third good choice for those who favor the motel-style life right in the heart of the city is the **TraveLodge** in New York City, 515 West 42nd Street (tel. 695-7171). Although Times Square is a long three blocks away, that's really no problem: a bus across the street from the hotel will take you there in about five minutes. All of the 155 units here have been newly decorated, and there is air conditioning, private baths, TV in every room, and free garage parking. The pool is a beauty and you can swim here year round, since the outdoor pool (a boon during the hot New York summer) also has an indoor enclosure. Use of two saunas, a solarium, and the lovely top-floor sundeck is free. If you've stayed at any of the other TraveLodges (they crop up everywhere, from Australia to Alabama to Alaska), you'll know they don't stint on extras, and the New York motor hotel is no exception: room service, direct-dial telephones, the privilege of taking your car in and out of the garage as many times as you like. All told, the value is excellent: singles rent from $38, doubles, from $44. Children under 17 may stay free in the same room with their parents, but each additional adult is charged $5.

We're accustomed to seeing **Howard Johnson's Motor Lodges** on highways, but here in New York you'll find a member of this famous family right in the midtown area. It's located on Eighth Avenue, between 51st and 52nd Streets (tel. LT 1-4100), within walking distance of Broadway theaters and all the cultural attractions of the west 50s. The 300 rooms here are all very attractive, with modern decor, wall-to-wall carpets, air conditioning, large bathrooms, color TVs that also show first-run, in-house movies ($4.75 per movie). Right on the premises, naturally, is a Howard Johnson's Restaurant (the kids can indulge in a different flavor ice cream every day) and a cocktail lounge. You can choose a studio room (with two studio couches) at $34 for a single, $42 for a double, or a more traditional room. Singles run from $38 to $46; doubles or twins, from $46 to $54; and family rooms, with two double beds, at $50 to $58. A third person staying in the room is charged $9. There is no charge for children not requiring an extra rollaway bed. Parking is included in the above rates, plus a $2 in-and-out service charge each time the car is used.

THE EAST SIDE: New York's East Side is traditionally known for being a bit more peaceful, a bit less frenzied than the West Side. Some—especially women—feel it's safer late at night. Some of the most elegant hotels—like the Waldorf-Astoria, the Pierre, and the Carlyle are East Side addresses. But there are also less expensive hostelries here, and the location couldn't be better. You're near Grand Central Station, the East Side Airlines Terminal, the United Nations, and the Fifth Avenue department stores. The posh specialty shops of Madison Avenue and the swinging boutiques of Lexington and Third Avenue are all nearby.

A big favorite on the East Side is the shiny, splashy **Loews Summit,** at Lexington Avenue and 51st Street (tel. 752-7000). This one features an in-hotel garage, a well-equipped shopping arcade, Maude's Restaurant and Bar for good dinners and good-sized drinks, and an attractive coffeeshop; in short, it's the kind of hotel that has enough so that one could just stay in on a rainy day and be well provided for. The Summit offers a luxurious lobby and rooms in attractive modern decor, all with color TV, direct-dial phones, bar-refrigerators, and that extra phone in the bathroom, too. Central air conditioning, of course. Now for the rates: From $45 to $54 for a single; $55 to $64 for a double or a twin. Suites, some with balconies, go from $80 to $120 for

The Literary Life—An Off-the-Beaten-Path Choice

We know of no hotel lobby in New York that is so full of fascinating ghosts as that of the **Hotel Algonquin,** 59 West 44th Street (tel. 687-4400). Every time we sit down at one of the plush little sofas in the oak-paneled lobby-lounge and ring the bell for a glass of Scotch —or a spot of tea—we are reminded of the generations of actors and writers and celebrated wits that have held forth here since 1902. But although Robert Benchley and James Thurber and H. L. Mencken and Laurette Taylor are part of the Algonquin's storied past, the current crop of celebrities is equally as bright: you might find Jean-Luc Godard or Sir Laurence Olivier or Truman Capote or Simone Signoret engaged in heated conversation or being interviewed by the *Times,* for the Algonquin is as much a literary and artistic club as it is a hotel. But it is a hotel, very much in the European manner of an inn, where the management tries to know each guest and make each one feel at home. And you really needn't be a celebrity to stay here. The 200 rooms and suites, comfortably furnished and with all the modern amenities of private baths, TV, direct-dial phones, guest-controlled air conditioning, plus the extraordinary security of *Cardgard* room entry in place of keys, are open to all comers. They range in price from $41 to $51 for a single, from $44 to $54 for a double, from $49 to $59 for a twin-bedded room. Most one-bedroom suites are $87, and two-bedroom suites are upward of $140. There is free parking on weekends for those staying at least two nights. Once you get to the Algonquin, do have a meal at the celebrated Rose or Oak Rooms or, at least, a drink in the lobby. Could that be Peter Ustinov over there to your right?

one-bedroom arrangements, $120 to $165 for two bedrooms. A third person in the room is $10 additional, and there is no charge for children under 14 sharing their parents' room.

There's a quiet, calm feeling about the **Hotel Beverly,** Lexington Avenue and 50th Street (tel. PL 3-2700), refreshingly unusual in the hubbub of the city. Also unusual is the fact that almost all rooms and suites here have kitchenettes—complete with refrigerator, cooking unit, dinnerware, and utensils—enough for any meal. Many corporations keep permanent hold on rooms here for the use of their executives; it seems they find the location and ambience congenial. So, too, do visiting families, and for the same reasons. In addition, children of any age can stay in the same room with their parents, free. All the rooms are air-conditioned and have TV and radio. Singles rent from $45, double or twin-bedded rooms, from $55 to $65, two-room suites, from $75 to $100, and three-room suites, from $125 to $150. All the suites have kitchenettes, but if you wish one with your room, be sure to specify in advance. A parking garage directly opposite the hotel is convenient at all times.

The same people who run the lovely Doral Hotels in Miami Beach are in charge at the **Doral Inn,** Lexington Avenue at 49th Street (tel. PL 5-1200), long one of our favorite hotels on the East Side. The location couldn't be more convenient, since it's smack in the midtown shopping area, across the street, in fact, from the Waldorf-Astoria. It's a busy, with-it hotel, the only one in New York, in fact, that has indoor squash courts on its premises, available to guests at a nominal fee. When you're not chasing the ball around the court, you can enjoy the feeling of quiet comfort in the well-appointed rooms, all with their own private baths, air conditioning, and color TV. Rates, for single rooms, depending on size and location, run from $40 to $48; doubles and twin-bedded rooms go from $48 to $56. An extra person is $8 more. Two-room suites, perfect for family living, run from $85, three-room suites from $125. Downstairs, The Pantry coffeeshop serves from 6 a.m. until late, and the Nicholas Restaurant and Cocktail Lounge offers lunch, dinner and supper until 1 a.m. Contact Trudy Cohen, Sales Manager, for reservations, and you'll be well taken care of.

One of the more relaxed, easy-going, and more reasonable hotels on the East Side is the **Roger Smith,** Lexington Avenue and 47th Street (tel. 755-1400). If you can't bear to leave the family pet back home, this is one of the few hotels that won't complain or refuse to accommodate you: they understand the attachment you feel for your pet. The rooms are spacious and well-furnished, all with automatic coffee-makers, bath, air conditioning, and TV, some with ice-cube machines. Singles run from $35 to $43; doubles, from $43 to $51. The suites all have serving pantries with cooking units, and some, since this is an older hotel, boast the presence of terraces or even wood-burning fireplaces. These one-bedroom, huge living room suites, which range in price from $60 to $95, could be perfect for families since children under 14 are free, and the pantry allows for eat-in meals; enjoy them family style, in front of a good wood fire, in the company of the family dog! Another nice feature is the free continental breakfast available to house guests on weekends and holidays in the breakfast room on the mezzanine floor. It's self-service, and you help yourself to as much as you want. Weekdays, however, you'll have to pay for your breakfast. The "La Quiche, Etc." restaurant serves lunch and breakfast at popular prices and is so popular, in fact, that at lunchtime the waiting line usually extends out to the street. Those with cars can use the adjoining garage at an extra charge, or join the New Yorkers who scramble for curbside spaces on 47th Street, free from 7 p.m. until 7 a.m. the next morning.

If you'd like a bit of turn-of-the-century ambience to go with your room for the night, then the **Prince George Hotel**, 14 East 28th Street (tel. 532-7800), might be just the place. This handsome old hotel, newly refurnished and brought up to date with all the modern conveniences of air conditioning, private bath, and TV in every room, still retains its early 1900s charm with its crystal chandeliers, antique clocks, and intricate wood paneling. The rooms are good-sized, well-furnished with individual decorative touches, and are a good bargain: singles go from $37 to $41; doubles or twin-bedded rooms, from $43 to $47; and suites from $75. Downstairs, there are a variety of restaurants, from the informal coffeeshop to the elegant Regency Room.

CENTRAL PARK SOUTH: This fashionable strip facing the greensward of the park has long been a favorite place to stay in New York, and it's convenient to all the theaters, restaurants, shops, and activities of both the East and West Sides. One of the most charming hotels in this area is the **St. Moritz**, 50 Central Park South (tel. PL 5-5800). The lobby suggests a place both elegant and exciting and, for further proof, take a look at the famed Rumpelmayer's, which is a combination old-world restaurant, soda fountain, candy-and-toy shop, and probably the most sophisticated place in New York to take your moppets for an ice-cream soda. You can also enjoy the leisurely life at Harry's New York Bar or the Café de la Paix, one of New York's few sidewalk cafes. Upstairs, the guest rooms are spacious, very well appointed, and all have air conditioning, color TV, and private baths. Rates run from $45 to $65, single; from $55 to $75, double or twin. One-bedroom suites go from $85 to $200; two-bedroom suites range in price from $175 to $300.

THE WEST FIFTIES: MUSIC, ART, AND EXPOSITIONS: Still very close to the center of things, but a bit removed from the hustle and bustle of Times Square, the West 50s are an ideal place to stay. The big attractions here are Rockefeller Center; Carnegie Hall and New York City Center; the Coliseum, home to many expositions; Lincoln Center, nor far north; the art galleries and elegant shops of 57th Street and Fifth Avenue. One of the nicest hotels here is the **Hotel Gorham,** 136 West 55th Street (tel. CI 5-1800). Walk into the lobby and you'll immediately get a feeling of quiet, unhurried comfort. It's a small hotel with just 116 rooms and suites, each styled for easy living, with serving pantries in all. All double rooms are large, and priced from $37 to $47, with the higher rates for rooms so large that they accommodate two queen-sized beds. All have private bath, air conditioning, TV, direct-dial telephone, and a blessed feeling of space. Singles go from $36 to $44. Very attractive single suites are available from $36 to $46. Each extra person is charged $8. But you need pay no more than $60 for a family suite which can sleep up to six persons. Theatrical people, tourists, buyers, and many Europeans all seem to feel comfortable at the Gorham.

Just two blocks from Carnegie Hall, the **Hotel Wellington,** 55th Street and Seventh Avenue (tel. CI 7-3900) is another good choice in this area. There's a modest but attractive lobby and nicely furnished rooms, all with private baths with tubs and showers, TV, radios and air conditioning. Your fellow guests might include performers from the Broadway theater, the members of the Boston Symphony, or Andre Previn and the Pittsburgh! Single rooms run from $26 to $34; deluxe singles go for $40. Standard doubles and twins run from $32 to $40; deluxe go for $46. Then there are parlor suites with one bedroom, from $55 to $75, and parlor suites with two bedrooms, from $80 to $110 single or double. A third person in the room is charged $6. A family of four could fit nicely into a double or twin room with two rollaways for $50.

A slight increase in prices is expected at the Wellington.

Modest But Comfortable: from $25 to $40

If the lure of the theater has brought you to New York, you can't pick a more convenient headquarters than the **Hotel Piccadilly,** 227 West 45th Street (tel. CI 6-6600); there are seven Broadway theaters on this street alone! The Piccadilly is a friendly, hospitable old-timer that has recently redecorated its 600 rooms; they are homey and cheerful, and all have private bath, TV, and air conditioning. Singles, small rooms with one double bed, go from $26 to $30; doubles run from $35 to $39, and twins from $37 to $42. Rooms with two double beds, from $38 to $42, can comfortably accommodate a family of four; a fifth person can be put up in a $5 rollaway bed. The parlor and one-bedroom suites are well priced from $50 to $70 for up to four guests. A triple combination of one double-bedded room and one single is also available at $38.

The Piccadilly's lobby has been nicely redone in smoky mirrors and red fabric walls, and now boasts the attractive Ziegfeld Restaurant, bright and cheery with its handsome plants, serving fine quality American food and drinks. There's a coffeeshop too, for quick meals. Advance reservations are recommended, especially during the busy summer season and on weekends and holidays.

Right in the heart of the Rockefeller Center area, the **Hotel Taft**, Seventh Avenue between 50th and 51st Streets (tel. 247-7000), is one of New York's more venerable hotels. Slightly down at the heels at this writing, it is awaiting a promised renovation from its new international owners; but the 1,500 rooms are still clean and comfortable, with air conditioning, TV and private baths in all rooms. Guest rooms of various sizes and locations go from $30 to $40 in a single, $38 to $48 double and twin, $150 to $158 suites. There's a big, sunny 24-hour coffeeshop in the lobby, as well as the Brewery, fine for beer and snacks, lunch, and light dinners. You might inquire before you make reservations here as to whether or not the renovation has taken place.

Just a few steps away from the Hotel Taft is the smaller, refreshingly old-fashioned **Abbey-Victoria Hotel**, Seventh Avenue at 51st Street (tel. 246-9400). This quiet, modestly mannered establishment once consisted of two neighboring hotels: the Abbey and the Victoria. Now they have been brought together under one roof and redone from top to bottom. The result: some 1,000 attractive rooms, all air-conditioned, with full bath and television. And the prices are especially easy to take: from $25 to $30 for a single, from $28 to $32 for a double, from $29 to $33 for twin-bedded rooms. Suites start at $50. Children under three using cribs are charged $1 extra a night; rollaway beds are $5. There's a Chinese restaurant, Confucius, plus a bar and cocktail lounge downstairs. A most pleasant choice.

The **Century-Paramount**, 235 West 46th Street (tel. 246-5500), certainly ranks as one of the best mini-priced hotels in the city. The Paramount Hotel was taken over a few years ago by the management of the Century, one of the pioneering budget hotels in New York, when its old building was razed to make way for a new Rockefeller Center office building. Now the Century people have 700 rooms to work with, and they are still maintaining their high-quality, low-price standards. The entire hotel has been refurbished, new bathrooms have been installed everywhere, and the rooms are nicely done with fairly modern furniture. All rooms are air-conditioned and have TV and private bath. Prices are easy to take: double-bedded and twin rooms go from $28 to $30; singles, from $22 to $26; with an extra charge of $4 for a rollaway bed. A family of four might choose a large room with two double beds from $28 to $32. Housekeeping is good. The clientele is fascinating: you might run into an airlines captain in the elevator, or a South American diplomat's family in the lobby or coffeeshop. Especially nice is the courteous and helpful attitude of the management. Advance reservations are always advised, especially if you plan to be in New York between Easter and October, high season for the Century-Paramount.

Quite close to Fifth Avenue, the 230-room **Hotel Seymour**, 50 West 45th Street (tel. MU 2-5940 or 682-0937), also offers a surprising amount of comfort for its small prices. The hotel is an attractive place, from the lobby with its elaborately carved ceiling to the well-furnished and unusually spacious rooms. There are high ceilings, big closets, pretty floral spreads on the beds, desks, large dressers, good (but sometimes slightly worn) walnut furniture. And most of the rooms are on the inside, so they are quiet. Naturally, air conditioning, cable color TV with built-in radios, and private baths, are all included in the price tab: from $20.50 to $29.50, single; $25 to $31 for a double-bedded room; $25.75 to $33.50 for a room with twin beds. One-bedroom suites run from $26.50 to $42. Two-bedroom suites go from $45 to $65. Many Japanese businessmen and U.N. people favor the Seymour.

Popular with foreign visitors to New York, the **Hotel Holland**, 351 West 42nd Street (tel. CI 6-0700), is one of the city's older hotels that has lately been completely refurbished and now ranks as an acceptable budget choice. It's opposite the new extension of the Port Authority Terminal in a busy block just a short walk from Times Square. While some of the halls need repainting and recarpeting, the 300-plus rooms here are okay if not glamorous, pleasantly furnished, with black-and-white or color TVs, private baths or showers, and air conditioning in summer. Singles go from $20 to $24, doubles from $24 to $28. Suites and adjoining rooms are available for families. Summer weekly rates are seven days for the price of five; winter weekly rates are $75 single, $115 double. Color TVs cost $10 more per week or $2 more per day. Kitchenettes, available only on a weekly basis, cost $10 more per week. Children under 12 can stay free with their parents if they do not require a rollaway bed, which is $4 per night. There's a coffeeshop and bar on the premises, plus dozens of restaurants a few blocks away. Special consideration is given foreign visitors. For reservations, contact Mr. T. Weiss, General Manager, well in advance.

EAST SIDE: Modestly priced accommodations are not exactly easy to come by on the East Side of New York, but if the discerning traveler makes an effort, he can come up with a few good choices. The **Hotel George Washington,** Lexington Avenue at 23rd Street (tel. GR 5-1920), is, to be sure, a bit off the usual tourist circuit, but what you lose in a slightly out-of-the-way location you make up for in savings. This 600-room Carter Hotel has many long-term guests, but there are at least 250 rooms for transients, all recently refurnished, and all with smart furniture and accessories, and air conditioning. The hotel's twin-bedded rooms (reconverted from two small ones), have two closets and two bathrooms, a real feeling of spaciousness, and are a good buy at $30 to $40. Doubles, $30 to $40, are smaller but still attractive. Singles run from $22 to $30. No charge for children under 14. Weekly rates start at $63 in a single, on a minimum stay of two weeks. And there are special rates for students, faculty, theatrical people, government personnel, and "Visit USA" guests from overseas. Some of the rooms have a view of nearby Gramercy Park, one of the loveliest spots in the city. A 24-hour coffeeshop and a bar are at the ready, and within a block are bus and subway lines to take you, in about ten minutes, to 42nd Street and the heart of the city.

Although we don't suggest you skip a visit to the United Nations, it sometimes seems to us that the sightseeing in the lobby of the **Hotel Tudor,** 304 East 42nd Street (tel. YU 6-8800), is almost as good, especially during the sessions of the General Assembly, as African chiefs in tribal costumes and Indian ladies in silk saris parade through. But, besides being the nearest hotel to the United Nations and the home of many delegates, the Tudor is also a nicely run tourist hotel and a good bargain, considering its midtown location (the crosstown 42nd Street bus takes you in minutes to the department stores, East Side Airlines Terminal, and the Broadway theater area), smartly styled rooms, and fine service. Singles at the Tudor run from $24 to $28, a room with a double bed is $30 to $32 for one person, $32 to $34 for two; a twin-bedded room is $34 to $45. Triples are $40, and family rooms with four single beds and two full bathrooms are $48. A marvelous arrangement for a big family or small group is the King Suite, which is actually a lovely apartment with a living room, three bedrooms, no less than four bathrooms, a huge color TV, and a fully equipped kitchen with dishes, glassware, et al. It rents for $120 a day, much cheaper than anything comparable in the midtown area. The hotel is constantly redecorating and upgrading itself. The lobby is an attractive one, with its stained-glass panels, heraldic shields, wrought-iron chandeliers, rich red carpet, and large paneled wooden front desk. The Tudor Olde-English mood (the hotel is part of Tudor City, a large residential complex done in a similar architectural motif) is also carried out in the handsome Three Lions Pub, which does a brisk business for medium-priced breakfasts, lunches, and dinners.

There's a gracious, old-world feeling about the lobby of the **Hotel Seville,** Madison Avenue and 29th Street (tel. 532-4100), complete with Spanish architectural details, an antique fireplace, red drapes and carpets, and a grand piano. The rooms could be a bit more modern and spruced up for our taste, (some are a bit musty), but considering that the average price is only $21 single, $25 double (with some single rooms without bath starting at $17; these are only occasionally available), it's a good buy for New York. A good choice for a large family is the two-room-with-kitchenette $53 suite for six people. All rooms have color TV, air conditioning, and full hotel service. About 50% of the 400 rooms here are available to transient guests.

A modest budget hotel that is currently undergoing extensive renovations, the **Hotel Latham,** 4 East 28th Street (tel. 685-8300), is another good choice for families with children watching the pocketbook. The Latham has simple one-bedroom suites that can sleep four at $25 to $30 a night, plus $2.50 for each extra person. Doubles average $20 to $23; singles, $18 to $21. All rooms have TV and air conditioning. Be sure to ask for one of the renovated rooms, with flowered wallpaper, new bedspreads, and acceptable furnishings. This is a large, older hotel that caters mostly to permanent guests (many refugee groups put people up here), but there are always some transient rooms available, and, in summer, it's frequented by many families. A bit off the beaten path, but very close by bus or subway to all tourist activities.

LINCOLN CENTER—AND POINTS NORTH: You can't get much closer to all the excitement of Lincoln Center than the **Hotel Empire,** just across the street from the main plaza, at 63rd Street and Broadway (tel. 265-7400). The Empire is, in fact, the "official" Lincoln Center hotel. It is an older, 600-room hotel, recently refurbished and brought back to its former standards by the savvy Carter Hotel chain (which also owns the Carter and George Washington mentioned above). All rooms are attractively decorated (patterned shades, nice bedspreads and furniture), most have color TV, air conditioning, and free parking (except for a nominal service charge) is included in most rates. Prices range from $24 to $28 for standard singles, from $28 to $34 for deluxe singles; from $26 to $32 for standard doubles or twins, from $34 to $40 for deluxe doubles or twins (please specify the category you wish when making reservations). An extra person is $6; children under 14 staying in their parents' room are free. Families will also do well in the small, two-bedroom suites (no living rooms) which can comfortably house four or five, at $40 to $50; rooms with two double beds, suitable for four are the same price (the latter are all outside rooms). Special guaranteed rates for students, faculty, overseas guests, clergy, theatrical and government visitors. And if you're a view nut, request one of the suites that commands a view of the Metropolitan Opera House, Avery Fisher Hall, and the Hudson dropping off into the distance.

Those who are diligently watching the budget may be interested in some of the Empire's older, plainly furnished rooms with private toilet and sink, bath down the hall. They come without air conditioning, TV and free parking, but rates are $20 single, $26 double, from $70 a week single, $90 a week double.

Although there are scads of good restaurants within walking distance of the Empire, you might find the hotel's own coffee-shop amusing, considering the interesting people who stay here. We once came in on a Saturday night for an after-concert cup of coffee, met a whole group of Whirling Dervishes from Turkey staying at the hotel, and spent a pleasant few hours cementing Middle East relations. Ballet buffs seem to make this place a special hangout.

One of the best choices in the Lincoln Center area is a hotel that few visitors have ever heard of. That's the **Hotel Olcott**, 27 West 72nd Street, right off Central Park West (tel. TR 7-4200), and the reason most out-of-towners don't know this place is because it's largely a residential hotel, and most of its guests are either longtime residents or entertainers, diplomats, U.N. people, and the like in New York for a few months. But at any one time, there will be at least 25 suites available to transients, and, as anyone who's discovered the Olcott will tell you, they are among the top buys in the city for the money. These are full, one-bedroom apartments, comfortable enough to live in for a long time (which most of the guests do), and their size ranges from large to enormous. Each has a living room, a twin-bedded bedroom, a private bath, and that great money-saver, a kitchenette, complete with dishes and utensils. The prices range from $26 to $30 a night for a single; suites for two people go from $34 to $40 a night, plus $5 for each additional rollaway bed needed (up to four people can be comfortably accommodated). On a weekly rate, the apartments go from $185 to $210, which is about what you'd pay *per day* for suites in some of the fancy midtown hotels. All rooms have air conditioning, direct-dial phones; color TV is available for $3 per day, $15 per week. Furniture is comfortable. Your fellow guests may well be Metropolitan Opera singers, Broadway actors, South American and European business and government people, as well as an occasional resident of the two-doors-away Dakota (New York's most famous and celebrity-studded apartment building), here while their apartment is being redecorated. Sea Breeze Off The Park, an excellent, mostly seafood restaurant off the lobby, is a softly-lit, modernistically decorated room with a piano lounge (à la carte entrees

United Nations

about $6.50 to $11). Seventy-second Street abounds with coffee-shops, restaurants, and gift boutiques and is one of the most interesting thoroughfares on the West Side. It's a short bus or subway ride to midtown.

The management states that weekly rentals, reserved in advance, are given preference; however, with luck, you may get a room or suite for a night or two on short notice.

For Budgeteers Rooms for $25 or Less

TWO COED Y'S: New York City boasts several YMCA accommodations, and while some are good and some are not-so-good, there is one that is so superior that many business and professional people—as well as tourists and students—stay here whenever they're in town. We refer, of course, to the **Vanderbilt YMCA,** 224 East 47th Street (tel. 755-2410), which boasts an excellent East Side location not far from the United Nations, a very cordial staff, and small but scrupulously clean rooms. Most of the rooms have TV, some have air conditioning, but none have private baths. Singles rent for $10 to $12 per day; doubles, at $7 per person; and this includes Y membership. Weekly arrangements are sometimes available after a personal interview. The physical facilities here match those of any health club, and are frequented by many of the big names of New York; you might find yourself sharing the swimming pool, sauna, and gymnasium with U.N. personnel, entertainers, and other VIPs. As for women, the Y is not chauvinistic; facilities are now fully co-ed. Advance reservations are requested.

Anyone who's been to the **Sloane House Y,** 356 West 34th Street (tel. 760-5850) in the last few years is in for a big surprise. The venerable old building (the largest residential Y in the world, and the first to go coed) has undergone a major facelift, and it's more than just cosmetics. Changes include a bright new lobby, electronically-controlled double doors, a full-time doorman, a computerized registration system and three completely renovated floors, reserved exclusively for travelers. Sloane House used to be a mecca for student travelers in the old days, and it looks as if it will be again; 2,000 British students stayed here recently, inaugurating the residence's "new era." Single rooms are $8.50 per night, with air conditioning, TV and private baths available at rates up to $16.50. A limited number of twin-bedded rooms is available at $13.50 ($19.50 with private bath). Group rates are even cheaper: $7 per night for 10 or more; and student rates (semester only, ID card required), are lowest of all: $35 per week. There's no pool at Sloane House, but the convenient mid-town location, spacious lounges, gamerooms, a gym and a beautiful new cafeteria (with an excellent lunchtime salad bar) and carpeted dining rooms are all pluses. Be sure to present this book when you register, and you will be assigned to one of the newly renovated floors.

For those who would like a Y facility uptown near the Lincoln Center area, the **West Side Y**, 5 West 65th Street (tel. 787-4400), is a first-rate choice. This very attractive building, right off Central Park (and around the corner from New York's famed Ethical Culture Society and School), has only single rooms, some with private bath and TV, some without. These go from $11.50 to $17.50 on a daily basis, from $41 to $71 on a weekly basis. Add $1 per day for Y membership dues. The place is perfect heaven for sports enthusiasts: it has no less than two swimming pools, four handball courts, two squash courts, three gyms, three weight rooms, and a running track (so the joggers can run either indoors here or outdoors in Central Park). Residents can use them all. Off the tiled Spanish lobby is a good cafeteria. Yes, women are allowed, but only if they are students; both men and women students are accepted on a semester basis at special rates. Be sure to make advance reservations.

MOSTLY FOR WOMEN: The all-women's hotel is a vanishing breed in this country, but fortunately, New York City still has a few. Women traveling alone looking for suitable inexpensive accommodations can still do well at the following two semi-residential hotels which do accept nightly and weekly transients.

There's a feeling of quiet and well-bred elegance at the **Barbizon Hotel for Women**, Lexington Avenue at 63rd Street (tel. TE 8-5700), known for almost half a century as the finest women's hotel in the city. Most of its 650 rooms are occupied by permanent residents—young working women and students from all over the country—but some 200 rooms are usually available to transients. They are bright, cheery, and attractively furnished, albeit very small (about nine feet by 14 feet). Rates are $17 and $19 for rooms with running water; $24 for those with semiprivate bath; and $29 for rooms with private bath. Special weekly and monthly rates are also available. The hotel is proud of its excellent security system (elevators are attended) and considers itself "the safest hotel in New York." Young men waiting for their dates are permitted only in the hotel's attractive lobby or in its comfortable lounge rooms on the 18th floor, which boast color TV sets. Laundry facilities are available. Guests have free use of the large and lovely swimming pool, and reduced rates at the health club. There's a coffeeshop and restaurant right in the building, and the address—right in the middle of the Lexington Avenue boutique neighborhood and a few blocks from famed Bloomingdale's Department Store—is eminently respectable. Summer is a slow season here, but advance reservations are always a good idea.

There's more of a college dorm feeling at the **Martha Washington Hotel**, 30 East 30th Street (tel. MU 9-1900), and although many students and young career women do live here permanently, many transient rooms are also available. It's a pleasant looking place—its attractive Colonial lobby contains early American furniture, yellow walls, a striking black ceiling, huge tableaux of Martha Washington and Mount Vernon on the walls. The rooms are small but cozy, most of them have kitchenettes and air conditioning, some have radios, and TV sets can be rented. Singles with bath are $18; twins with bath, $25; and if you're willing to share a bath with a few other girls, prices go down to $11 for a single, $18 for a double. Conveniences dear to the hearts of traveling women: a second-floor laundry with turquoise washers and dryers and a nylon-stocking machine; irons and ironing boards brought to your room on request; a sundeck on the roof, with beach chairs and an open view. Your fellow transient guests will probably include airline stewardesses, traveling business women in their 20s and 30s, and maybe even a lone youngster (the only male guests allowed are boys under ten) traveling with his mother.

Chapter IV

THE BEST BUYS IN NEW YORK RESTAURANTS

SOME YEARS AGO, a friend of ours determined that he was going to eat his way through every restaurant in New York City. To approach the task systematically, he opened the pages of the classified phone directory, turned to the restaurant listings, and began proceeding from the Acropolis Restaurant to the Zoevetta Luncheonette. About five years and more than a thousand meals later, he gave us a triumphant progress report: he was all the way down to "H". All of which is by way of saying that there is no shortage of restaurants in New York. But, unless you have time on your hands, money to burn, and a nonstop compulsion like our friend's, you will obviously have to be a great deal more selective. Restaurants surround the visitor on every side. Which are the best? Which offer the most value for the dollar spent? Where are the unusual, the off-the-beaten-path "finds" that the natives adore and that tourists seldom find? Here's where we come in.

To help you make your way through the perplexing maze of the New York restaurant world, we have set forth some very simple guidelines. We have chosen those restaurants which, in our opinion, offer the best buys in dining in New York, regardless of how much you spend. (Some other New Yorker might come up with a very different selection; but no matter—getting two New Yorkers to agree on their list of favorite restaurants is like getting Yankees fans and Mets fans to agree on their favorite ballplayers—and that's part of the fun.) And, because the price range in New York restaurants is so enormous—you could easily spend $60 or more for a romantic dinner for two, or $15 for a family meal for four—we have grouped these selections into various price categories. You should first know, however, that thanks to inflation, the cost of dining in New York is at an all-time high. New Yorkers expect to pay around $15 for what they consider a good dinner, and that's even before considering cocktails, wines, taxes, and tips; if they get by with less, they consider themselves lucky. Our price categories, then, are set forth as follows: (1) Haute Cuisine: Dinner for $30 and Up; (2) Expensive: Meals Averaging $20; (3) Moderately High: Meals Averaging $14; (4) Modest: Meals Averaging $10 and Under; (5) Fast Food and Friendly Prices: Meals from $2 to $6.

LUNCH: You will note that we have, for ease, broken these categories down in terms of dinner prices. A good way to stretch your food budget is to occasionally eat your main meals at lunch, when the values are always best. Even some of the most expensive restaurants, where dinner is all à la carte, offer prix-fixe lunches for reasonable fees. In most places, lunch runs 15% to 20% less than dinner.

BEVERAGES: If you want cocktails before lunch, plan on spending at least $2 per drink. Be careful when you buy wine: a prize year vintage in a luxury restaurant could skyrocket your bill to the tune of $25 or $35 or more. The cost of a bottle of wine will vary in each restaurant, depending on vintage and cachet. If you are not familiar with the subtleties of wines, put yourself in the hands of the waiter or wine steward and ask him to suggest the proper wine to accompany your dinner. In most cases, he'll stay away from the expensive vintages and select a good, moderately priced wine. For four people, order a full bottle; for two or three, a half-bottle will do nicely. To save on the tab, order the "vin de maison" or house wine, good and less expensive than bottled wines; it can be bought by the glass or in a carafe.

DRESS: Yes, women can now wear pants, even at the most posh preserves (but dressy pants, not sporty slacks), and casual dress for men is permitted in most places. However, if you're going someplace really elegant, double-check on the dress requirements when you phone for your reservation.

RESERVATIONS: The more expensive the place, the more imperative the need for a reservation. A few places do not accept reservations and, if so, they will tell you when you phone. But it never hurts to phone in advance and reserve, especially at dinnertime.

TIPPING: Leave your slide rule at home and relax. At the most modest or the most elegant place, the rule is to give the waiter 15% of your check (an easy way to approximate this is to, roughly, double New York's 8% tax added to all meal tabs). If a captain is involved, he should receive 5% more.

WHERE AND WHEN: Most of the restaurants are in the prime tourist areas of either midtown (East and West Sides) or Greenwich Village, but a few are slightly uptown or downtown; none of them, however, will be more than a 15-minute ride from midtown by bus, subway, or cab. Hours of operation are listed for each restaurant, and you can safely assume that lunch is served from noon to 2:30 or 3 p.m. almost everywhere; and dinner from 5:30 or 6 to 10 or 10:30 p.m. Many restaurants also serve after-theater suppers on Saturday night. Many are closed on Sundays and, during summer, some take rather long vacations. So, best always to check before you go.

PLEASE NOTE: Although we have made every attempt to be accurate, menu prices are always subject to change, and, in times of inflation, there is no telling where prices will go. In any case, the restaurants mentioned will still, we feel sure, be offering the best values for the money.

Now, then, let's begin.

Haute Cuisine: Dinner for $30 and Up

One of the ultimate French restaurants in New York must certainly be **La Grenouille**, 3 East 52nd Street (tel. 752-1495). Owner-host Charles Masson, who spent many years with the late Henri Soulé at Le Pavillon, opened his restaurant in 1962, and since then the "Frogpond" (as the regulars call it) has served what many consider the finest haute cuisine in the city. The restaurant is small, with practically no decor other than the fabulous fresh flowers which are everywhere. The menu at both lunch and dinner is prix-fixe only, $15.75 for lunch, $29.75 for dinner (not including coffee); add cocktails and wine, however, and your bill can go way up, depending, of course, on the wine you choose. Our favorite dinner appetizers are the Bili-Bi, an elegant cream soup with fresh mussels, seasoned with a touch of white wine ($2.75 extra), and the superb pâté du chef. For the main course, the poularde à la creme au champagne, a beautifully prepared roasted chicken with champagne sauce, the frog legs Provençale, and the bay scallops à la Nage, are excellent. All the desserts are beautiful, from the fresh fruit tarts to the best chocolate mousse you'll ever have. And the soufflés, an additional $7.50, are spectacular. Luncheon entrees run to brains in brown butter sauce, a very good striped bass, and a delectable spinach soufflé. You might have a drink at the tiny bar before your meal. La Grenouille is open for lunch from noon to 3, dinner from 6:15 to 10:45, Mondays to Saturdays. Closed Sunday.

Roger Fessaguet's kitchen at **La Caravelle**, 33 West 55th Street (tel. JU 6-4252), has an equal number of ardent devotees who claim that this is the grandest of the French restaurants in New York and that its haute cuisine ranks with the finest in the world. We, personally, have never been less than enchanted with the experience of dining here: the pretty, spring-like room, the celebrated crowd, the appropriate Parisian *hauteur* of the waiters, and the food, the food, the glorious food. M. Fessaguet's standards are arduous, and his dishes do not disappoint. Dinner is prix-fixe at $26.75, and the specialties change every day. You might have a very fine duckling Smitaine with white wine and sour-cream sauce, or perhaps the côte de veau Washington, a veal chop with a cream sauce of bourbon and cognac, served with corn fritters on the side. The fish dishes are always incredible: imagine the likes of brochettes de quennelles, a feathery light mousse of pike in the most delicate of sauces; cold salmon in summer; the broth of mussels (Bili-Bi); seafood au gratin and the crabmeat. All are memorable. And although the desserts are beautiful enough, we think it would be a shame not to partake of the soufflé glâcé, $2.75 extra at dinner. Lunch is prix-fixe at $15.75, and, again, the specialties change every day. Coffee extra. La Caravelle serves lunch from 12:30 to 2:30, dinner from 6 to 10:15, Mondays through Saturdays. It is closed Sundays, holidays, and for the month of August.

La Côte Basque, at 5 East 55th Street (tel. 688-6525), has long been one of the great dining places for the Beautiful People, and beautiful it is. The Bernard Lamotte murals make you feel you're dining by the seaside in a French cafe; the service is gracious and courtly, and the company is heady. Again, it's far from inexpensive, but the menu is prix-fixe: $16.25 at lunch, $28.50 at dinner. Salad and coffee are not included. The food is classic and superbly prepared: you might try the anguille fumé (smoked eel) among the appetizers, or choose from the likes of caneton rôti aux pêches (roast duck with peaches), filet de boeuf sauce Perigueux or sole grillée for your main course (fish is always special here). For dessert, fromage and coffee are perfect. The wine cellar is one of the best in New York, so expect to pay accordingly. Lunch and dinner are served Mondays through Saturdays, closed Sundays, holidays, and all of July.

Lutèce, 249 East 50th Street (tel. PL 2-2225), is one of the last holdouts in this era of failing palaces of haute cuisine and we, personally, hope it will last forever. We like to sit in the greenhouse-like setting where the city landscape is reflected hazily under the mylar dome or, in colder weather, upstairs in the elegant dining room typical of many of the formal dining rooms in New York's private townhouses. The food can be as unreal as this gracious setting. Lunch is prix-fixe at $16, and this may well be the meal to choose, since dinner can be expected to go upward of $30 per person. Among the appetizers, the fish pâté, or any of the pâtés en croûte are superbly flavored. For your main course you might have boeuf à la mode (beef in wine), délice de veau (veal with cheese and ham), or the beautifully delicate filet of sole almandine. Everything is prepared in a grand manner and served with flair. For dessert, what better than soufflé glâcé framboise (frozen raspberry soufflé) or success à l'orange (frozen orange mousse with almonds)? If you do come for dinner, you may want to try the house specialty, the mignon de boeuf en croûte Lutèce, a variation of beef Wellington, $16.50, or the poussin Basquaise (baby chicken), $15. And for dessert, the classics, crêpes flambées or white peaches flamed with Kirsch. Open for lunch from 12 to 2, Tuesdays to Fridays, for dinner, from 6 to 10, Mondays to Saturdays.

Although the menu is continental rather than strictly French haute cuisine, **The Four Seasons,** 99 East 52nd Street (tel. 754-9494), ranks right up there with the best restaurants in town. One of the great showplace restaurants of New York, it is seasonal in mood, with changing floral displays and art work (the Picasso, however, is there year round). You can dine in either the more formal Pool Room with its bubbling marble pool in the center of the room; or in the more casual (and slightly less expensive) Grill Room, an informal hangout greatly favored by people in the wine trade. The menu at the Four Seasons is costly—$2.75 cover charge and everything à la carte. You might start your feast with the house special, the crisped shrimp with

For the most rarified of New York dining experiences, nothing equals **The Palace**, 420 East 59th Street (tel. 355-5150). Certainly, its price is the most rarified in town: $80 prix-fixe, before wine, tips (suggested at 23%), and taxes. But many share restaurateur Frank Valenza's conviction that there is no establishment anywhere that meets The Palace's standard of quiet elegance, privacy, superbly attentive service, and a repertoire of haute cuisine magnificently prepared, with each course presented triumphantly as a work of art. Valenza's passion for perfection is evident in every detail; the finest stemmed crystal for the rarest of wines, the gold-rimmed plates, the brocaded silk chairs, and silver pots filled with fresh flowers on each table. Only 40 guests are seated each night—with a staff of 27 to provide the service!

To prepare yourself for the sybaritic adventure to come, an eight-course banquet that will take at least three hours to savor, eat very lightly or not at all during the day. Then, put yourself in the hands of the maître d' and let him advise you. The finest vintage wines are available from the cellar, and they are costly. You might begin, as we did, with a superb lobster and artichoke heart salad in tangy vinaigrette, and a fish pâté centered on goose liver and truffles. Soups are extraordinary, especially the mussel soup lightly seasoned with saffron and the winey, robust lobster bisque. Then comes a small entree or "releve," we can recommend the famous angel-hair pasta with a basil-flecked tomato sauce and the oysters on the half shell dotted with red caviar. Now it's time to clear the palate with a perfectly balanced tart-sweet fresh grapefruit sherbet doused with vodka. By now you should have strength for the main course, perhaps a roast of milk-fed baby veal with the lightest of potato puffs and artichoke hearts, or fresh Long Island fish, or filet of roast lamb. After that, a lightly tossed green salad, followed by a splendid pyramid of the freshest of seasonal fruits—perfect strawberries, cherries, peaches, grapes—presented with an array of cheeses, which included an unusual Roquefort Napoleon. This would be enough for any normal glutton, but for those who can manage it, there are at least three desserts to follow: the chef's specialty of white chocolate mousse, feathery chocolate cake, and apple cake—not to mention the miniature French pastries, and the tiny cookies passed around in a big wicker-like basket spun entirely of sugar. Desserts are incredibly sweet, best sampled in very small portions. Then chocolates (frozen truffles) and beverages, and, about three hours after you've sat down, a final, reluctant, good night.

The Palace is open for dinner only, Monday through Saturday, with seating from 7 to 9:30. Reservations essential.

mustard fruits, $8.50 or the salmon and pike pâté, $6.25. Then, perhaps, the mousse of trout with leeks, $15, or the roast squab with oysters and sage, $15, accompanied by the raw mushroom salad, prepared tableside, $4. The wine selection is superb, and the pastry wagon irresistible: so are the cappucino and Grand Marnier soufflés, $3 each. Luncheon prices are a little less steep, but the cover charge ($2) remains. If you're going to the theater and don't have all night to luxuriate over dinner, then take advantage of the pretheater dinner, served from 5 to 7, Monday to Friday, and prix-fixe at $17.50. You get a cold appetizer or soup, a choice of eight entrees, vegetable, salad and dessert.

The Four Seasons is open for lunch from noon to 3 and dinner from 5 to 11:30, Mondays through Saturdays. Closed Sunday and holidays.

Expensive: Meals Averaging $20

Now we move from the temples of gastronomy to the places where we ordinary mortals feel a bit more at home. Described below are ten restaurants that are among our favorites in the city. All of them are special—in atmosphere, in food, in value. None are inexpensive, but for the value received they are extremely good buys. The price range, for dinner, goes from about $15 to $25, or an average of $20 per person, before wines, tips, taxes, etc. The restaurants are listed according to nationality group or special interest.

DINING IN THE SKY: The quintessential New York restaurant experience? We'd say it's at **Windows on the World,** that dazzling showplace in the sky, 107 floors up, up, up above the city at the top of the World Trade Center, the almost-tallest building in the world. Windows on the World is one of those magic, mind-blowing places that leaves even jaded city sophisticates gasping, a place that reaffirms the greatness and glamor of New York. Encompassing a veritable acre of glass, the various dining rooms, cocktail lounges, and private rooms that make up master restaurateur Joseph Baum's crowning achievement afford 360-degree views of the city, the bridges lacing the rivers, the busy traffic of sea and sky; on a clear day, one can see 50 miles. Within, the decor is almost as stunning as the ever-changing floorshow outside. Using muted tones of gold and beige and pale rose, lavish touches of mirror and brass and wood, exquisite plants and fresh flowers everywhere, architect Warren Platner

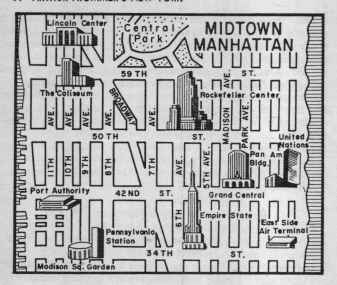

has created an ambience that is futuristic yet warm, a brilliant tour-de-force of almost science-fiction-like splendor. Walking along a mirrored reception chamber lined by huge, semiprecious rocks, being greeted by waiters in white uniforms with flashing gold epaulets, seated in a multitiered dining room where ingenious use of mirrors affords full views to every diner, one gets the feeling of gloating in a gigantic luxury liner, suspended in a sea of sky.

With so much going for it, it really wouldn't matter what the food at Windows on the World was like, but it happens to be good—very good, in fact, which is more than one can say for most skyscraper restaurants, although it is not in the same league as at one of the city's mighty temples of haute cuisine. Actually, there are two distinct dining areas which must be considered separately. Up until 3 p.m., Monday through Friday, the main dining room is a private club; nonmembers may dine by paying a surcharge of $7.50 per person. After 3 p.m., it becomes The Restaurant, for which weeks-ahead reservations are usually necessary on Friday and Saturday nights, Monday through Thursday reservations are available on short notice. On weekends, The Restaurant is open to the public without a cover charge. It's then, from noon to 3 on Saturday and from noon to 7:30 on Sunday (including a 7:30 seating) that you can enjoy the Grand Buffet at $13.95 per person. (Reservations are available on short order for Saturday; there's a longer wait for Sunday.)

As for dinner, served from 5 to 10 Mondays through Saturdays, it is prixe-fixe at $18.50, and there are also à la carte selections from $11.75 to $17.95. The classic Russian coulibiac of salmon is excellent as is the rack of spring lamb James Beard. Talmouse with ham is a succulent beginning to the meal, and the desserts are impeccable, worth every last calorie. Choosing between the golden lemon tart, with slices of lemon baked right into it, the mango and macadamia nut sundae and the frozen soufflé Amaretto is simply too painful; best to come with a group of friends and sample a little bit of everybody's dessert! The wine list is sensibly priced. Weekday lunch has similar à la carte dishes at lower prices, and you can also partake then of the Grand Buffet table, either as an appetizer, for $4.50, or as an unlimited meal, for $11.50. If you come on weekends for the Grand Buffet, you avoid the cover charge, and, for $13.95, take a taste trip around the world: bulghar wheat salad with cumin, marinated shrimp with huge peppercorns, Japanese noodle salad with mushrooms, smoked chicken, mountains of cold meats and fishes, hot curries, etc., suggest the lavish fare.

Another part of the restaurant that's both charming and popular is the Hors D'Oeuvrerie, which requires reservations only for lunch and Sunday brunch; other times, you'll wait in line a bit, but it moves quickly. The Hors D'Ouevrerie is an internationally minded cocktail lounge and grill, most romantic, where you can nibble on hors d'ouevres like baked sesame clams, coconut fried shrimp, a sushi and sashimi platter, or taramosalata with hot pita bread as appetizers, or order enough of them, or of the grilled entrees, plus dessert, to make a full meal. They are, however, expensive, and an average bill here runs $15. Sunday brunch at the Hors D'Ouevrerie is special fun, since it's then that you can have the Cozumel Breakfast (from papayas and tortillas to cafe con leche), at $8.50; the Chinese Tea House Lunch, at $9.95; or the Scandinavian Sunday, a variety of pickled, baked, and soused herrings, salads, eggs, at $7.50, à la carte, there are omelets, brioches, food from the grill, desserts like pears and Brie, the fudgy chocolate pastry cake, and the toasted Gugelhopf. At night, when the sun goes down and the lights wink on over the city and the music begins at the grand piano, the Hors D'Ouevrerie (with the adjoining City Lights Bar), is one of the most idyllic spots in town for dreaming and dancing.

Parking is free for Windows on the World patrons in the basement of the World Trade Center. By subway, take the IRT Seventh Avenue local to Cortlandt Street, or the IND AA or E train to Chambers Street. Reservations: Write Windows on the World, No. 1 World Trade Center, New York, NY 10048 (tel. 938-1111).

AND ON THE GROUND: Down on the concourse on the ground level of the World Trade Center, there's also excellent dining available at **The Market Dining Room and Bar** (tel. 938-1155), a restaurant that recaptures the spirit of the old Washington Market that once occupied the site. It is now dedicated to serving market-fresh products in hearty American portions, with the emphasis on the little extras, like free dishes of carpaccio (thin slices of raw beef) or lentil salad before your meal, or fresh fruit juices in the drinks, and fresh eggs given to departing dinner guests. A turn-of-the-century clublike atmosphere prevails, with globe lamps, large wooden booths, enormous napkins with a buttonhole to secure it to your shirt, and baskets of fresh produce standing about. Steaks (20-ounce sirloin for $16.95), charcoal-grilled butterflied leg of lamb, $11.95; pan-fried shrimp and oysters, $11.75, are typical of the hefty, all-American fare. At lunch you might try a platter of seasonal vegetables for $6.50, or a freshly ground steak tartare at $7.25.

Market Dining Room & Bar serves lunch weekdays from 11:30 to 2:30 and dinner Monday through Saturday from 5 to 10:30, Sundays 12:30 to 7 with "sweet market jazz."

If you step out of the Bar Room and onto Market Square you'll find the **Cafe** with waitress service but lighter fare, like great sandwiches at $2.75, chili, and stews. Open Monday through Saturday from 11:30 a.m. to midnight.

STEAK HOUSES: Those of you who have come to New York in quest of the perfect steak need search no further. Some of the best steak and lobster houses anywhere are right here, and all you need is a well-stuffed wallet (or a generous expense account) and an enormous appetite. For the New York Steak Experience, don't miss **The Palm**, 837 Second Avenue (between 44th and 45th Streets; tel. 687-2953). It's noisy, it's crowded, there's sawdust all over the floors, the waiters are rushed and can be curt.

But the true trencherman overlooks all such indignities, for those thick grilled steaks, those succulent fried onion rings and hash brown potatoes, those monstrous lobsters can be duplicated in few other restaurants. Prices are not for the timid: an average meal runs $25 per person at dinner, a few dollars less at lunch. At a recent meal, filet mignon and steaks were $14; and lobster, $24! (We always find one order of four-pound-plus of lobster perfectly adequate for two—it's almost big enough for three.) There's no menu, but the waiters will tell you about the clams Casino (baked clams with bacon) among the appetizers, $4, and the terrific cheesecake, $2, for dessert. That is, if you have room for anything else after those steaks!

If there's no room at the Palm, you'll be just as happy at **Palm Too,** at 840 Second Avenue, just across the street (tel. 683-7630) —same mood, same food, same madness. The Palms are open from noon to 11, Monday through Friday, Saturday 5 to 11. Closed Sunday and on Saturdays during July and August. You can reserve at lunch only.

Whether the Palm or **Christ Cella** is the city's greatest steak house is a question that's been hotly debated by New York's beefeaters for eons now. Suffice it to say that both are memorable. Christ Cella (pronounce it Krisella if you want to sound like a New Yorker), located at 160 East 46th Street (tel. OX 7-2479), is perhaps a trifle more genteel than its counterpart, the noise level a few decibels less, and the service can be more leisurely. Its prices are also rarified, as expensive as the well-heeled crowd that gathers to consume lobsters that go for about $25, steaks for $16.50. Hash browns, baked potatoes, or french fries come with the entree. The menu also offers a wide assortment of fish as well as other meat dishes, and the freshly made soups (cream of asparagus, onion) and the salads—especially the spinach salad with bacon, $4.50—are excellent. French pastries, cheesecake, and delicious Napoleons are among the desserts. Like the Palms, Christ Cella caters mainly to a business crowd, and is open weekdays from noon to 10:30, Saturdays from 5.

If you have a hearty appetite for steaks and you're going to be in the theater district, the **United States Steakhouse Company,** 120 West 51st Street (tel. 757-8800), is a good place to know about. It's a big place with a bright atmosphere—red buntings hanging from the ceiling, amusing graphics on the walls, wooden floors and comfortable seating—and the accent is on really solid American fare. Service is cordial and to the point. At lunch, the executive crowd keeps the food bar where they serve meat sandwiches up front busy, not to mention the handsome 42-inch oak bar, where the three-martini lunch is still in style. Lunch, dinner, and after-theater fare in the main dining room all feature choice cuts of meat as the specialty of the house. All cuts—from the chopped steak with sautéed onions at $5.95 to the 24-oz. T-bone at $17.95—are expertly prepared to your order. Since the house prides itself on regional American specialties as side dishes, it's fun to sample the cream of peanut soup (a bit bland for our taste) to start, corn fritters (crispy and luscious dunked into maple syrup) along with your meal, and the six-nut pie for a grand finale. Fish dishes—like the filet of sole with walnuts or almonds, $8.25—are nicely done. Crisp, greasy and altogether irresistible, homemade Saratoga potato chips, prepared right in the kitchen, are brought to your table as soon as you order.

The United States Steakhouse Company is open weekdays from 12 noon to 3 for lunch, every day but Sunday for dinner, from 5 to 11:30. All major credit cards accepted.

ITALIAN EXCELLENCE: Tops on the long list of Manhattan Italian restaurants is **Barbetta,** 321 West 46th Street (tel. 246-9171). Forget all your assumptions about Italian restaurants; this one is decidedly different, an experience best compared to dining in a wealthy friend's villa. Barbetta's century-old brownstone on the theater district's Restaurant Row exudes refined elegance. There's a small, gracious cocktail lounge where you might sip an aperitif before dinner in the stately dining room with its tall draped windows and classic table settings. In summer months, tables in the city's prettiest restaurant garden are highly prized.

As for the food, it's definitely northern Italian with hardly a tomato sauce in sight. The seasonal menu features Italian white truffles during their short Christmas-time season, and in summer, a true culinary delight is available: vitello tonnato, pure white cold veal in a piquant tuna sauce, $9.75. In spring try the fresh pesto Genovese, the pounded garlic, basil and pine-nut paste that tops fresh pasta, $5.75. But year-round Barbetta's menu glows with intriguing fare, from succulent whole squab to crisp fritto misto. Risotto, $6, can replace pasta here (in true northern Italian fashion), and this rice dish is available in several varieties, including a chicken-liver flecked version. You might accompany your entrees with the excellent salad of paper-thin sliced mushrooms.

Barbetta is open for lunch, which costs about $9 to $12, from noon to 2:30, and for dinner, with entrees from about $6 to $10 (plus 75¢ cover), from 5 to midnight. It's very popular before and after theater.

TIFFANY TRIUMPHS: Imagine an Art Deco palace, gleaming with mirrors and brass and signed Tiffany glass and antique chandeliers, touches of brilliance and beauty wherever you look. Imagine the most affluent and gregarious singles in town—singles of the category of say, Governor Carey or Princess Lee Radziwill—congregating at the bar and the tables. And imagine a first-rate kitchen that members of New York's food establishment rate among the best in town. No need to just imagine it: **Maxwell's Plum** is there, at First Avenue at 64th Street (tel. 628-2100), and it's one of New York's most stunning watering holes, a winner on every count.

Restaurateur Warner LeRoy (the son of film director Mervyn LeRoy), scoured the world to furnish Maxwell's with authentic turn-of-the-century art works, reproductions that fit in beautifully with the originals, and daring innovations like the ceiling of Tiffany glass behind the bar and cafe in the Back Room. It's here that the food is the most exciting: on the all à la carte menu, you can choose from entrees like veal piccata sauteed with lemon butter, English Dover sole, shrimp curry, steak tartare, or roast rib of beef with Yorkshire pudding and roast potatoes, in a price range from $5.95 to $14.75. Each day there is a plat du jour, usually for $7.25. Appetizers like Scotch smoked salmon, $6.85 and fish soup, $2.45, can indeed, be special. Desserts are among Maxwell's specialties; pecan pie with schlag, $2.55 and chocolate soufflé with whipped cream and chocolate sauce, to name a few.

The Back Room is Maxwell's gourmet dining room, and prices here are the highest. The Cafe offers a wider range of specialties—every thing from omelets and very good hamburgers on, and the Back Room lunch menu is also widely priced, starting with fancy burgers for $3.45. Weekend brunch, Saturday and Sunday, noon to 5, is a great time to bring older children, who'll enjoy the ambience as much as any adult. Maxwell's Plum is open every day, from noon to 1:30 a.m.

Ten years after he dazzled New York with Maxwell's Plum, Warner LeRoy encored with the re-creation of **Tavern on the Green**, New York's venerable restaurant right in Central Park, 67th Street and the Park (tel. 873-3200). Again, the decor is fantasy-land come to life. Rooms of crystal and frosted mirrors, of glass and sparkling lights reflected from the trees in the park, of dazzling chandeliers and Tiffany-style lamps, of carved wood statues and carved plaster ceilings create a kind of modern rococo that LeRoy has made famous. Eating here is an experience in escaping reality. And the menu is vast—everything from salads, sandwiches, and hamburgers to (in the Crystal Room), Dover sole stuffed with lobster with Mornay sauce, $16.50, or a rack of lamb for two, $28.50. Appetizers and desserts are about the same as at Maxwell's Plum, so if you missed Maxwell's chocolate cake, or banana fritters with cinnamon sauce and schlag, you can try them here. Saturday and Sunday brunch is a perfect time to enjoy the splendid setting here, although even egg dishes— scrambled eggs, omelets, eggs Benedict, eggs Florentine and the like, served with croissant, brioche or muffins and jam are a pricey $6.95.

We'd rate the food good here, if not up to the level of Maxwell's. But for sheer splendor of setting, it's hard to beat Tavern on the Green. And if you dine in the Elm Room on a Tuesday through Sunday night you'll also have piano music as a background, $2.50 cover. Open for lunch Mondays to Fridays from 12 to 2:30, Saturday and Sunday from 11 to 4; for dinner from 5:30 until 2 a.m. daily (kitchen closes at midnight).

THE THIRTIES REVISITED: Stepping into the **Rainbow Room**, 30 Rockefeller Plaza (tel. PL 7-9090), is a bit like going back into the time machine, since it's a classic Art Deco room—all glass, chrome and multilevel—where the swing-time ambience of the '30s still lives. Perched 65 floors above the crowds, the Rainbow Room is *the* place for dinner-dancing in the sky, and the food, while not quite as glorious as the ambience, is always commendable. The dinner menu is à la carte, with entrees like filet of beef Wellington, breast of chicken Kiev and roast Long Island duckling, priced from $9.95 to $12. The seafood crêpe Napoleon is a tasty appetizer, the watercress salad refreshing, and the dessert specialties like Grand Marnier or chocolate soufflés ($7.50 for two people) memorable. Dinner is from 5 nightly, with pre-theater (prix-fixe at $13.50 and à la carte) and supper (after 11 p.m.) seatings. A band plays for dancing nightly, and usually it's the justly popular Sy Oliver. There's a music charge of $2, Sundays to Thursdays; $2.75, Friday and Saturday. The $9.75 Sunday brunch, 11 to 3, is lots of fun, with dishes like hot Bloody Mary soup, crêpes, omelets, beef Stroganoff, and fancy desserts.

VILLAGE PERFECTION: The best restaurant in Greenwich Village? Our vote would go to **The Coach House**, 110 Waverly Place (tel. 777-0303). Owner Leon Leonides is always on hand to see that everything goes perfectly here, and, as a result, you have the feeling of being a guest in a country home. Banquettes line the walls, the tables are large, and fresh flowers of the season grace the reception table. There is no bar here, and reservations are an absolute must; you can usually plan on a 15-minute wait. Once you're seated, however, no one will rush you, even if other guests are waiting. The menu offers both complete dinners and à la carte choices. Available on both is the black bean soup Madeira, $2.50 à la carte, thick, full of beans with just the right touch of sherry. All entrees come with a potato and the freshest vegetables available. In fact, everything here is utterly fresh: the striped bass, served in a delicate wine sauce, tastes as if it had been caught that morning; it's $22.50 on the dinner. The medallions of veal, small and very tender pieces sauteéd in wine sauce, $20.50, are very fine, too. On the à la carte selections, the triple-cut lamb chop, huge and cooked to perfection, is the best we've ever tasted, $13.50. Weight-watchers are advised to throw caution to the winds here and indulge in dessert; both the pecan pie and the Viennese chocolate cake are worth every calorie. The Coach House is open for dinner only from 5:30 to 11, Tuesday to Saturday; Sunday, from 4:30 to 10:30; closed Monday.

Moderately High: Averaging $14

WEST SIDE: Times Square is, alas, no longer the glamor magnet it once was, but from your table at **Act I**, high up at 1 Times Square (tel. 695-1880), the view is dazzling. The 15th floor, a contemporary room done in a theatrical theme, boasts a handsome cocktail lounge and dancing and entertainment at night; the 16th floor reminds us of an old-fashioned porch with its wicker furniture and potted plants everywhere. Food is unspectacular American, but the complete dinners are a good buy at $9.95. You can begin with fresh fruit cocktail, then choose, perhaps, flaming roast duck or breast of Cornish hen, chicken Dijon or halibut Portuguese for your main course. The house specialty is bone-in-ribs of beef with Yorkshire pudding. All entrees are served with vegetables and a salad, plus coffee and a choice of desserts. You may also order à la carte, from $9 to $15.25. A "Businessperson's Lunch" at lower prices is served weekdays. Lunch is served 11:30 to 3, dinner from 5 to 10. Mondays through Saturdays. Keep this place in mind, too, for after-theater supper, served from 9:45 to midnight. Closed Sundays and major holidays.

The **Promenade Cafe** at Rockefeller Center (tel. PL 7-5730), is a gracious lady among the city's restaurants, very popular with natives and out-of-towners alike. It's so pleasant to dine in the outdoor cafe in the summer or indoors in winter, since the dining room directly overlooks the ice-skating rink at Rockefeller Center. You can sit back and relax with good continental food while you watch the brightly clad skaters whirl by. Complete dinners at $12.50 include entrees like roast prime ribs of beef or prawns fried in ale batter, appetizer and soup, potato and salad, plus tempting desserts like lemon mousse or whiskey cream pie. A la carte entrees average $7 to $9. At lunch, there are salads, sandwiches, quiches, and specialty main dishes from $5.50 to $8.75. The Promenade Cafe serves lunch from 11:15 to 4, dinner from about 4 to about 10:30, every day of the week.

Celebrity Stuff

The words "show business" and "Sardi's" are practically synonymous in our town, since **Sardi's**, at 234 West 44th Street (tel. 221-8440), is undoubtedly the most famous theatrical restaurant in the world. But the food is good, too, the service cordial and friendly, and that's the reason you're likely to spot Dustin Hoffman or Betty Bacall or Barbra here as you look up over your spaghetti or antipasto (the Sardis are Italian, and so is much of the menu). Our favorite appetizer is the house special, the hot shrimp à la Sardi. For a main course, everybody seems to love the cannelloni au gratin, large crêpes stuffed with meats and cheese in a spicy tomato sauce. Supreme of chicken, served with asparagus tips and duchesse potatoes, is also good, and there's a crispy spinach-and-bacon salad. We love the frozen cake with zabaglione sauce for dessert. Price range is wide, with dinner entrees from $6 to $20. Lunch, less expensive, features "nine special dishes at a special price." You'll have fun here anytime, but if you can, try to come after the opening night of a Broadway play. Then it's traditional for the star of the show to make a grand entrance—to cheers if the show is a hit, to polite applause if it's a bomb. Broadway openings or not, Sardi's keeps serving from 11:30 a.m. to 2 a.m. (the bar stays open later), every day. A special late-dinner menu goes into effect at 9 p.m.

There's a gracious, old-world feeling about dining at the **Hotel Algonquin,** 59 West 44th Street (tel. 687-4400). Located just a few steps away from the Broadway theaters, the Algonquin has long been host to the great names of the English and European theater who couldn't imagine staying anywhere else when they have an engagement in New York; dining with them here, you have the feeling of being in a very special English club, where the food is always excellent, the service impeccable, and the mood warm and mellow. Good conversation comes naturally in such a setting, which is perhaps why the celebrated "Round Table Luncheons" were held here in the 1920s by Dorothy Parker and Robert Benchley and Alexander Woolcott, and why current-day celebrities are always being interviewed here by the newspapers and magazines (wasn't that Mike Nichols you just passed on your way into the dining room?). But good food also comes naturally here, like everybody's favorite, the roast prime ribs of beef au jus with Yorkshire pudding, $12.95. Also recommended: poached rainbow brook trout stuffed with shrimp mousse and hollandaise sauce, $8.75; and the curried shrimps with rice and chutney, $9.95. You can have a cocktail (or afternoon tea) at a cozy sofa in the lobby, take lunch or dinner in the Rose Room, or lunch and pretheater dinner (starting at 5:30 p.m.) in the Oak Room. The marvelous after-theater buffet is held in the cozy Victorian lobby. We can't think of a nicer way to end an evening than supping on, say, chicken salad with kumquats, or Welsh rarebit, or just on a fine assortment of cheese and fresh fruit. And the dessert buffet is irresistible: who could withstand the temptation of the Vicar's Folly (lemon mousse with a cherry sauce, laced with gin) or the pot of bittersweet chocolate au rum—not to mention the Irish coffee?

The Algonquin serves lunch every day from 12 to 3; dinner, Monday through Saturday, from 5:30 to 9:30; and after-theater supper, Monday through Saturday, beginning at 10. An important note to motorists: Parking is free for dinner guests, even if you come for pretheater dinner at 5:30 and don't pick up your car until 12:30 a.m. Parking is also free for Saturday luncheon guests.

New York's most celebrated artistic "salon" is the venerable **Russian Tea Room,** located "slightly to the left of Carnegie Hall," at 150 West 57th Street (tel. CO 5-0947), and as famous for its loyal following of musicians, dancers, and performers as it is for its borscht, caviar, and blinis. It's an incredibly warm and cozy place, always heady with excitement (could that have been Bernstein—or Nureyev—over in the corner?) and good talk and the aroma of those marvelous Russian favorites. Here's your chance to feast on steaming bowls of borscht (perfect on a cold New York winter day), delicate blinchiki (crêpes stuffed with cottage cheese and preserves and topped with sour cream), rich beef Stroganoff, shashlik Caucasian (marinated leg of lamb, skewered and broiled with vegetables), or the unusual pelmeny Siberian (dumplings of chopped beef and veal, floating in consommé with dill, mustard sauce, and sour cream) to mention but a few. Desserts are special, and we often come here just for some hot tea, served steaming in a glass, and some kissel (cranberry puree) or kasha à la Gurieff (hot farina with fruit sauce), or halvah. Entrees are priced from $6.25 to $14.75 on the à la carte menu. Lunch is usually served from 11:30 a.m. to 4, dinner from 5 to 9, and after-theater supper from 9:30 to 12:30 a.m. On Sunday, it's dinner only (à la carte or table d'hote), from noon to 1 a.m. It's fun to arrive at the Russian Tea Room about 6 in the evening to see the people who make this place so special; or come after the performance and join them as they reminisce about the high notes or the grand jetés over a glass of vodka or a bowl of borscht.

French Treat

One of New York's oldest French bistros and still one of its most deservedly popular, **Pierre au Tunnel** charms everyone who passes through its narrow doorway at 306 West 48th Street (tel. 582-2166). So do Jacqueline and Jean-Claude Lincey, the daughter and son-in-law of Pierre and Jane Pujol, the original owners, who now run this family business. White napery, good wine, courteous waiters, and flowers on the table set a convivial mood. Everything is à la carte. You could begin with a plate of hors d'oeuvres variés, proceed to a hot onion soup or a cold vichysoisse, then on to classics such as scampi Escoffier, $10.75 or les mignonettes de boeuf bordelaise, $11. If it's Friday, don't miss the bouillabaisse à la Marseillaise, $11.50. Our favorite dessert here is the mousse au chocolate, $1. Lunchtime prices are quite reasonable, from $5 to $7 for dishes like calf's liver sauté, tête de veau vinaigrette or broiled lamb chops.

Pierre au Tunnel serves lunch from 12 to 3, Mondays to

Saturdays, dinner from 5:30 to 11:30 regularly, from 4:30 Wednesdays and Saturdays. Closed Sundays.

Hearty Eating

A favorite gathering spot for the television crowd (it's right near CBS), **The Slate Steak House,** 852 Tenth Avenue at 56th Street (tel. 581-6340) is a discovery: try it when you're near the Coliseum, Lincoln Center, or the 57th Street area. A convivial crowd gathers at the big bar downstairs, and upstairs, against a paneled wood background, the mood is mellow, the service friendly, and the food hearty. The specialty here is carefully aged prime beef, served up in a perfect prime ribs of beef, $12.95; a beautifully done sirloin, $14.95, or junior sirloin, $9.95. You can feast on a whole Maine lobster for $16.95, or on veal parmigiana, shrimp scampi or fresh fish of the day for much less. The homemade appetizers are too good to miss, especially the scampi in a delicate garlic sauce, the chopped liver, smoked trout, and quiche—there's a different one every day. Along with your entree comes a bountiful fresh salad with lots of tomatoes and onions and a very good house or Roquefort dressing, plus a choice of vegetables or crispy homemade cottage-fried potatoes. Save some room, too, for dessert, especially the outstanding homemade cheesecake or chocolate pudding pie. Lunch features moderately priced specials every day, in the $3.95 to $5.25 range —perhaps omelets, goulash, or meat loaf.

The Slate serves lunch from 12 to 4:30, dinner and supper from 5 to midnight, every day but Sunday.

Steak, Japanese Style

Like to dine in a Japanese steak house, just the way you would in Tokyo? You need go no further than to one of the handsome **Benihana of Tokyo** restaurants; you'll find them, on the West Side, at 47 West 56th Street (tel. 581-0930), and at 15 West 44th Street (tel. 682-7120, where the official name is Benihana Palace). There's an East Side Benihana at 120 East 56th Street (tel. 593-1627). These fabulous Tokyo-based restaurants feature the original teppanyaki-hibachi-style cooking, meaning that everything you eat is cooked at your table, which also happens to be the stove. You and your party will sit on three sides of the table, and your own Japanese chef will take command of the fourth side. While you're having say, a sake Martini or perhaps a Tokyo Bloody Mary, he'll begin working on the hibachi shrimp, and then, while you're having your onion soup and salad (all included in the price of the complete meal), he'll be slicing and sizzling the mushrooms, onions, bean sprouts, and squash that go along with the hibachi chicken, $7.50; the sukiyaki steak, $9.25; the hibachi steak $10.25; or the filet mignon, $10.25. Delicious! Rice and green tea come along with the meal. The luncheon menu offers the same dishes à la carte, from $3.95 to $5.95, as well as a complete lunch of hibachi steak, Japanese vegetables, and a salad bowl for $5.95. Whenever you come, you'll enjoy the gracious setting, the folk crafts, and the remarkable skill of the chefs! All the Benihanas have bars, but Benihana Palace offers free hors d'oeuvres with your predinner drinks. All the Benihanas serve lunch (from 12 to 2:30) and dinner (from 5:30 to 1) daily; Sundays, it's dinner only.

Italian

A huge crowd of very substantial New Yorkers and suburbanites is unswervingly loyal to **Patsy's**, 235 West 56th Street (tel. CI 7-3491), and they would rather fight than switch to any other Italian restaurant in town. They don't care about what restaurant is "in" or "out" at any particular moment: they simply know that, for almost 40 years now, Patsy's has been dishing out delicious, lusty Italian fare, in huge portions and in a warm family atmosphere (on weekends, people come here with the kids and the mother-in-law and the visiting relatives and . . .). The setting is simple, neat and well-lit: mirrored walls give the narrow room a feeling of spaciousness, and white tablecloths and white-jacketed waiters compliment the blue floors and golden appointments. The quality of the cooking should please the most demanding of Neapolitan gourmets. Everything is à la carte, and not inexpensive. We particularly like the seafood dishes: tender squids in a tomato-based cassuola, $6.25, and mussels à la marinara, $4.90, are our favorites here, but we also like the shrimp marinara, $6.95, and the cassuola di pesce, $7.95. And then there are all those delicious spaghetti, chicken, and veal dishes, and the daily specials. Don't miss one of Patsy's pastries for dessert. Patsy's serves from noon until 10:45, Tuesday through Thursday and on Sunday; from noon until 11:45, Friday and Saturday. Closed Monday.

The time to come to **Mamma Leone's**, 239 West 48th Street (tel. JU 6-5151), is when you are truly hungry. Mama's claim to fame rests now, as it has since 1906, on her old-fashioned habit of feeding massive portions to insatiable appetites. Although Mama's complete dinner is now $10.95, a bit more than it was back then, it is still one of the best buys in town . . . considering. As soon as you are seated (and unless you make a reservation that will take some time), you are brought a big hunk of cheese and a loaf of Italian bread, plus tomatoes, celery, and peppers—and that's before you start to order! Then comes the huge antipasto, followed by a steaming plate of pasta (the homemade lasagna is our favorite), followed by main dishes like chicken cacciatora or veal cutlet Parmigiana or a whole roast chicken or filet of sole, followed by crunchy, deep-fried and sugar-dipped bugie, followed by homemade ice cream or rum cake, followed by coffee, followed by the vow not to eat again for at least three days. There are also steak and lobster dinners at slightly higher prices, and an à la carte supper menu from 9:30 on. Kids can have a special dinner for $5.50. Lunch is fun, too, for it's then that you are challenged to eat all you can of the "heroic" Buffet Italiano luncheon, $4.95. The atmosphere at Mamma's, like the menu, is overgenerous: there are numerous rooms, filled with fountains and statuary and paintings and theater folk and celebrities and hungry New Yorkers and starving tourists and. . . . Mamma Leone's serves lunch from 11:30 to 2:30, Monday through Friday; dinner, from 3:30 to 11 daily; from 2 to 10, Sunday.

Jewish-Roumanian

Time was when you had to journey all the way down to the Lower East Side to get classic Jewish Roumanian food. But all that has changed, now that the venerable **Parkway Restaurant,** which has drawn the crowds for over half-a-century to Christie and Delancey Streets, moved uptown to 345 West 46th Street (tel. 765-0578), in the heart of the theater district. And that's great news for anyone who fondly remembers—or has never experienced—this unique cuisine. Karl and Susan Oberwager, both Europeans, are the most gracious of old-world hosts, and they've made their restaurant a delight, sparkling white tablecloths, photomurals of old-time New York Jewish life on the wall, courteous service, and a true atmosphere of old-time hospitality and hearty Jewish (but not kosher) food.

The big problem here is deciding *what* to eat: there are so many delicious specialties. It's most fun to come with a few people and sample many different dishes. As soon as you sit

Indian Adventures

New York's Indian restaurants, once tiny holes-in-the-walls catering to the Indian colony and adventurous young people, have lately gone glamorous; eating Indian is definitely "in" these days. The showpiece of them all is **Raga,** 57 West 48th Street (tel. 757-3450), a branch of India's Taj hotel chain. This midtown palace that occupies the site of the old Forum of the Twelve Caesars, decorated in the most elegant Indian fashion yet to hit New York, boasts thick, richly colored striped carpeting, lush silk banquettes, and antique Indian musical instruments on the walls. Service is solicitous and selections are above the ordinary run of Indian fare, featuring seldom-seen choices like an appetizer of highly spiced oysters, $5.50. Dinner entrees range from about $6 to $12. Live music accompanies dinner.

Nirvana, 30 Central Park South (tel. 752-0270) is an Indian penthouse close to heaven, festooned with reams and reams of colorful print fabric, forming a dramatic tented ceiling. Broad windows offer treetop views of Central Park. In the evening, Nirvana is one of the city's most romantic hideaways. Food is consistently good and often innovative, featuring excellent lamb curry ($8.95 for a complete dinner) and a rare fish called pomfret, $7.95. A la carte entrees at dinner range from about $5 to $10, complete dinners from $7.75 to $12.95.

Gaylord, 50 East 58th Street (tel. 759-1710), enjoys a superb reputation for very good Indian food and is responsible for introducing tandoori (clay oven) cooking to New York. Through glass walls you can view the expert tandoori cook at work, producing moist, succulent clay-baked chicken and other meats. If you've never sampled this style of Indian cooking, try the tandoor combination of meats and shrimp at $9.50. A la carte dinner entrees are about $4 to $9.

down, bowls of grated radish, chopped onion, chicken-shmaltz and greeven, sour pickles and broiled peppers are brought to your table, along with a basket of challah, compliments of the house. While you're nibbling (or, more likely, devouring), and sipping a glass of seltzer water (be sure to order a bottle), you have time to decide among such appetizers as stuffed cabbage, eggplant Roumanian style, gevetch (baked mixed vegetables), or even pitcha (frozen calf's feet). Appetizers range from about $1.75 to $2.50. Or you might start with matzoh ball or kreplach soup. Specialties of the house are the Roumanian broilings, like Mushk steak (the eye of the rib), $11.75; the highly garlicky karnatzlach (chopped meat sausages), $7.25; and broiled chicken livers with unborn (yes!) eggs, $7.25. Or you might have roast Long Island duckling, chicken fricassee, boiled beef flanken—or more lightly, fresh fish of the day. All entrees are accompanied by tasty kasha varnishkes and fresh vegetables.

Desserts? Again, the problem is a wealth of riches. You might settle for warm apple strudel (home-baked, of course), or tender ruggelach, or poppyseed cookies, washed down with some hot tea or coffee served old-world style, in a glass. Wine and liquor is available. Particularly if you have children with you, don't miss treating everybody to an authentic egg cream. It's not on the menu, but just ask, and they'll bring out a bottle of seltzer, milk and chocolate syrup, for you to mix and spritz on your own.

Parkway Restaurant is open every day, serving lunch from 11 to 3 (similar dishes, plus sandwiches, slightly lower-priced); dinner from 4 to 12 Monday to Saturday, Sunday from 1, Wednesday, Friday, and Saturday nights, there's an Israeli singer and a $1 music charge.

EAST SIDE: Moving crosstown to the East Side, there is an equally impressive selection of eateries, but of a slightly different nature and ambience.

Two Great Bistros

Le Veau d'Or, 129 East 60th Street (tel. TE 8-8133), has long been hailed as one of New York's best French bistros. Its robust, hearty, bourgeois fare is responsible for drawing what seem to be unmanageable crowds night in, night out. And no wonder: food and service are impeccable, and you can have a complete meal, from pâté to fromage, for the price of the entree, averaging $11 to $13. Rarely have we been disappointed in any of the house specials—and that includes the filet of sole almandine, $11.50; the veal kidneys with mustard sauce, $13.30; the sauteed veal à l'Indienne, $12.30; and the spring chicken in casserole "Grand-'Mère," $12.30. You may begin with appetizers like artichoke vinaigrette or boeuf en gelée, have onion soup or cold vichysoisse, and end with lovely desserts like crème caramel or pêche melba. This is not the place for a quiet, hand-holding dinner—it's too crowded and tends to get noisy. For more relaxation, come at lunchtime, when it's not quite as frantic, and when the prices are much lower: complete lunches are mostly in the $8 to $9.30 category.

Le Veau d'Or is open Monday through Saturday, serving lunch from 12 to 2:30; dinner, from 6 to 10, closed Sunday.

Even a brief visit to Provence does wonders for the palate and spirit, but a trip to **La Colombe d'Or,** 134 East 26th Street (tel. 689-0666) is the next best thing. The great majority of New York's French restaurants are Lyonnaise, but this one is strictly Provencal, from the traditional print fabric used for chairs, banquettes, and waitresses' aprons to the ratatouille and soupe de poisson on the menu. The foods of southern France are marked by an imaginative use of garlic and tomatoes, and, of course, seafood is a highlight. Provence is the home of bouillabaisse, and La Colombe d'Or's version, $11.50, does not disappoint. You might start a Provencal meal here with one of the homemade pâtés, $2.75; which range from a coarse country variety to a creamy pork rillettes; for a lighter beginning, try spinach dressed with olive oil, sesame, and garlic, $1.85. Soups are so hearty and filling that only the biggest eaters should start with one of these. Main courses include a hearty winter cassoulet, a robust white bean stew with sausages and a variety of meats, $8.75. Batter-dipped strips of extra-crisp fried fish, $9.25, are served with zesty aioli (garlic mayonnaise). Coq au vin, a rich Provencal beef stew, or sirloin of lamb with a delicate herbed sauce serve meat lovers nicely. A tempting dessert cart offers a luscious array of homemade pastries.

La Colombe d'Or provides a livelier, more aggressive fare and a sunnier ambience than most French restaurants. Open for lunch weekdays from 12 to 2:15 with entrees from about $5 to $9 and for dinner Mondays through Saturdays (closed Sundays) with entrees from about $6 to $10.

European Charm

Step into **Monk's Court,** 244 East 51st Street (tel. 935-9208), and you have in effect, left the city for a charming European inn. You're seated in a cozy nook or corner of the dark, candlelit room and, from your table, you can look up to the 30-foot-high brick walls, the wooden chests and antiques, the three huge wine barrels, a tiny balcony, and the figure of a monk. It's especially nice in winter, when the two fireplaces are working. Monk's Court specializes in European entrees, like quiche Lorraine, Welsh rarebit, duckling à l'orange flambée, veal Cordon Bleu, and Dover sole Meuniere, averaging about $6.75 to $10. Lunch prices are about $1.25 less. Summer features are huge natural salads like alfalfa salad homestyle or spinach salad mimosa, plus cold fruit soups. Everything is à la carte, but apples and cheese come along with the French bread, served as soon as one sits down. The onion soup is done the way it used to be at Les Halles, and the desserts are special treats, like the strawberry cheesecake with Kirsch or the fruit sherbet sprinkled with champagne, each $1.75. Monk's Court is a good spot to remember after the theater, since it's open from noon to midnight, *tous les jours.* There's a special "Lincoln Center Supper" every day after 10 p.m., and $3.95 brunches Saturdays and Sundays 12 to 4.

Pub Scene

Charlie Brown's, in the Pan Am Building at East 45th Street (tel. MO 1-2520), is another of the English pubs so popular on the New York restaurant scene. Its big time is lunchtime, when the advertising and publishing execs congregate to meet and greet and eat and drink. Come in the evening if you want more peaceful surroundings in which to enjoy the delicious dishes, all à la carte. The roast ribs of beef with Yorkshire pudding, $11.95, is outstanding; so is the fried shrimp in ale batter with pungent orange sauce, $8.25. Other good meat and fish entrees, as well as Charlie Brown's terrific grills and skillet steaks (the latter smothered with onions or in red wine), are priced at $13.75. Desserts carry out the English mood: have your choice of English sherry trifle or Oxford chocolate cake, among others. Luncheon entrees include great big beef sandwiches, hearty omelets, curries, and daily specials like shepherd's pie or roast loin of pork, plus the steaks and grills, all from about $4.75 to $9.50. You can "talk it over at Charlie Brown's" anytime between 11:30 to 3:30 for lunch, from 5:30 to 10 for dinner, Mondays through Saturdays.

Chinese Adventure

Except for old China hands, few westerners—certainly few New Yorkers—had ever sampled the glories of the celebrated cuisine of China's Hunan province. But all that changed when Hunan opened its doors a few years back at 845 Second Avenue at 46th Street (tel. MU 7-7471). The gourmets have flipped for this one, and rightly so, since the food is really unusual, the setting is both comfortable and elegant, the service excellent, and

Dining at the City

Food can make even cold glass and steel lovable, as the new **Citicorp Center** at Lexington Avenue at 53rd Street demonstrates. A multi-level international bazaar of restaurants and retail food shops called The Market surrounds a stunning sky-lit atrium, well-stocked with tables and chairs where you may eat (bring your own or buy some light food and carry it to the tables), often watch free entertainment, lounge, or just plain people-watch.

Should you want to dine indoors, a bevy of international restaurants, awaits you.

Hungaria (tel. 755-6088), where famed food consultant George Lang has created a Hungarian inn, with gypsy violinists serenading nightly. Whose focal point is a sausage "tree" displaying the varied selection of European sausages served cold or skillet-fried. The menu lists not only goulash, $3.95 at lunch, but several exotic choices, like pork scallopine served on a fresh-baked garlic scone, $10.75 at dinner. Dinner entrees go from $8 to $14. For a budget luncheon choice: a platter of the previous day's leftovers, called a student's meal, at $4.75. You can even ask for a free plate of bones to chew on, old country style. Of course there are Hungarian pastries galore, $2.25. Tables are close together here and service can be erratic, but the food wins out.

Avgerinos (tel. 688-8828) is a dazzler of a Greek taverna (white stucco walls, artifacts everywhere, tile floors) which, with its haunting Greek music and its delectable food, will convince you you're back in Athens. An amazing open kitchen dishes out the lightest of spinach pies and dolmades (stuffed grape leaves), a classic moussaka ($5.25 at dinner, $3.25 at lunch), wonderful souvlakis, and other traditional favorites. Greek wines, luscious breads, modest prices, and cordial service make a meal here a special treat. Don't miss the baklava for dessert!

Slotnick Daughters (tel. 935-1744) is a winner in the pastry department. There are just a few tables in the back of this fragrant coffee emporium, but they are *the* place in The Market for a coffee and something luscious like chocolate mousse cake, chocolate zucchini cake, mocha cheesecake, or zucchini crumb layer cake. There are also a few imaginative sandwiches and salads on the small menu.

Richoux of London (tel. 753-7721) is the first American branch of the 24-hour British chain of coffeeshops with class. Here you can get an English brunch of eggs, bacon, grilled tomato and fried bread at $5.50, or a selection of rarebits at $4, any hour of the day or night, served by Edwardian-costumed waitresses amid a sedate, very English atmosphere.

Auberge Suisse (tel. 421-1420) is a sleekly decorated, intimately lit Swiss restaurant serving, in addition to cheese fondue, at $16 for two, specialties from all of Switzerland's diverse regions. Entrees average about $10.

Les Tournebroches (tel. 935-6029) is a tiny pink gem of a restaurant run by one of the city's master French chefs, Charles Chevillot. From any table in the house one can view the huge rotisserie (the turning spits or *tournebroches*), custom-made in France, on which such delicacies as veal shanks, carre d'agneau and various brochettes —of seafood, grilled sausages, kidneys, etc.—are done to just the right turn. Entrees range from $7.50 (for brochettes of kidney) and $8 (for fish of the day) to $13 for filet mignon. Don't miss the patisseries—tarts made of the freshest raspberries, oranges, or strawberries, or le dessert du jour—perhaps creme caramel or a lovely chocolate mousse.

Nyborg and Nelson (tel. 223-0700) is a new version of a famous New York gourmet shop. Knowledgeable New Yorkers have long been shopping at N. & N. for the finest Scandinavian herrings, salads and pâtés. The restaurant serves open-face sandwiches from $2.50 to $3.50, gravlax (smoked salmon with mustard-dill sauce) at $4.95, and good homemade soups.

Alfredo's (tel. 371-3367), a U.S. branch of Rome's most famous restaurant, is an up-to-the-minute Italian-modern place, decorated with natural woods and bright colors. Their most renowned dish, of course, is fettucine Alfredo, $7.95, rich with cream and cheese—and calories. There's a full menu of pastas, $3.95 at lunch, your best choice, and other Italian dishes, as well.

Healthworks (tel. 838-6221) is another outlet of New York's extremely popular self-service salad restaurant chain that's become a mecca for dieters and health food fans. Salads are between $3.50 and $4.50.

Clam and Oyster Bar (tel. 838-1133), a quick-service facility, is dedicated to all forms of fresh seafood, like raw clams at 35¢ each or oyster stew at $2.95, served with no frills.

the prices are not high. But we must issue a warning: the food of Hunan is spicy and hot (even more so than in Szechuan cooking), so, unless you thrive on this sort of thing, advise the waiter beforehand, and he'll stay the cook's hand, at your request. For those who crave something fiery, General Gau's duckling, $7.75, is prepared with a red-hot sauce: for more cowardly palates, there's Neptune's Platter, $9.75, a delicious array of seafood and Chinese vegetables. Vegetarians can find a satisfying Buddha's Delight at $5.50 here, and dessert lovers will find the stuffed honey crisp bananas a welcome change from the usual fortune-cookie-and-pineapple Chinese desserts. Lunch is served from 11:45 to 3; dinner, from 3 to 11:30 on weekdays. On weekends, it's dinner only, from noon to 1 a.m.

Swiss Surprise

It's a little bit of the Swiss Alps transplanted to New York. **Chalet Suisse,** 6 East 48th Street (tel. 355-0855), has white stucco walls, wooden beams, waitresses wearing native costumes, and beautiful and authentic Swiss food—the makings of a perfect evening. You can choose from either the à la carte menu or the prix-fixe dinner at $16.25. At a recent dinner, both the cheese-and-onion pie and the cervelat salad (smoked pork and beef sausages) were very good. So were the breaded veal cutlet à la Holstein and the escargots bourguignonne among the entrees, and the Swiss apple tart for dessert. For neuchâteloise (cheese) fondue, $7.25, order from the à la carte menu. And for dessert, what else but the classic chocolate fondue! It's $6 for two, and a delight. The lunch menu is completely à la carte, and prices range from $7 to $14.50 for steak. Open Mondays to Fridays; lunch, from noon to 2:30; dinner, from 5 to 9:30. Closed Saturday and Sunday.

Two Japanese Favorites

The atmosphere is ah-so-harmonious over at **Nippon,** 145 East 52nd Street (tel. 355-9020), one of the first and finest of New York's Japanese restaurants, where everything—from sculptures to the indoor garden to the wood used in the booths to the kimonos worn by the waitresses—is authentic, done in classical Japanese manner. So, too, is the food, which includes some rare Japanese dishes as well as those most appealing to American tastes. For a complete dinner, try the tempura (deep-fried fish and vegetables), $9.80; or the teriyaki (steak marinated in a sweet Japanese sauce), $11.80; or beef or chicken sukiyaki, $10.30. All these dishes come served with miso soup or consomme, rice, pickled vegetables, various side dishes, green tea, and desserts. A la carte entrees include shabu shabu (prime ribs and fresh vegetables); hama nabe clam casserole, and a yosenabe seafood casserole. It's fun to order a jug of warm sake, $2.20, to go with your meal. Lunch is also pleasant, and prices are a bit lower. If you wish to sit western style, i.e., on a chair—be sure to make a reservation at both lunch and dinner. Otherwise, your choices will be floor seats in one of the numerous tatami rooms off the main western-style room, or at the tempura bar up front where you can get a delicious tempura—and only tempura—meal.

The Nippon serves lunch from noon to 2:30, Monday to Friday; dinner, from 5:30 to 10, Mondays to Thursdays, until 10:30 Fridays and Saturdays; closed Sunday.

There's a serene Oriental mood about **Rock Garden of Tokyo,** 34 West 56th Street (tel. 245-7936), that we find altogether refreshing in the midst of busy New York. A Japanese rock garden in the foyer and outside the building, handsome ceramics, rice paper screens and lanterns, plus the kimono-clad waitresses put one in the mood for a new kind of experience. Rock Garden is a Japanese steak house, and when you dine here, your meal is cooked right at your table on a hibachi grill. Entrees on the all à la carte menu average $6.50 to $9.50 for the likes of yakinuki liver or salmon teriyaki, but can go as high as $12.50, for the live lobster. At lunch, the prices go from $4.50 to $7.25 for entrees served with salad, rice, and tea. How about a Tokyo Bloody Mary, some Japanese plum wine, or a glass of warm sake with your meal? Rock Garden of Tokyo serves lunch from noon to 2:30, Monday through Saturday; dinner, from 5:30 until about 10:30 or 11, every day.

Italian Elegance

Exceedingly smart and chic, **San Stefano,** 322 East 14th Street (tel. 473-5953), serves stylish cuisine to equal its stunning decor. Attractive orange print fabric graces tables and banquettes, nicely set off by natural brick walls and fireplaces and sheets of shining copper that cover two walls to striking effect. The northern Italian fare is consistently fine and service is always flawless.

You might start with an imaginative hot antipasto that contains enormous shrimp and very good mozzarella in carrozo (a sort of deep-fried mozzarella sandwich) in addition to the usual eggplant, clams and mushrooms, $4. Ordering a Caesar salad, $5 for two, guarantees an elaborate production, but it's serious business, not just showmanship, and the result is a fresh, crisp salad with the perfect note of pungency. Pastas are not to be missed; a good idea is to share one order as a first course. Try the excellent canneloni or manicotti in rich tomato sauces, $5.25;

the more delicate linguini in clam sauce, or a superb tagliatelle verde, $6.50. Main courses include a hearty stuffed veal chop Valdestan at $9.95; milk-white veal Francese; elegant roast capon or plain, robust veal and peppers. Light potato croquettes accompany most entrees, which range from about $5 to $10 à la carte. For dessert, there's an exquisite, although most un-Italian, sinfully rich chocolate cake, $2.75.

Graceful atmosphere, fine food, and attentive service combine to make San Stefano the rival of any of uptown's renowned Italian eateries. Open for dinner only, from 5:30 to 11, Sundays 3 to 9. Closed Mondays.

GREENWICH VILLAGE: Here, again, another switch in ambience. With 14th Street as the very obvious boundary, a step into the Village will reveal a combination of past, present, and future, aptly depicted in the vast array of restaurants.

One of the favorite Village steakhouses is an unpretentious and deservedly popular spot called **Peter's Back Yard,** 64 West 10th Street (tel. 473-2400). In the center of the main dining area is an enormous charcoal pit which accounts for most of the decor, and a dining balcony rings the main room. (The one-time backyard has been enclosed, but the name still remains.) Steaks and beef dishes are, as expected, the main attraction; all beef is prime and properly aged. The filet mignon, at $13.95, with a very good Bordelaise sauce, is one of the most tender cuts of beef we've ever had. And how they manage to cook the sirloin so that it is blood-red in the middle, yet very warm and moist, we will never figure out: no matter, it's terrific, also $13.95. This is one place where we *do* recommend you have the dessert; the cream cheesecake, $2, is something special. An endless cup of coffee is 75¢. Open for dinner Mondays to Fridays from 4:30 to 11; Saturday, to 12. Open (hurrah!) Sundays and holidays from 2:30 to 11.

Spanish

To many aficionados, there is no better place for Spanish food in all New York than **El Faro,** an out-of-the-way restaurant at 823 Greenwich Street (corner of Horatio Street) in the Village (tel. WA 9-8210), but it's worth the effort to get to. For years, this restaurant has been packed with its fans, so make a reservation before you go, and then be prepared to wait. All entrees are à la carte, all served with Spanish rice or Spanish potatoes and salad, and the most sensational are the seafood dishes: the paella à la Valenciana, with lobster, of course, $9.75, but the crab meat with green sauce, $10, and the shrimp à la diablo, $6.75, are also memorable. Have a pitcher of sangria, or some imported Spanish wine, to go with your meal. At lunch, prices are cheaper, from $4 to $7. The salad dressing is so good that you'll probably want to take home a bottle. El Faro is thoroughly unpretentious, with no attempt at decor to relieve the formica-table-and-bare-walls look, save for a few murals, but this, interestingly, is an atmosphere itself. At any rate, it's the food and not the ambience that count here. (There's a much more elegant El Faro, El Faro 72, uptown at 40 West 72nd Street, open for dinner only; tel. EN 2-2050. Menu and prices are similar to downtown). Lunch is served from 11 to 3, every day but Sunday; dinner, from 3 to midnight, Friday and Saturday to 1 a.m.

A Meal in the Middle East

If you're a lover of Armenian food (and if you're not yet, you should be), you'll find **The Dardanelles**, at 86 University Place (between 11th and 12th Streets—tel. CH 2-8990), a love of a place. This nicely decorated little restaurant has comfortably spaced tables so that you can enjoy your exotic fare in privacy. The menu is both à la carte and table d'hôte, and every dish is completely explained. For your main course on the dinner, you might choose the patlijan karni yarik, baked stuffed eggplant with chopped lamb, onions, tomatoes, $9.50; the stuffed vine leaves, yaprak dolma, also $9.50; or go with the old standbys—shish kebab at $10.50; moussaka, $9.50. A tasty shrimp casserole with feta cheese is $6.95 and every night there are special fresh

Central Park

fish dishes. The appetizers are adventures all to themselves: we like both the spicy midia dolma, mussels stuffed with rice, pine nuts, and onions; and the boerek, layers of thin dough filled with cheese, egg, and parsley. And Armenian yogurt soup is unusual and good. Desserts in Middle Eastern restaurants are definitely not for the weight-conscious, but you will be excused, this once, if you order the bourma, chopped nuts rolled in thin dough and served with a honey syrup, or the more usual baklava. You can also order dinner à la carte, with prices starting at $5.50 and going up to $8.50, for filet mignon shish kebab. Lunch is à la carte only, entrees from $3.45 to $7. Open for lunch, Monday to Friday from noon to 2:30; for dinner, from 4 to 10; Saturday, 4 to 11; Sunday, 4 to 9. Closed summer Sundays.

WATERSIDE DINING: To dine like a real New York insider and maybe spot a few "Beautiful People," to boot, travel to the tip of exotic Brooklyn (yes, Brooklyn), and the new **River Cafe**, 1 Water Street (tel. 522-5200). Since its summer 1977 opening, this swank waterside spot has been *the* see-and-be-seen restaurant. Built on a barge underneath the Brooklyn Bridge (you approach it through a service building on land and then up a gangplank to the restaurant itself), it commands a truly spectacular view of lower Manhattan and New York Harbor. Perfect for a romantic rendezvous at night, it has a special daytime appeal, too, as you watch the river busy with waterborne traffic. Beautifully appointed in pale tones, with each table sporting a tiny shaded lamp evocative of a '30s supperclub, the River Cafe is movie-star glamorous. But the food is not to be ignored. The continental menu offers a variety of dishes, from calf's liver at $8.25 to veal chops at $12.50, with fresh fish offerings that vary with market availability: filet of sole is $8.75. Pastas with light homemade sauces are a specialty here; these are $6 to $7 for a full order, $3.25 to $3.75 for a half-order. At lunch, lighter fare includes omelets at $4.50 or the fish du jour at $8.25. And Sunday brunch, 11:30 to 3, offers a wide range of choices, from scrambled eggs at $4.50 to elegant Beluga caviar with buckwheat blinis at $17.50.

Lunch is served daily from 11:30 to 2:30, and dinner from 6 to 11. You can also just drop by for a drink at the Cafe Room or at the bar of the dining room, to enjoy the same view and piano music as the diners do.

Modest: Meals Averaging $10 and Under

WEST SIDE: It's easy here—easy on the purse, easy on the palate. And minimal funds will not limit what you eat, only where you eat it!

The Neighborhood Crowd

There's a very relaxed feeling at **Teacher's,** Broadway at 80th Street (tel. 787-3500), a hangout for many of the city's artists, writers, and other members of the intelligentsia who live on the West Side. Since it's just about 15 blocks (a short bus ride) from Lincoln Center, it makes sense to enjoy a delicious, reasonably priced meal here before or after a Lincoln Center event. Walk past the big mahogany bar up front and you'll find a dining room with natural-wood walls, butcher-block tables and booths, and a feeling that manages to be both intimate—so you can really sit and talk—and yet lively. The paintings and photographs on the walls were all done either by customers or by the aspiring artists and performers who wait on table with good cheer and courteous attention. Teacher's specialties are the work of its artistic Thai cook, Sam for short, who turns out a lightly spiced chicken gai yaang, marinated and broiled in a special sauce and served with a cucumber salad, $4.95; a hotter Thai beef salad, $3.95; and a flavorful pork sate Indonesian, served on a skewer with a peanut-butter sauce, $4.95. For those whose taste runs to French food, there are five dishes on the blackboard every night, including the likes of bouillabaisse and duck à l'orange; and they always have two broiled fresh (never frozen) fish dishes every night. These are superbly done, and cost from $4.95 to $7.95. Teacher's is also known for its tasty spinach-and-bacon salad (if you find sand in it, your meal is on the house!), great appetizers like guacamole and toasted tortillas or homemade country pâté, and luscious desserts of which the praline ice-cream cake and the apple pound cake are standouts. Lunch is a bargain, from $2.15 to $4.75. Come on Sunday between 11 and 4 and indulge in one of the liveliest brunches in town—eggs Benedict, eggs rancheros, caviar and sour cream, and the like, from $3.95 to $5.60, with a cocktail thrown in for good measure.

After your meal, saunter next door to Zabar's, the city's prime appetizing emporium (open practically all the time), and try to resist the heady aromas of fresh breads and cheeses and spices and coffees and smoked fish and caviar and lox and bagels—and maybe come home with some gourmet kitchen equipment at the best prices in town.

Mexican

Since it's right in the heart of the theater district, **El Tenampa,** 304 West 46th Street (tel. 586-9039) has become somewhat of a hangout for theater folk: one well-known Broadway star frequently eats in the kitchen here. It's fun, too, if you're on your way to the theater, and even more fun after the theater crowd clears out and you can spend a whole evening pretending you're in Mexico. This cozy little Colonial-style place, cheerfully decorated, is a husband-and-wife operation, with the friendly Marco Holderbaum, an auto-racer by passion and restaurateur by profession, presiding out front, while Olivia Holderbaum cooks up marvelous traditional dishes in back. Go with all sorts of combination plates at $5, or try some of the specialties like pollo mole poblano (chicken with Mexican chocolate sauce) or chiles nogada estilo Pueblo (peppers stuffed with cheese and covered with cream and nut sauce), $6.25. Be sure to tell Marco whether you want your food mildly seasoned, moderately seasoned, or positively mouth-burning; he'll oblige. We can't resist the spicy appetizers like nachos and quesadillas, a good glass of wine or beer to cool it all off, and some refreshing fried bananas with honey for the finale. Lunch, priced even more modestly, is served weekdays only, 12 to 3; dinner, Monday to Saturday from 5 to 11:30. Closed Sundays.

Don't be put off by the very plain appearance of **Xochitl,** 148 West 46th Street (tel. PL 7-1325). Those who know their Mexican food know that Xochitl is one of the very best Mexican kitchens in town. And since very little seems to have been done to glamorize this place in the almost 40 years it's been here, the prices have managed to stay very low indeed. All the Mexican classics you've heard of—enchiladas, tacos, tostados, chicken mole, chile con carne—are here, plus some you may not have heard of, like baby cactus with eggs or chilaquiles, which are little pieces of toasted tortillas in chile sauce and cheese. Whatever you order, it will be delicious. Watch out, though, for the red sauce on the table—it's muy caliente! Dishes run from about $2 to $6, with a big combination plate going for $6. You should be able to come out of here happy and well fed for $5 or $6 or less—which is not easy in New York today. Xochitl is open every day but Sunday, from noon to 11:30.

Seafood

We sometimes wonder if New Yorkers—or at least New York seafood lovers—could continue to survive without **Paddy's Clam House**, 215 West 34th Street, (tel. CH 4-9123). Since 1898, it's been drawing huge crowds (it serves between two and four thousand people a day), it always manages to keep its prices ridiculously low, and everybody goes home happy. They must be doing something right.

Paddy's, however, is no place for romantic dawdling over your meal; ravenous seafood lovers are always waiting for a table, and the atmosphere is far from intimate. It *is* the place for delicious, absolutely fresh fish, beautifully prepared and promptly dispatched to your table. The atmosphere is noisy, friendly, and lots of fun, with no frills at all. Lunch is a bargain at Paddy's: for $3.52 you can have a fish or clam chowder appetizer, an entree of fresh fish that changes every day, french fries or boiled potato, and coffee. There's a similar dinner special every night at $5.46. Some of Paddy's other crowd-pleasing specials: broiled lobster dinner, with fish chowder or clam broth, a whole Maine lobster with french fries, dessert, and coffee, for $10.50, a bargain considering today's lobster prices; the Fried Fisherman's Delight, a plate of scallops, oysters, shrimps, clams, fish filet, and french fries, $7.75; and the broiled scampi with garlic butter, $7.25. Many kinds of pies, 85¢, are featured for dessert; beer and ale, but no liquor, are available.

Paddy's is open from 11 to 9:30, Mondays through Saturdays, and from noon to 8:30 on Sundays and holidays.

A Theater District Landmark

Since 1899, **Rosoff's**, 147 West 43rd Street (tel. 582-3200), has served the theater-going public with wholesome American-style cooking. Its handsome Victorian mood is reflected both in the Barrymore non-smoking room with its stained glass ceiling and intimate love seats and at the spacious booths. The "Eat, Eat" mood of Rosoff's begins in the cocktail lounge, where you can enjoy a lavish cocktail buffet between 5 and 8. Complete dinners are well priced: $8.50 for the house special of barbecued breast of spring lamb; $9.50 for roast breast of turkey, $10.50 for the fresh lemon sole. Also featured are lobster tails, steaks, and poultry. Appetizers are traditional and delicious; try the chopped chicken livers or gefilte fish or pickled herring, and then the chilled borscht. The main course comes with potato and vegetable, and you are urged to "indulge yourself often" at the salad and relish "Take-More Table." And as if all this weren't enough, there are desserts like the fluffy whipped cream nessel-rode pie laced with rum—a triumph of calories over common sense. A la carte and snack menus are available, as are special children's menus and free birthday or anniversary cakes. Lunch is another bargain, from a $2.75 sandwich to about $8 for a complete meal. Rosoff's serves lunch Mondays through Fridays from 11:30 to 3:30, dinner from 3:30 to 9 Mondays through Thursdays, until midnight Fridays and Saturdays; from 11:30 to 9 Sundays.

Spaghetti

An extremely popular, usually jam-packed Italian restaurant in the heart of the theater district is **Johnnie's,** a small and intimate place at 135 West 45th Street (tel. CI 5-9667 or JU 6-9192). If you have to wait for a table, you can do so comforta-bly in the friendly bar, and if you're planning to dine before the theater, we suggest you make reservations. In addition to the à la carte menu, Johnnie's offers an old-fashioned bargain dinner at $5.95, and hearty and complete it is. You begin with mine-strone, piping hot, and thick with fresh vegetables. For your main entree, you can choose between lasagne, fish of the day, spaghetti with meatballs, and eggplant parmigiana. There's rum cake, tortoni, or spumoni for dessert, and coffee, too, for the one price. Lunch at Johnnie's is another bargain: daily specials, served with soup, dessert, and beverage, cost $3.95. Lunch, from 11:30 to 3, Mondays to Fridays; dinner, from 3 to 3 a.m. daily (Sunday, noon to midnight).

Fondues and Fromage

It's a cheese-lover's idea of Paradise, and even if you don't know your Emmenthal from your Esrom, we think you'll still enjoy a visit to **La Fondue,** at 43 West 55th Street (tel. 581-0820). Owned by one of the largest cheese importers and retailers in the city, La Fondue is a brick-walled, provincial-looking French place, crowded and noisy at the busier times of the day, with small, too-close-together tables, like so many of the restaurants dispensing good food in New York. But if you come late-ish for lunch, or on a weekday for dinner, you'll really have the time and comfort for enjoying the quality food. There are three kinds of fondues—the classic Swiss cheese fondue, $4.95; the prime filet

Eating Italian Style

One of our favorite spots for dining before or after the theater, or just on an evening out—in other words, anytime—is **Trattoria,** a big, bubbly, high-spirited Italian cafe in the Pan Am Building on East 45th Street (tel. MO 1-3090). The mood is ever young, the service efficient, and the pastries and gelati (homemade ice cream) are among the best in town. (Don't miss the chocolatey, creamy Tartufo!) Complete dinners, with entrees like scampi, quiche with prosciutto, chicken Tetrazzini, and scallopine of veal are $10.50, and are served with soup, spaghetti or salad, homemade ice cream or cake, plus espresso and coffee. At lunch, there are main courses like striped bass with mussels and clams, eggplant parmigiana, and veal cutlet mozzarella, from $4.50 to $7.95. Salads, marvelous antipasto, and soups, plus wines, and goodies like cappucino or caffe cioccolato to go along with those scrumptious desserts. A new outdoor cafe makes Trattoria more fun than ever. Trattoria is open every day but Sunday, from 11 a.m. until 1 a.m.

mignon fondue, $6.95, and a heavenly chocolate fondue, $3.45—plus a variety of cheese and sausage boards, excellent quiches and croques, even le cheeseburger, all modestly priced à la carte. Five-course dinners have plenty of cheese choices (from quiche Lorraine to cheddar cheese soup to fondue to cheesecake), and most are under $9. For noncheese-eaters, there's prime broiled filet mignon, sirloin, chicken, and burgers. Lunch is all à la carte, with plenty to eat from $2.95 to $4.25. Cider, beer, and wine, plus Swiss grape juice are available, as well as cocktails. On your way out, you can stop at the retail store and take some cheese—or a fondue pot—back to your hotel! La Fondue is open seven days a week, from 11:45 to 3 for lunch; from 3 to 1 a.m. for dinner and after-theater snacks.

Jewish Dairy Foods

The classic Jewish dairy dishes—blintzes, potato pancakes, kashe varnishkes, and the like, are no longer known only in cities like New York; cultural assimilation and food technology being what they are, blintzes are now frozen and sold in supermarkets as far away as Honolulu! And by a kind of reverse process, the famous dairy restaurants of New York are dwindling in number. Only a few are left, but happily, one of the best of these is found right in the heart of the busy midtown area: that's the 50-year-young **Farmfood Vegetarian Restaurant**, at 142 West 49th Street (tel. 757-4971). It's a big, busy, noisy place, and if you're in a hurry you can sit up at the counter and feast on a big bowl of soup (it may be borscht or schave or the great cabbage soup the day you're there) and black bread. Take one of the tables in the big back room for more relaxed dining. No meat is served at Farmfood (roasts and cutlets are made from nut meats), and no animal fats are used, but fish and cheese dishes are very much in evidence. Many of the famous Jewish classics are here: cheese kreplach or potato pirogen (a kind of dumpling), $3.75; matzoh brei (fried matzoh) with apple sauce, $3.50; kashe varnishkes with mushrooms, very filling, $2.90; and, of course, blintzes: we like the pineapple cheese kind at $3.75. Of the meat substitutes, protose steak, $3.75, and broiled Salisbury steak, and carrots, $3.75, are both interesting. And since you're in the heart of smoked-fish country, you might want to try a lox omelet, $3.95; a chopped herring sandwich, $2.45; or a platter of smoked whitefish, $4.95. The Farmfood people are also health oriented, and they attract the local health-food addicts with huge salads like the "Max Warmbrand"—grated carrots, beets, watercress, and baked potato, $3.75. The menu changes daily, but everything you eat here will be fresh, tasty, and old-fashionedly inexpensive. Farmfood is open from 11 a.m. to 9 p.m. on weekdays, until midnight on weekends.

The uptown star of the sour-cream circuit is the **Famous Dairy Restaurant**, 222 West 72nd Street (tel. 874-8607), which is not far from the Lincoln Center area, and is fine for a blintz before or a strudel after the Philharmonic. All of the pastries are home-made and delicious.

Should you find yourself downtown, bargain hunting on the Lower East Side (an activity we heartily recommend), you can have a great dairy-vegetarian-fish meal at **Ratner's** 138 Delancey Street (between Norfolk and Suffolk Streets; tel. 677-5588). Prices are moderate and the food is fresh and delicious. Don't miss the pastries!

Note: Any of these restaurants is a fine place to make the acquaintance of that New York phenomenon, the Jewish waiter, who is often more temperamental, if less haughty, than a French maitre d'. You may practically have to shout across a crowded room to get his attention (he is continually in motion), but be persistent. He is apt to be bossy and may want to make your selections for you, but be resolute. Actually, he is really a Jewish mother and only wants to help; he'll feel terrible if you don't enjoy your meal and eat it all up. So eat.

Getting in on the Ground Floor

What the Brasserie is to the East Side (see ahead), another Restaurant Associates' establishment, **Ground Floor Cafe**, on the ground floor of Eero Saarinen's C.B.S. Building, 51 West 52nd Street (tel. 751-5152), is to the West Side: a smartly casual, open-almost-always restaurant dispensing good food at moderate prices. The decor is futuristic-calm rather than provincial, and the food American-continental rather than French, but the mood is similarly animated in both. If you're alone, you can be comfortable up at the counter or bar, or you can sit down and relax at the tables or in the unusual pipe-rack-enclosed booths. You can order anything from a pancake-style omelet ($5.50) to a quiche ($5.95), or fried shrimp ($7.95) on the imaginative à la carte menu. You can also do well with the complete dinners ($9 to $10.95), with main courses like roast prime ribs, veal Cordon Bleu, steak, or fish; these come with raw vegetables; gazpacho soup or appetizer platter; baked potato and vegetable; and beautiful desserts from the dessert cart. The Apple Grunt, a baked apple with raisins and ice cream (free with dinner, $1.50 à la carte) is one of our favorites. There's also a special lunch every day, an entree plus salad, at $6.50. Ground Floor is open from 11:30 to 11:30, Monday through Saturday in winter; Monday through Friday in summer.

Two Popular Bistros

Over in the French neighborhood (Ninth Avenue in the 50s) is a small, attractive, and enormously popular restaurant heavily frequented by the local French population, the sailors off the French ocean liners, and knowledgeable New Yorkers who want a good and inexpensive French dinner. We refer, of course, to **Brittany du Soir**, 800 Ninth Avenue (at 53rd Street; tel. 265-4820). Everything is à la carte. We could make a meal just on their delicious homemade soup, the potage fermier, $1.10, the wonderful French bread, and a carafe of red wine. On the main courses, we usually take the moules marinières, mussels in wine sauce, $7; but we can also vouch for the filet of sole, $6; the lamb chops, $7.75; and the shrimps Provençale, $8. There is always a chicken dish on the menu at $6. Desserts range from simple cheese with toasted French bread to a lovely mousse, $1.50.

Entrees at lunch go from $3.75 to $7.50. Dinner is served Monday through Thursday from 5 to 10:30; until 11:30, Friday and Saturday. Lunch is from noon to 2:45, Monday through Saturday. Closed Sunday.

One of the most difficult things to find in New York is a reasonably priced, reasonably good French restaurant. **Larré's French Restaurant,** 50 West 56th Street (tel. 974-9170), a large, simple place so similar to many to be found in France, is one of these. The decor is simple, with no money wasted on nonessentials, but the pleasure of crisp white tablecloths and napkins is there. Dinners can be table d'hôte, priced from $6 to $9.75 (without appetizers), and the choices are varied, from appetizers like pâté maison, celery remoulade, or egg à la Russe; to such main courses as striped bass, ragout of beef bourguignon, or coq au vin; on to desserts like chocolate mousse and peach melba glâcé, and coffee. Lunch is even cheaper: $3.25 to $6, with, again, many choices, but no appetizers. Larré's has been popular for over 30 years with budget-minded diners who dislike the factory-like atmosphere of most inexpensive places. Open Mondays through Saturdays, from 11:30 to 2:30 for lunch; from 5 to 9:30 for dinner, until 10 on Saturday.

THE EAST SIDE: There are many interesting and modestly priced eateries up and down the main thoroughfares and little side-streets of the East Side—a hole-in-the-wall here, a super-slick, glossy speakeasy there.

Mexican

No need to fly to Mexico City for a great meal—the aficionados consider **El Parador,** 325 East 34th Street (tel. 679-6812), on a level with the best anywhere. El Parador is done in a Mexican Colonial motif, but it's so jammed with people that you probably won't notice the decor; they do not accept reservations, so be prepared to wait on line weekends. But you will notice the food; the fresh shrimps in salsa verde, $7.50; the chile rellenos, $6.50; the superb chicken El Parador (one of the three Spanish dishes on the menu), steamed with onions and heady with garlic, $7.50. Hefty combination plates are $6.50. The appetizers are almost as good as the main dishes: we find it hard to choose between the guacamole, the baby cactus, and the nachos (refried beans topped with melted cheese) each $3. The classic Mexican and Spanish desserts, flan and natilla, are here, as well as mango and guava shell preserves. And of course you'll want a cooling pitcher of sangria or some Carta Blanca or Moctezuma XX, imported Mexican cerveza, to go with the hot and spicy delicacies. El Parador serves dinner only, from 5 to 11 every night except Sunday.

French Fun

It's always open, it's always fun, and the food does not disappoint at **Brasserie**, 100 East 53rd Street, in the Seagram Building (tel. PL 1-4840), one of midtown's most popular informal restaurants. The decor is brightly French Provincial, the menu a combination of French and Alsatian dishes, plus some French-American hybrids like fromage burgers. *Le dejeuner, le diner,* and *le souper* menus are mostly à la carte: omelets piperades, $4.50; choucroûte Strasbourgeoise, $7.25 (a house specialty); onion soup, $1.95; croque madame or monsieur, $4.95. Complete dinners, too, with entrees like duckling with black cherry sauce, range from $8 to $10, served with hors d'oeuvres or soup, vegetables, dessert, and beverage. Lunch, with main courses like quiche Lorraine and cold poached salmon, goes from $4.95 to $5.95. Lunch is from 11 to 5; dinner, from 5 to 10; and supper, from 10 p.m. to 6 a.m., perfect after an evening's entertainment. Open every day, 24 hours a day.

Fancy, Unlimited

We doubt if there's another place in New York—or anywhere else, for that matter—quite like **Serendipity**. Located at 225 East 60th Street (tel. TE 8-3531), a block behind Bloomingdale's, Serendipity is a way-out kicky country store that sells Tiffany shades and cinnamon toast, Hebrew eye charts and Zen hash, frivolous hats and frozen hot chocolate drinks. The prettiest people lunch and meet here for afternoon tea and after theater, over the marble-topped coffee tables, and while the food is on the whimsical side, there are times when fantasy is more fun than meat-and-potatoes. Personally, we have long found Serendipity to be one of the city's happier happenings. The "Serious Food" side of the menu features very good casseroles (curried chicken, burgundy beef, shepherd's pie) from $4.75 to $5.50; omelets from $2.75 to $4.75; a foot-long chili hot dog at $3.75; hamburgers, and the enticing Ftatateeta's toast, $2.95. Zen hash and a variety of open-faced vegetable sandwiches are there for those on natural-food trips. But we wouldn't dream of coming here without indulging in the desserts: perhaps the heavenly apricot smush or the frozen mochaccino or the lemon ice-box pie or the dark-devil mousse. . . . Not to mention the glorious espressos and hot chocolates and spicy teas and chocolaccinos—but come and see for yourself. Serendipity is open daily from 11:30 a.m. to 12:30 a.m., Friday to 1 a.m., Saturday to 2 a.m.

Soul Food on Third Avenue

Since it's not too easy to find a really good soul-food restaurant in Manhattan south of Harlem, it's a treat to discover **Jack's Nest** at 310 Third Avenue (near 23rd Street; tel. 260-7110). Here, in large and comfortable, indeed, almost elegant, surroundings, you can feast on delicious Southern fried chicken, bar-b-que ribs, chicken smothered in gravy, whiting, croakers, or porgies, smoked ham hock, or, of course, chitlins (pig intestines), all with your choice of black-eyed peas, candied yams, collard greens, etc., and all at prices to quiet your soul: $2.65 to $3.90 at lunch, $4.25 to $5.65 at dinnertime. And although the portions are more than filling, such good home cooking almost cries out for second helpings, which are available at reduced rates. For that special celebration, you could have the chitlins and champagne, $7.85 at dinner, a rather royal Carolinian treat. Desserts include an exceptionally mouth-watering sweet-potato pie. Open for lunch, Monday through Friday from 11 to 3; and dinner, Sunday through Thursday, 3 to 11; Friday and Saturday, until 1:30 a.m.

Greek

Stepping into the narrow entrance of **Z,** the Greek restaurant at 117 East 15th Street (tel. 254-0960), you find yourself suddenly whisked away to that bright, sunny land, miles away from the grayness of the Union Square area outside. Waiters in black and white rush frantically through the crowded, white-stuccoed rooms, and Greek music fills the air. Sit long and leisurely at your small wooden table (you'll have to; such busyness makes the service slow) and sip some Greek wine. Tempt your palate, if you like salty dishes, with the marvelously stimulating saganaki, a baked cheese dish, $2.15. We also like the antipasto, $2.15, and the dolma (stuffed grapeleaves), $1.55. The delve into the entrees or daily specials, all from $3.55 to $4.25, including Greek salad for dinner, 10% less for lunch. Our favorite is the traditional moussaka, Z's specialty of eggplant, ground beef, and feta cheese, moist and delicately seasoned with cinnamon. Lamb is slightly on the overcooked side here, but both the exochiko (pastry-covered lamb chunks baked with feta cheese) and arni spanaki (sauteed spinach on a joint of lamb) are good; so, too, of course, is the shish kebab. If it's lunchtime, try the souvlaki, a pita bread sandwich of broiled beef and lamb, lettuce, and tomato, $1.85. Choose a dessert from the pastry table; the incredibly rich and honey-sweet baklava is perfect with a cup or two of Greek coffee. Z serves lunch every day, from 11:30 to 3; dinner, from 5 to 11:30.

Czechoslovakian

A trip uptown to eat at **Ruc,** 312 East 72nd Street (tel. 650-1611), allows you to work in a little sightseeing with a good meal. For this is New York's Yorkville neighborhood, longtime home to thousands of Germans, Hungarians, Czechs, and Ukrainians. Now the population is changing as the high-rise, high-price apartment buildings of the Upper East Side move relentlessly north and east, but there are still plenty of Mittel-European beer halls and cafes, intriguing butcher shops, and fragrant spice and cookery emporiums to wander through (Paprikas Weiss, one of the best, at 81st Street and Second Avenue, stays open until 6:30 p.m. for predinner browsers). Almost all of the restaurants are good here, but Ruc is one of our favorites, especially in the summer, when there's a large, attractive garden for quiet dining. The place is usually crowded with neighborhood countrymen feasting on the likes of wiener schnitzels, stuffed cabbages, the house special of boiled beef with dill sauce ($7.95) and those ubiquitous dumplings—for something special try the apricot dumplings with cheese and cinnamon. Full dinners of soup, main course, dessert, and coffee average $5.25 to $9.95 (for steak), and there are plenty of à la carte items: omelets, cold plates, cheeses. Start your meal with a glass of Slivovice, the native brew, and end with palacinky, the Czech version of crêpes suzettes. Dinner from 5 to 10 p.m., until 11 on Friday; and from noon to 11, Saturday and Sunday. Also recommended: **Hungarian Rendezvous,** 2262 Broadway at 81st Street (tel. TR 4-9444), which enjoys an excellent reputation for its fine home-cooked food at moderate prices. It's also an espresso shop, with delicious pastries.

Bargains Around the Clock

For some of the most generous meals in town at some of the most generous prices, it's hard to beat **The Green Kitchen**, First Avenue at 77th Street (tel. 988-4163), still going strong after almost half-a-century under the same family management. There are lots of comfortable booths inside amidst the plants and Tiffany-type lamps, but it's fun to pick a seat at the glassed-in sidewalk cafe and watch the Upper East Side world saunter by as you dine on very good Greek and fish specialties at prices that went out of style back in the '50s. You might try the eggplant moussaka at $4.15 or the boiled striped bass at the same price, or go for the London broil with mushroom sauce for $4.65; the price for these and other entrees (from $4.15 to $8.95, for steak) includes, amazingly enough, not just a complete plate, but a complete meal: soup, salad, vegetables, potato or rice, and homemade desserts. The side dishes are standard, the main courses excellent. Splurge a little bit and order the extraordinary Black Forest cake for an extra $1.20; it's baked right on the premises, as are all the pastries and the luscious soft bread that is brought to your table as soon as you sit down. Not only is The Green Kitchen easy on the pocketbook, but it also stays open every day, 24 hours a day, so it's perfect in the midst of a day of sightseeing or at the end of a night on the town.

GREENWICH VILLAGE AND POINTS SOUTH: Perhaps the largest variety of inexpensive restaurants is in this area. Along with your food, enjoy the unique ambience that makes the Village so special.

Italian Favorites

A colorful former speakeasy that still retains the old-time Village ambience that is fast disappearing in the wake of highrise apartment buildings, kitschy craft shops, and throngs of people, the **Beatrice Inn**, 285 West 12th Street (tel. 989-9351) is a tiny basement restaurant that has been dispensing good, homemade Italian food forever—or at least for some 50 years, with the same family still in charge. Choose a table near the fireplace, order a cocktail and definitely a bottle of vino, and relax. You can order à la carte or have a most reasonable complete lunch or dinner. Complete dinners, including appetizer or soup, entree, dessert, and beverage, run from $6 for the baked ziti (all pastas are homemade and very good) to $9.25 for filet mignon. Chicken parmigiana, $5.50, and frog legs Provençal, $6.25, are good choices. Wine is moderately priced. The luncheon tab is slightly lower. Beatrice Inn is open for lunch from 11:30 to 2:30, Mondays to Fridays; for dinner from 5 to 10, Mondays to Saturdays. Closed Sundays.

Newer on the Village scene and already with a reputation as one of the best Italian restaurants in town, **Trattoria da Alfredo,** 90 Bank Street (corner of Hudson; tel. 929-4400), has a delightfully European flair. The atmosphere is very relaxed, with butcher-block tables and simple, spare decor, but a touch of elegance in the linen napkins pyramided on the tables: glistening silver and glassware. And the food—bellissimo! We could sing a few arias about the delicious spinach-and-bacon salad, $3.75; the exquisite pastas (fettucine verdi all' Alfredo is one of the best at $4); the unusual veal, meat, and chicken dishes which change every day and are usually priced at $7. Everything is beautifully fresh and made to order, and the portions are large enough so that just pasta and salad (plus your own bottle of wine, since no liquor is served) make more than an adequate meal. Don't miss the homemade cheesecake at $2.25. Trattoria da Alfredo is open every day but Tuesday, serving lunch from 12 to 2, dinner from 6 to 10:30. On Sundays, dinner only, 6 to 10:30. Reservations are always necessary.

Village Eclectic

Bare brick walls and plain wooden tables topped with black glass give the **Star Thrower Cafe,** 2 Bank Street (Seventh Avenue at 11th Street; tel. 924-9450) a quintessential Village look, but one that's enhanced by enormous expanses of windows which bring the eclectic street scene inside. This Village newcomer is often crowded and always abuzz with interesting conversation. Close-together tables make eavesdropping easy, but intimate tête-a-têtes awkward. Choose Star Thrower when you're in the mood for a slice of choice New York people watching, accompanied by very good food.

Fresh seasonal ingredients prepared with innovative flair keep the crowds coming for dishes that are just a bit different. For instance, a vegetarian lasagne at $5.50 uses the traditional layers of broad noodles, but assorted fresh vegetables make up the filling. As an appetizing change from first-course escargots, you can select mussel-filled mushroom caps. Outstanding entrees include a chicken breast wrapped in pastry and filled with cream cheese at $6.50; homemade green noodles in creamy cheese sauce at $4.50; ragout of squab at $9.50, and ethnic selections like Cuban-style tenderloin with black bean sauce. Homemade cakes are available for dessert, but be warned, main courses are huge and you'll probably have little room left.

At lunch, choose from omelets, $2.75; quiche and salad, $3.50; or a fish of the day, $4.75. Sunday brunch (except in summer) is served from 1 to 4 p.m., with eggs and such starting at $3. Star Thrower Cafe is open for lunch from noon to 3 and dinner from 6 to midnight, Tuesdays through Sundays. Closed Mondays.

Steaks

Generations of hungry Villagers have soothed their appetites for steak at one of the most pleasant and unpretentious of restaurants, the **Blue Mill Tavern,** 50 Commerce Street (tel. CH 3-7114). Almost hidden amid century-old houses in a quaint and quiet part of the Village, it is still within walking distance of many off-Broadway theaters. Come in for a drink and sit at the bar, or arrive for lunch or dinner and sit in the main room where bluish walls, small tables pushed together, and white tablecloths outline the warm simplicity of this place. There are no fancy menus: the waiter simply brings the house copy of the menu, handwritten on a wood-backed easel, and leans it against an empty chair near your table. The menu has slight, occasional changes, but you can always count on the small steak at $5.75; it is excellent, well-seasoned and done to perfection, and adequate for all but the largest of appetites. Other good choices are the broiled blue fish, $3.95; the chopped sirloin, $2.95; and the sirloin, $7.95. All meals come with salad, vegetables, and home-fried thick potato chips, all served family style, so this is a place where you can really save those dollars. Blue Mill Tavern is open for lunch Monday through Friday from noon to 2; and for dinner, Monday through Thursday from 5 to 9:30; until 10:30, Friday and Saturday. Closed Sunday.

Spanish

Open the door on **Un Rincon de España** at 226 Thompson Street (tel. 260-4950) and, sure enough, you're in a little corner of Spain, complete to the bullfight paintings along the wall, the wrought-iron candlesticks on the white tables, the tiles bordering the tiny bar, and the Flamenco guitarist giving out with plaintive melodies. The Village regulars keep this place jammed, not only for the *muy autentico* mood, but for the top-notch, modestly priced food. Salad with a spicy house dressing arrives as soon as you sit down, and while you're dipping your crusty French bread in the sauce and sipping a glass of wine, go ahead and order the mejillones a la Carlos—mussels in a pungent garlic sauce, $3.50 and enough for two. Seafood, fish, and meat entrees are priced in the $5.50 to $7.50 range, with an outstanding paella Valenciana (again, enough for two), just $6.75. Mariscadas—seafood stews—are another specialty of the house, and for those who dare, the broiled octopus is considered among the best in town. Desserts? Nothing special, but sip your coffee slowly and drink deep of the very special mood.

Un Rincon de Espana serves dinner only, from 5 to 11, Fridays and Saturdays until 12, Sundays from 1 to 11. The same management runs Un Rincon de Espana downtown at 82 Beaver Street, open from 11:40 to 8:30, Mondays to Fridays, tel. 344-5228.

Olde New York

A Colonial gem tucked away in a quiet corner of Greenwich Village, with small, oak-beamed rooms and a pleasant garden, **Ye Waverly Inn,** 16 Bank Street at Waverly Place (tel. CH 3-9396), has been serving very good home-style American cooking (not so easy to find in New York) to its crowds of regulars and out-of-towners for many years now. Prices are surprisingly low, considering the quality and the candlelight charm of the place. Dinners average $8.50, but the famous chicken pot pie and Southern fried chicken are only $7.50. The entree is served with appetizers, two vegetables, a salad, plus such pleasant desserts as Southern pecan pie and chocolate Charlotte Russe, and coffee. Cocktails are available, and so is Irish coffee. Lunch is an especially good bargain: entrees, priced from $3.85 to $5.25, are accompanied by two vegetables and either appetizer or dessert. Ye Waverly Inn serves lunch from 11:45 to 2 Tuesday to Saturday; dinner from 5:15 to 10 or 11 daily, from 4:30 to 9 on Sunday. Sunday brunch, too.

Mexican

Mexican Village, 224 Thompson Street in the heart of the busy Village scene (tel. 677-9706), is one of those restaurants that's *always* busy, even on a cold winter weeknight when everyplace else is practically empty. And with good reason: not only is the food authentic and good, but the atmosphere is muy simpatico (lots of wood and brick, a beamed ceiling, Mexican glass lanterns), and the prices are surprisingly cheap for New York. One of their specialties, for example, the tasty flautas con guacamole, a kind of Mexican grilled-cheese tortilla sandwich, is just $4.75; arroz con calamares (rice with squid—delicious!) is $4.45; and chicken molé, a classic Mexican dish with a chocolate sauce, is $5.75. Combination dinners average $4. On weekends, there are dinner specials not offered anywhere else in New York, like pepino rellano (stuffed zucchini), enchiladas Jalisco (sliced steak enchiladas) and enchiladas Suizas (boned breast of chicken in sour cream sauce), each $7. Vegetarians can enjoy the vegiteria Mexican style. There are terrific appetizers, too—nachos, chilled avocado soup, cactus salad. The chile sauces on the table are hot, so use them sparingly; to cool off, you can always order some iced mint tea; or a bottle of Carta Blanca cerveza—the ideal accompaniment to a Mexican meal. There's often only one waitress, so service can be a bit spotty when the place fills up, but it's pleasant enough to linger over your tequila while you're waiting for the delicacies to emerge from the hole-in-the-wall kitchen, presided over by a native chef. Open 4:30 p.m. to midnight, until 1 on weekends; closed Tuesdays.

East-West Success

Dine like a real in-the-know New Yorker at the Lower Manhattan "in" spot—**Hisae's Place**, 35 Cooper Square (near the Public Theater; tel. 228-6886). Throngs fill the place every night, and with good reason. An eclectic establishment, Hisae's offers market-fresh ingredients in Oriental style, though not strictly Oriental, preparations. You can, for example, feast on exciting East-West combinations like trout dressed with ginger, $6.95, or shrimp enlivened with black beans and vegetables, $7.95. Enormous appetizers include a mound of marinated octopus or a seasonal treat like crunchy asparagus with real blue cheese dressing. A platter of raw vegetables with dipping sauce precedes appetizers. Portions are large, so order sparingly.

Everybody comes to Hisae's, from local types to serious food lovers. Reservations are accepted only for four or more, but if you're just two, you can wait at the friendly bar. Hisae's Place is open for dinner only, from 5 to midnight, Friday and Saturday to 1 a.m., with entrees from $4.95 for chicken Hawaiian to $8.95 for steak and shrimp.

Hisae's popularity spawned an offshoot called **Hisae's Fish Place,** serving only fish, at 570 Hudson Street in the West Village (tel. CH 3-4212), and yet another, **Hisae's Lobster House,** at 13 East 37th Street (tel. 889-9862).

Health Foods for Gourmets

Brownie's, 21 East 16th Street, at the top of the Village (tel. AL 5-2838), is the kind of endearing place that has devotees rather than customers. Some are devoted health-food types, some devoted vegetarians, some devoted dieters—but most are just devoted to good food. And that's what you get plenty of here at the most reasonable prices high quality will allow, served either at a long, busy counter up front, in the country-style, antique-filled dining room in back, or in the newer, no-smoking dining room on the side. The atmosphere is tea-roomy warm, the service pleasant and to-the-point.

Sam Brown (there really is a Brownie), who's been at this stand for almost 40 years, is finicky about using natural ingredients whole-grain flours, vegetable oils, ultra-fresh spices, honey instead of refined sugar), never save leftovers, and are constantly creating new and delicious recipes for the likes of African couscous or breaded vegetable cutlet or chopped liver that tastes just like grandma's—except that it's made of vegetables. Although meat is tabu here, fish is not, and every night, in fact, Brownie's offers a choice of five fresh fish specialties (Polynesian platter with fish filets and fruits; planked fish, baked fish, fish served with artichokes, roasted peppers, and the like) at $9.95, served with soup and salad. On the extensive à la carte menu, there are many salads, sandwiches (including tasty stuffed pita platters), vegetarian and fish entrees. Lunch entrees, with a choice of soup or salad, run from $3 to $4.25, and you can always have a drink at one of the best vegetable-juice bars in town. Brownie's, by the way, is something of a celebrity hangout, Danny Kaye, for one, is frequently in attendance at his own special corner. Brownie's is open weekdays until 8, Saturdays until 4; closed Sundays.

After your meal, saunter around the corner to Brownie's gourmet-and-health food store at 17th Street and Fifth Avenue, stocked with an international array of healthful goodies plus home-baked and mouth-watering cakes and cookies. Copies of Brownie's natural-foods cookbook are available. Children, by the way, adore both eating here and visiting the retail shop;

there's so much to look at—and even the candy bars are nutritious!

Chinatown

Manhattan is dotted with Chinese restaurants, and you can have an adequate Chinese meal almost anywhere in the city. But we think you should make the trek down to Chinatown, not only to combine a little sightseeing with your meal (see details in Chapter V), but because the city's best, most authentic Chinese kitchens are to be found here. And there seems to be some kind of unwritten rule that the plainer the restaurant, the more indifferent the waiters, the grander the cuisine. At least that's the case at **Foo Joy,** 13 Division Street (tel. 431-4931), a one-of-a-kind Fukienese restaurant in a city swarming with Cantonese restaurants and a sizable number of Szechuanese types. Atmosphere is minimal: Formica tables, bright lights, brusque service, but the food more than makes up for the lack of ambience. Start with our favorite, fish rolls, something like an egg roll, but rolled in caul fat and deep fried with a filling of fish and chopped greens. An order of several thin, crisp rolls serves four as an appetizer. Next we'd opt for the Fukienese pork chops, a mound of lean chops in a soy and scallion sauce, or a whole crisply fried sea bass at $6.50. There's also the typical lengthy menu of seafood, pork and chicken variations, with most dishes averaging $4. Try the chicken layered with ham and deep fried. Foo Joy is open daily from 11:30 a.m. until midnight.

China Royal, 17 Division Street (tel. 226-0788) is a big, bustling emporium serving excellent Cantonese food at low prices. These are not the ordinary run of Cantonese dishes, however. Here you'll find exotica like salt-roasted spareribs with fried milk. Fried milk, a soybean product, appears on the menu in several variations; it's a creamy, soft substance, not unlike bean curd, that's deep fried and crisp outside, warm and melting within. Orders of fried milk dressed up with meat or vegetables are all about $3. In fact, everything at China Royal is inexpensive, with a top price of $6.50 for roast squab. Portions are large and four hearty eaters can easily fill up and take doggy bags home for $20. Sea bass with Chinese vegetables presents a fried whole fish covered with crisp Chinese bok choy. Seafood makes up a great portion of the menu with oysters, scallops, and whelks plus the more common shrimp and lobster choices. Bean curd comes in several varieties and noodle dishes in generous portions are as low as $2.50. Service is surprisingly cheerful. Open daily from 11 a.m. to 11 p.m.

Happy Garden, nearby at 12 Bowery (tel. 349-9677), is simple, but it is pleasantly decorated, and the service is efficient. We have a long list of favorites here. The wor shu opp, fried duck with a coating of chopped almonds and sauce, is delectable, $4.15; so is the sub gum wonton with oyster sauce, little dumplings stuffed with a mixture of liver, vegetables, seafood, and topped with pork, chicken, and duck, $4.25, and the more simple noodles with spareribs and black-bean sauce, $1.75. Seafood is outstanding here: butterfly shrimp, $5.40; fantail shrimp, $5.15; and Cantonese-style crab, $3.95; are all heartily recommended. No liquor. Open from 11 a.m. to midnight weekdays, until 1:45 Fridays and Saturdays.

Another place the devotees swear by in Chinatown is **Hong Fat,** at 63 Mott Street (tel. WO 2-9588), a shrine to the wide noodle that is always open, always crowded, and cheap. **Sam Wo,** 39 Mott Street (tel. WO 2-8750), is another hole-in-the-wall with great Cantonese food. Again, cheap and open every day.

For a real experience in Chinese eating, choose a dim sum lunch at either **Hee Seung Fong,** or **H.S.F.** as it is familiarly known, 46 Bowery (tel. 374-1319) or **Silver Palace,** 50 Bowery (tel. 964-1204), two of the most "in" establishments in the city at this moment. Dim sum, in case you hadn't heard, is the umbrella term for dumplings and other exotic morsels that are served early in the day, always accompanied by pots and pots of tea. The correct procedure for a tea lunch is to choose whatever appeals to you from the carts and trays that are constantly whisked by your table (dim sum never offers a menu). Your bill is tallied by counting the number of empty plates you've amassed. It's perfectly proper to linger over tea lunch and continue eating until you're thoroughly sated. You'll be seated communal style with lots of other diners, all eating happily away. Both places are jammed on weekends. Individual selections at both average about $1 to $1.50 each. H.S.F. serves dim sum from 7:30 a.m. until 5 p.m.; at Silver Palace, the dumpling hours are 7 a.m. to 4 p.m.

Probably the best place uptown for Northern Chinese food is the **Harbin Inn,** 2637 Broadway at 100th Street (tel. MO 6-3450). Nearby, the **Szechuan Taste West,** 2332 Broadway (84th to 85th Street; tel. 873-6665), features the hot and spicy dishes of Southwest China that have lately become so popular in New York. The original **Szechuan Taste** is at 24 Chatham Square in

Chinatown (tel. 267-0672), and **Szechuan East** is at Second Avenue and 80th Street (tel. 535-4921). Midtown Chinese restaurants are apt to be lavishly decorated and expensive, and are usually avoided by the true believers.

On The Waterfront

An ideal stop if you're touring the downtown New York area or visiting the South Street Seaport, **Sloppy Louie's,** down in the Fulton Fish Market at 92 South Street (tel. 952-9657) is one of those places that is practically a New York institution, like the Brooklyn Bridge or the Staten Island Ferry. Its prices are cheap, its seafood is wonderful, but perhaps best of all, it is still as unadorned and unpretentious as it was 40 years ago when Louie took over (there had been a restaurant in this building since 1811). No attempt has been made at providing an atmosphere for gracious dining, but despite that (or maybe because of it) everyone seems to have a grand time, sitting at long wooden tables, feasting on succulent plates of hot fish, and brushing shoulders with Wall Street executives or truckdrivers or local stenographers who throng the place at lunchtime. At dinner, it's a typical motley New York crowd, who don't mind getting down here before 7:50 p.m. (you can, however, stay as long as you want), when the last customer is seated.

But the main attraction is, of course, the fish. Everything is à la carte, but the entrees come served with potatoes and vegetables, so they are almost a meal in themselves. A good plan is to ask the waiter what's in season before you order. The shad roe, when they have it, is delicate and lovely, and also good are the Florida red snapper, $6.60; the oyster fry, $5.45; and the New Orleans shrimp creole, $6.95. We are especially partial to Louie's famous bouillabaisse, a huge, steaming concoction, just as good as the last time you tried it in Marseilles, $5.95. The big, hearty bowls of fish soup, like Maine lobster soup and Long Island clam chowder are also a treat. Everything at Louie's is, in fact, good and absolutely fresh, since the fish comes right from the market and only the choicest selections are bought. So serious is Louie about freshness, for example, that he will not stock lobsters: if you order one, he will hop out to the market to buy it for you; the price depends on the size and season, but usually, it will run about $13 for a pound-and-a-half lobster. Liquor is not served, but you can bring your own bottle of wine.

Louie's opens its doors at 11 a.m. and stays open until after

8 p.m., Mondays to Fridays. Closed Saturdays, Sundays, and on all major holidays.

A Meal in Little Italy

For those who love lusty, truly ethnic Italian food, the greatest neighborhood in the city has to be Little Italy, a subway stop or two below Greenwich Village. The streets are lined with homey, family-style restaurants where they make the fried mozzarella, the lobster fra diablo, the clams in garlic sauce, the steak in hot peppers, and the fried zucchini the way they did back in Naples or Sicily, from whence most of the area's citizens descended. Come at lunch, after you've been touring downtown Manhattan, and join the local politicians and legal eagles (City Hall and the courts are just a few blocks away) wheeling and dealing over the steaming pastas. If you come for dinner on a weekend, be prepared to join the hungry throngs queued up in long lines, since most of these restaurants do not accept reservations. Prices are slightly lower than uptown, and you can probably get a good meal anywhere from $4 to $8. **Grotta Azzura**, 387 Broome Street, is the most popular of the restaurants, and the one where the lines are longest. Other delicious favorites: **Angelo's**, 146 Mulberry Street; **Antica Roma**, 40 Mulberry Street; **Forlini's**, 93 Baxter Street; **Luna's**, 112 Mulberry Street; **Paolucci's**, 149 Mulberry Street; **Puglia**, 189 Hester Street; **Raffaela's**, 134 Houston Street; **Villa Pensa**, 198 Grand Street; and **Vincent's Clam Bar**, 119 Mott Street, for the best Italian fish dishes anywhere. It's nice to walk around the streets a little bit beforehand, poke your head into the grocery stores and smell the marvelous cheese and sausages, perhaps listen to a strain of a Caruso record. Finish your evening with a heavenly pastry and espresso at **Cafe Roma**, 385 Broome Street, or at **Ferrara's**, 195 Grand Street, where, in summer, you can sit at the sidewalk cafe and pretend, perhaps, that you're on the Via Veneto.

SoHo

It's nice to spend a Saturday afternoon browsing through the galleries and boutiques of SoHo (below Greenwich Village; see sightseeing chapter for particulars), and it's also fun to stop off and have a meal with the local colony of artists, musicians, and creative types who keep this area hopping. Perhaps the most SoHoian of the restaurants down here, one which recalls the elegance of the days of Old New York when SoHo was a center of commerce and entertainment, is **The Ballroom, 458** West Broadway (tel. 473-9367). White walls, lots of plants, sheer white curtains, and odd-shaped mirrors provide a comfortable and classy atmosphere in which to partake of good food. An extraordinary mural depicts the best-known people on the SoHo scene. Meals here are basically continental with such offerings as pâté, quiche, fettucinne Alfredo or carbonara, and daily fresh fish baked in a parchment bag. A full and interesting variety of soups, salads, and omelets is also on hand, and the desserts are home-baked. Lunch usually runs about $5, a full dinner, about $10. Lately, the Ballroom has made a name for itself as an entertainment mecca, with top cabaret artists featured every night. Sunday brunch is a great treat, at about $4. Open for lunch Monday through Saturday from noon to 3:30, Sundays from 12 to 4; and for dinner, Tuesday through Saturday, 6 to 11, until 10 on Sunday.

Despite its name, **Mama Siltka, 468** West Broadway, (tel. 260-6779) is not a Hungarian restaurant; it seems that Mama Siltka was a gypsy spirit guide to a friend of owners Philip and Gail Merker. Well, whoever Mama Siltka was or wasn't, she must have been a good cook, for she's inspired the chefs here to turn out some marvelous creations, concentrating on very fresh seafood, chicken and meat dishes prepared with a gourmet's touch, and at very fair prices. Sit back and relax in one of the two huge dining rooms removed from the singles action of the bar up front (this is a big meeting place on weekends), sip a glass of wine and admire the SoHoian natural mood of wood and brick and plants and paintings. A few of you can share the mussels Dijonnaise, $3, done in a very light, mustard cream sauce. Don't miss the soups, especially the hearty fish broth seasoned with a touch of Pernod, or the mellow New England clam chowder. Entrees run from about $4.95 to $8.95; we'd recommend the broiled salmon or red snapper, $7.95 each, or the chicken Francaise—light slices of chicken, gently seasoned, with a lemon sauce, $4.95. Daily specials—like the mousseline of salmon and sole that we sampled—can be extraordinary. Desserts are too good to pass up, so save some room for the frothy strawberry zabaglione, the incredible honey walnut torte or the not-to-sweet cheesecake. Mama Siltka is open from noon to 1 a.m. for food, until 4 a.m. for drinks, every day of the week, including Sunday brunch.

Spring Street Natural Restaurant, 149 Spring Street (tel. 966-0290), is a great big airy place where wooden tables, exposed brick walls with paintings by local artists, many plants, over-hanging fans, and a relaxed atmosphere set the mood for dining on wholesome, unprocessed, really good food. Everything is homemade from all natural ingredients. There are many flavor-ful fresh fish and seafood dishes (salmon steak au vin with rice, shrimp in mustard sauce, mussels sauteed in spinach); gourmet vegetarian creations like leek casserole, zucchini tempura with parmesan sauce, bulghur croquettes with curry sauce; imagina-tive salads like the excellent tabouli topped with tahini sauce and surrounded with lemons and cucumbers, a huge meal at just $3.50; unusual homemade soups (avocado, spinach, or cream of cauliflower); and mouth-watering desserts like carrot layer cake, .cranberry pie, and praline cheesecake. Most entrees run $3.25 to $6.95. Sunday brunch, 11:30 to 5, is a special treat; that's when, in addition to the regular menu, crêpes (whole-wheat, of course) are served, stuffed with spinach and mushrooms and Florentine sauce or seafood; there's even a fruit de jour crêpe with sour cream and brandy sauce. Crêpes plus garnishes cost $3.75 to $4. You can have wine at your table or a drink at the big, friendly bar up front, crowded with local types. Open daily, from 11:30 until 2 a.m.

A great place for people-watching—its always-busy bar caters to a delightfully diverse mix of local artists, craftspeople, lovers, and tourists—the **Spring Street Bar,** 162 Spring Street (tel. 431-7637) is also known for terrific American-French food. Dinner specials like chicken Cordon Bleu, Mexican chile, swordfish, seafood crêpes, fresh ham with mustard sauce, run $4 to $10 à la carte. Lunch and supper feature all of the same, plus sand-wiches, omelets, and brunch-like egg dishes such as croque mon-sieur and eggs Benedict. Open daily from noon to 6 for lunch, from 6 to 11 for dinner, from 11 until 2 a.m. for supper. A fine place for good food and good talk—great for capping a night's adventures.

Fast Foods, Friendly Prices

Now we come to those places that seem to have been designed with budgeteers, visiting or otherwise, in mind. They are ideal for a quick, casual meal; they offer hearty, satisfying food, and in most you can put together a complete lunch or dinner from $2 to $5. And, best of all, since New York is a wonderfully cosmopolitan town, they offer a range that goes from quiches to crêpes, from sauerbraten to sukiyaki, from pita to potage. Some are one-of-a-kind places, others are the popular chain restaurants that you'll find all over the busiest parts of town. Wherever you are, you won't be far from one of these nourishing dispensaries. (Consult Manhattan's Yellow Pages classified phone directory for complete addresses.)

SOUP KITCHENS AND BREAD LINES, À LA FRANÇAISE: While McDonald's is becoming a way of life for millions of Parisians, the many new French soup kitchens and fast-food establishments that have invaded New York appear to be taking revenge. Over in the theater district, **Pot au Feu,** 123 West 49th Street, (tel. 765-4840), is but a cafeteria cleverly and pleasingly disguised by high ceilings, mobiles, balconies, waterfalls, and colorfully severe modern European-style furnishings. Get in line and try the house specialty, Pot au Feu, a clear broth with chunks of chicken, beef, and fresh vegetables, or any of the other fine offerings which include onion soup au gratin, Italian minestrone, crème à la reine, beef or chicken stew, chef's or health salad. The complete soup lunch is $3.66 and stew or salad lunch, $4.17, including bread, beverage, and choice of dessert: chocolate mousse, apple cobbler, cheese and fruit, or salad. Wine, either Chablis or Burgundy, is 85¢, and Michelob beer on tap is 93¢. Le Bar is open from 4 to 9 p.m., with hors d'oeuvres and music. And if you can't get your fill of soup within the restaurant, Pot au Feu will package it for you to take out at reduced prices. Open Monday through Saturday, 11 to 9, with outdoor dining from June to September.

At **Potagerie,** a fashionable Fifth Avenue soup-and-bread line (between 45th and 46th Streets; tel. 586-7790), a filling meal of bread and soup will cost you $4.15. The varieties of soup offered change daily, with onion soup, clam chowder, and cream of chicken as the favorites. As at Pot au Feu, your soup is dished out of metal tureens and served in deep ceramic bowls. It's fun to sit at the wooden tables near the plate-glass windows and watch the crowds sauntering down Fifth Avenue—unless it's winter when the steaming soup inevitably fogs the windows and makes the restaurant a beckoning refuge from the cold. Open Monday through Friday, 11 to 9; Saturday, 11 to 7:30.

There's more than just soup at **La Bonne Soupe,** 48 West 55th Street, (tel. 586-7650), and for relaxed dining, this is our favorite in this group. You relax in a French country atmosphere while waitresses serve thick-crusted bread and a choice of French onion, sweet-and-sour cabbage or paysanne soup for only $3.75, wine and dessert included. The onion soup with its thick cheese is particularly good. But if you're hungry for something else, you can also have ratatouille, paysanne, spinach or cheese omelets; these come with french fries or salad and are $3.50. Quiche Lorraine is $3.50. At dinner only, indulge in one of the special fondues for two; chocolate, cheese, or beef bourguignon, from $2.75 to $12.95. For dessert, don't miss the wonderfully rich and smooth mousse au chocolat, $1.25, or free with the soup meal. La Bonne Soupe serves from 11:30 to midnight every day. There's another La Bonne Soupe on the East Side, at 987 Third Avenue, in the fashionable Bloomingdale's neighborhood (tel. 759-2500).

It's quite likely that there's a **La Crêpe** restaurant in your own hometown, but here in New York is where this popular chain got started, and, at last count, there were six of them in Manhattan alone. These popular, Brittany-inn-style French pancake houses where the crêpes are made on an open grill for all to watch and where costumed waitresses serve you your food are fun for a light meal or snack. There are over 100 varieties of crêpes, and the price ranges from $1.15 (for a snail-butter crêpe) to $6.95 (for a caviar crêpe). Expect to pay an average of $2.75 for those filled with sausages, eggs, cheese, meats, etc.; about $1.35 to $1.75 for the dessert crêpes, with strawberries, ice cream, and the like. Besides crêpes, you may also dine on onion or fish soup or lobster bisque, quiche Lorraine, and lovely desserts like tarts, rum cake, and mousse au chocolat, all extra. One of our favorite La Crêpes is across the street from Lincoln Center, at 67th Street and Broadway; others are at 158 West 44th Street, 57 West 56th.

THE OTHER SOPHISTICATES—SAUERBRATEN, BROODJES, BABA GANOUSH: All gussied up with instant, old-world decor, **Wienerwald** is probably the fanciest of the quick-service restaurants, offering comfortable booths and tables for its hearty German-Viennese food. Most of the international specialties—like Hungarian beef goulash with buttered noodles, German knockwurst with sauerkraut and whipped potatoes, or the grilled chicken with home fries and vegetables—go from $4.25 to $6.25. Beef specialties are lower, veal dishes higher. Cold buffets and sandwiches are inexpensive. Strudels and such are standouts on the dessert list, and imported beers, wine, and cocktails go well with this type of food. All three Wienerwalds are open every day.

Visit the Vienna Woods at Eighth Avenue and 48th Street, Broadway and 51st Street, or Broadway near 46th Street.

The **Zum Zum** chain, which was originally dedicated to German sausages in endless variety, has changed its accent and its image recently. In fact, you now have to ask for the famous frankfurters, bauernwurst and bratwurst, 85¢ to 95¢; they're no longer listed on the menu. What is listed, however, represents good counter-restaurant value. Casseroles, like chicken chasseur, $3.25; boeuf à la mode, $2.95; shrimp cocotte, $2.95; and quiche Lorraine or Florentine, $3.25, come in ample portions that include a green salad. Salad Nicoise and shrimp Louis, each $2.95, are other interesting departures for Zum Zum. Bratwurst on a platter with good hot German potato salad is $2.75, and the Blue Max burger (with blue cheese) is $2.35. Great yogurt pies and a variety of fruit flavors are 85¢. Light and dark German beers are the best accompaniments.

There are Zum Zums all over the city, but you might try Lexington Avenue at 45th and 58th Streets; the Pan American Building at 300 Park Avenue; 24 East 42nd Street; and Eighth Street at University Place in the Village. Most are very crowded at lunchtime; before or after is much more peaceful.

Dutch Lunch

If the Delft tiles on the walls of this small, quiet, two-room sandwich shop didn't give it away, the "Broodje" roll, a Dutch tradition, will tell you that you are dining in the style of the low countries at **Broodje**, 246 East 51st Street (tel. 832-7188). Owner Bill Berensmann who lived in Holland for many years became captivated by broodjes over there, and decided to recreate them back here in New York. All the sandwiches—Edam cheese, Holland ham, Dutch salami, roast beef, etc.—are tasty and inexpensive, $1.15 to $1.45; but the beef tartare, at the highest price, is a real treat. There are also roast beef, shrimp salad, and cold cut platters, offered along with soups, salads, and desserts at special prices. And for dessert, don't miss the Dutch chocolate cake, 85¢, a particularly moist and scrumptious delight. Broodje also serves imported beers and wine, and plans to be open for dinner in the evenings, presenting a variety of entertainment, including jazz, chamber music, and one-act plays. Call for information.

Although there are frozen yogurt shops all around town, **Curds 'n' Whey**, a charming "yogurteria" at 4 East 45th Street (tel. 682-8876), is the only place we know that uses yogurt not just as a dessert, but as the basis for serious cooking. Yogurt is used in the cream base of the homemade soups, in the salad dressings, in the house's own yogurt cheese (try it on bagels!), and in a variety of dishes ranging from well-spiced yogurt calzone to a flavorful yogurt spinach quiche. There are plenty of other natural foods offerings, too—beautiful vegetable and fruit salads, "pitapatters" (whole-grain Syrian breads stuffed with assorted vegetables and spreads), banana bread, carrot-raisin cake, vegetable juices, and luscious yogurt desserts topped with fresh fruits, granola, honey, nuts, and the like. Prices are modest: large salads about $3.25; quiches, $1.75; combination soup-salad-quiche-pita meals from $3.25 to $4.75. This self-service eatery is decorated with antiques and plants, paintings on the wall, a ceiling fan overhead, butcher-block tables and ice-cream-parlor chairs, which makes lunch comfortable and the idea of lingering over a late-afternoon snack or light pretheater dinner particularly appealing. Then, when the tables are lit with candles, it's fun to sup on, perhaps, a quiche or green pepper stuffed with tabouleh, or the calzone, along with a salad, and a glass of wine. Open weekdays from 11 to 8; Saturdays, to 5; closed Sundays.

There are five **Amy's** in town—at Broadway and 62nd Street, in the Lincoln Center area; at 108 University Place, near the Village; at Bank and West Streets (in the Westbeth Courtyard) in the Village; at 210 East 23rd Street; and at 112th Street and Broadway in the Columbia University area—and wherever they open, people get turned on to the delights of Israeli-Middle Eastern food, served snackbar style at tiny prices. All of the Amy's are attractive, with brick walls and blond Formica tables, and a tempting counter which dispenses wonderful sandwiches —of falafel (vegetable burger), humus bitahina, (chick peas and sesame spread), grilled feta cheese, baba ganoush (mashed eggplant spread), kufta (chopped meat), hamburgers, fish filet, steak, and the like, served in toasted pita (round, flat Syrian) bread, $1.30 to $2.40—as well as various combination platters of these ingredients. The meatless combination platter—falafel, humous, baba ganoush, stuffed vine leaves, feta cheese, and black and green olives, with toasted pita—is a mouth-watering, high-protein meal for $2.70. Amy's dinner plates are excellent bargains ($4.90 the top price for a tenderloin steak), and they are served with all the Middle Eastern accompaniments. The University Place Amy's is open from 11:30 a.m. to 1 a.m.; the others close at 10 p.m.

For fast food with style and nutritional value, use your noodle and head for one of the **Dosanko Larmen** restaurants. These are Japanese noodle shops that are exceptionally clean, attractively decorated, and feature only larmen (soft noodles and vegetables in broth) in several varieties, as well as gyoza (Japanese fried dumplings). Service is brisk and friendly, and prices range from $2.25 to $3.50. There's one at Madison and 48th Street, another at 341 Lexington Avenue (between 39th and 40th Streets), and still another at 19 Murray Street in the financial area.

BEST OF THE BASICS—BURGERS, BAGELS, AND PIZZA: No need to tell you here about McDonald's: they're all around town and everybody knows how cheaply they can fill up hungry families. You may not, however, know about an almost elegant answer to the fast-burger syndrome: the numerous **Steak & Brew Burgers,** located at many places in the city (59th Street and Lexington Avenue, 57th Street and Avenue of the Americas, and many, many more: just look for the familiar logo). Dim lighting, pewter-like plates, and thick wooden tables all combine to hide the fact that this is, in essence, a fast-food chain operation. The hamburgers are large, tasty, done as you request, and arrive in a variety of styles (pizza, bacon, Swiss, regular) at reasonable prices ($1.75 to $3.15), in almost record time. The Idaho Spuds, 95¢, are a thick and welcome change from the usual shoestring variety of french fries. Salads, 95¢, are fresh and generous. Beverages come in frosty mugs. Simplicity being the motto of any fast-food menu, warm apple pie, cheesecake, and rum raisin ice cream, 95¢, are the only desserts offered. Hours, and in some cases prices, vary from location to location.

Since New Yorkers are absolutely mad about bagels, it's no wonder that the new chain called **Bagel Nosh** has caught on like wildfire. Bagel Noshes are most attractive, self-service places, with loads of greenery, butcher block tables, and a variety of bagels—like garlic, onion, pumpernickel, raisin—plus an even greater variety of toppings to put on them, from cream cheese to salami to burgers to brisket of beef. Prices run from 75¢ to around $2.50. There's a Bagel Nosh at Fifth Avenue and 35th Street, another at Broadway and 71st Street (near Lincoln Center), still another at Third Avenue and 36th Street. Most stay open early until quite late.

The first fast-food, natural-food restaurant anywhere has opened at 17th Street and Fifth Avenue, and **Dennis'** (tel. 741-

0770) is already a winner. Dennis' is a big, casual place with green-and-white chairs and tables and, at first glance, might almost be a McDonald's; you order your meal here just the way you would at McDonald's, and computerized service speeds it along to you. But instead of emerging with hamburgers and fries, you get a luscious array of natural mini-meals at very low prices. You might go with the "Inside Pizza," a wholewheat pita bread split and stuffed with veggies and melted mozarella, or pita stuffed with couscous, garbanzos, and salad, each $1.25; or try the all-natural taco at $1.15, the nitrite-, nitrate-free hot dog at $1.15, the spinach or tuna salads ($2.45 and $2.75), the sandwiches served on sesame-soy rolls, the homemade soups, fruit and vegetable juices, fanciful yogurts, and the carrot, orange, and walnut cakes imported from Brownie's, New York's famed full-service natural foods restaurant just around the corner (see above). In cold weather, home-baked wholewheat and honey doughnuts with steaming apple cider are a must. Besides lunch and snacks, Dennis' was planning to serve breakfast and dinner at the time of this writing. Open six days, 11 to 6:30, closed Sundays.

The former private club called The Lambs now houses one of the best eating bargains in town. **The Sanctuary,** 130 West 44th Street (tel. 575-0498), operated by The Church of the Nazarene, offers an open-to-the-public buffet that's brimming with good, wholesome food at rock-bottom prices, in a cool, comfortable quiet room, nicely furnished, with plenty of elbow room and a low-key atmosphere that makes conversation a pleasure. The daily buffet includes hot choices like roast beef or Salisbury steak, quiche Lorraine, and 13 different cold salads, plus a daily soup. The lunch buffet is $3.49, dinner is $4.49, beverages add 50¢ and desserts, like carrot cake (a treat!) or a brownie à la mode, $1.25. No smoking.

Pizza parlors are by no means a rarity in New York—there must be one on every other block—but we know of none that has such a fiercely devoted clientele as **Ray's Famous Pizza** at 465 Avenue of the Americas (corner of 11th Street) in Greenwich Village. Ray's pizzas have marvelously crusty bases, the thickest cheese toppings anywhere, and wonderful flavors—many aficionados have rated them the best in New York. Two pizza slices (it's hard to stop at just one—they're 65¢ each) and a cup of coffee make a satisfying lunch and a wonderful snack anytime you're in the Village.

Before or after catching the view from the top of the World

Trade Center, have a fine lunch or snack downstairs at **The Big Kitchen,** built on the site of the old Washington Market and one of the most imaginative fast-food dispenaries anywhere. Behind enormous checkerboard letters that spell out its name and which also serve as dividers and counters, loom acres of food stalls serving American specialties, almost all of them homemade and with an emphasis on the freshness and quality that make The Market Bar and Dining Rooms (on the same level) and the Windows on the World Restaurant (107 floors skyward) so special. Take your choice of the Delicatessen, which sells overstuffed sandwiches at about $2 and barrel pickles, plus all sorts of delicacies to take home or make a picnic out of right here; the Bakery, which uses no additives or preservatives, and turns out an enormous variety of fresh and fantastically good breads and pastries at low prices; the Oyster Bar, which serves up raw clams and oysters for about 45¢ each and fried fish and chips; a health food section, which serves salads, yogurt, and pita bread sandwiches; a barbecue area which roasts chicken and ribs on spits; and the Grill, which is known for its excellent freshly grilled burger at $1.40. You should be able to put a meal together here anywhere from $2 to $6. Open weekdays from 7 a.m. to 7 p.m., weekends until 5 p.m., The Big Kitchen is a self-service facility, but there are more than enough pleasant tables to seat the lunch-hour throngs.

The stylish Coffee Exchange outside The Big Kitchen sells coffee and pastries to morning commuters, becomes a soup bar at lunch, and a retail coffee bean shop for homeward-bound workers.

Chapter V

SIGHTS OF NEW YORK: THREE ONE-DAY TOURS

IT OFTEN seems to us that New York tourists fall into one of two categories. The first are the compulsive sightseers who feel that if they *don't* get to the top of the World Trade Center, visit the United Nations, have a meal in Chinatown, and take the boat to the Statue of Liberty, they might as well have stayed home. Then there is the other school, the lazy ones who like to know that the World Trade Center is *there* if they really want it, but are perfectly happy just walking around the city, absorbing the sights, the sounds, the sensations as they find them.

Our own feeling is that both have a point: the major sights of New York *are* exciting and important, and you should see as many of them as you comfortably have time and energy for. But you should also allow yourself plenty of time to let New York sink in by osmosis: to rummage through a Village antique store or watch the lovers stroll through Central Park or sip a martini at some cocktail lounge in the sky as the city shimmers below you. A holiday in New York, we think, ought to be made up of equal parts of doing and dreaming—with enough leisure for both.

But fitting everything in can be quite complicated, especially if you're here for just a short time. The quickest way to see the city is, of course, to take a guided tour: **Gray Line** (tel. 397-2600) runs a bevy of excellent ones that will take you uptown, downtown, to Harlem, for a night on the town or an excursion up the Hudson River. You'll get plenty of information and an overall view of where you're at. For an even more overall view, plus a sensational thrill, take a helicopter trip. **Island Helicopters** (tel. 895-5372) leave every day from the Heliport at 34th Street and the East River and skim over the highpoints of New York—the Empire State Building, the Statue of Liberty, the United Nations. Flights range from $9 to $20 to $30 per person, depending on the length of the flight. Similarly exciting flights are conducted on the 30-passenger helicopters of New York Airways for $15; they're the same company which runs more than 150 flights daily from the World Trade Center/Battery Park City Heliport to the three New York airports and back. If you really get turned on to helicopter flying, you can get a wild, unlimited travel card for $162, which permits all the helicopter flying you want for any 31-day period. Reservations: 661-5100.

If, however, you have the time for the in-depth approach, the best way to see the city is to get out and walk. We have, therefore, devised three one-day walking tours (taxis, subways, or buses will get you to each area to explore quickly and economically) that you might use as basic guideposts for seeing the city. If you have more than three days, break the tours up: follow a suggested activity for the morning; spend the afternoon shopping or going to the Central Park Zoo or catching a matinee.

The first tour concentrates mostly on the sights in the midtown area and then takes you downtown to see the Statue of Liberty: it would be ideal if you have just one day in the city. The second tour sends you exploring the financial and shopping district of Downtown Manhattan, takes you to the top of the World Trade Center, then directs you to the Staten Island Ferry, the United Nations, and proposes an evening dining and browsing in Chinatown. On the third day we suggest you see the city from the decks of a "round-the-island" boat, take in a few of the important museums, and explore the shops and sights of Greenwich Village. There are, of course, numerous other places that are important and fun to visit which we'll describe in other chapters. But we think that once you've completed the three main tours, you'll be able to say, "We've seen New York." And if you have children with you, you'd better *not* leave without having seen them: these are the experiences youngsters remember all their lives.

Note: You'll be doing plenty of walking, so be sure to wear comfortable shoes. You should also carry with you two maps, both free. The first, the **New York Visitor's Guide and Map,** is available at the offices of the New York Convention and Visitors Bureau at 90 East 42nd Street, or in an information booth right in the middle of Times Square. (The Bureau will also answer questions by phone: 687-1300). Unfortunately the Bureau does not carry a subway map, so head down to any subway change booth for one of these.

The First Day
(The Empire State Building, Macy's, Rockefeller Center, Radio City Music Hall, then downtown to the Statue of Liberty)

THE EMPIRE STATE BUILDING: You might as well start this tour at the top: the top of the Empire State Building. You'll have plenty of company: some 1,500,000 visitors a year, from all over the world, make the pilgrimage to the world's once-highest building: 1,472 feet above sea level, 102 stories high, a sleek, modernistic monument that well typifies the skyscraper city in its boldness, daring, dominance. The real excitement starts when you reach the 86th-floor Observatory; from the outdoor promenade deck, it's a 360-degree view, and if the day is clear, you can see as far as 50 miles into the distance. But the big show lies below you: Manhattan, an island of steel and concrete and glass rising out of the sea, looking from this height like a Lilliputian landscape until you start to pick out the landmarks: the lacy spires of the New York skyline, the Statue of Liberty, the United Nations, the green expanse of Central Park, the great ships

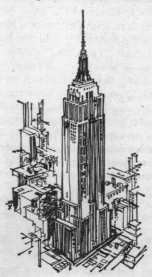

Empire State Building

heading out of the Hudson, bound for Europe. For a view from an even higher vantage, you can go up another 16 stories, to the 102nd floor. From either observation tower (this one is enclosed), the effect is spellbinding: you may forget to leave. But do get down to earth again, to explore at close range the wonders you've glimpsed above.

The Empire State Building, Fifth Avenue and 34th Street, is open every day from 9:30 a.m. to midnight. Admission: $1.70 for adults, 85¢ for children.

While you're here, stop in at the **Guinness World Record Exhibit Hall** on the concourse level to see who and what broke all the records. This multi-media display is great fun for kids and adults alike. Open daily 9:30 to 6:30, admission $1.50 adults, $1.25 children, (tel. 947-2339).

MACY'S: Since you're already on 34th Street and you'll have to see Macy's sooner or later, you might as well catch it now. Walk just a block west from the Empire State Building to Herald Square and visit the world's biggest store. You can shop here for anything from hams to hammocks to haute couture; if you're lucky, you might catch an Irish Festival or a Mideast Bazaar or some other international fiesta of the kind that Macy's frequently presents. Be sure to visit "The Cellar" downstairs, a veritable street of little shops—a pastry shop, a candy shop, a produce area—selling gourmet foods and cookware from all over. There's even a branch of P.J. Clarke's famous bar-restaurant down here. Take the kids to "Growing Up On Five," a new floor for children that completely outfits youngsters from infants to pre-teens and has a toy shop, shoe department, pet store, book store and decorative fabrics store to boot. Also on this floor is the greenery-filled, mirrored Fountain Restaurant, for old-time ice cream treats and light meals. After you've exhausted Macy's (could that be possible?), or yourself, you might consider Gimbels and Korvettes, next door. Proceed or ignore, as you please, and then hop a bus going uptown on Sixth Avenue (Avenue of the Americas) to your next destination, Rockefeller Center, which runs from 48th to 51st Streets, observing the new office-building skyscrapers that line the Avenue. Somewhere between Macy's and Rockefeller Center, you could schedule a stop for lunch (see Chapter IV on restaurants).

ROCKEFELLER CENTER: It's noted as one of the architectural marvels of New York—and of the United States, a high-water mark of urban design. Although it is one of the busiest, most heavily trafficked areas in the city, this 24-acre, 21-skyscraper complex gives the feeling of old-world gentility and beauty, thanks to the masterful use that has been made of open space. You'll appreciate this as you approach the Center from the best vantage point, the Channel Gardens, which begin between 49th and 50th Streets, across Fifth Avenue from St. Patrick's Cathedral and Saks Fifth Avenue. Depending on the season, the gardens will be abloom with chrysanthemums or lilies or roses or tropical plants, and you'll see scores of other tourists and natives stopping to sit on the benches and maybe munch a lunchtime sandwich here. On either side of the walk is a continental array of shops and services. Continue down the promenade to the central sunken plaza, the focal point of the complex. In winter, the plaza is an ice-skating rink, a Brueghel canvas in the heart of the city; in summer, an open-air restaurant. Directly behind the plaza is the massive statue of Prometheus by Paul Manship, with its fountain in back; and behind that the RCA Building soars skyward.

However, in order to really appreciate the intricacies of Rockefeller Center, you should take a guided tour, which also takes you backstage at Radio City Music Hall. Tour groups leave frequently from the RCA Building from 10 until 5 every day, and cost $2.35 for adults, $1.50 for children five to 11. The tour also includes admission to the Observation Roof, another stunning vantage point from which to view the vista of New York. If you've already seen the view from the Empire State Building, you will be forgiven for skipping this one, but better yet, come back some evening for a trip to the Observation Roof alone (admission is $1.60 for adults, 85¢ for children), to see one of the original—and still the greatest—of the city's light shows. Or combine sightseeing with a romantic drink sky-high in the Rainbow Room, where the view is included in the price of your cocktail (see Chapter VIII on nightclubs). There's also a tour which includes lunch at the famous Promenade Cafe, the movie and stage show at the Music Hall, in addition to the usual tour. Price ranges from $12.95 to $14.95 (tel. 489-2947).

RADIO CITY MUSIC HALL: Since you've already seen one of the world's tallest buildings, its biggest department store, and its biggest privately owned complex of office buildings, you might as well see the world's biggest theater—which is, of course, the famed Radio City Music Hall. In fact, if all the sightseeing has worn you out, now may be a good time to stop (it should be about midafternoon) and relax for two or three hours. Even if you continue the tour as we outline below, remember to come back here another time. The Music Hall is currently living on borrowed time: at the time of this writing, it had been given a reprieve, but it is likely that it will close within a year or so. See it while you can. The Music Hall, the ultimate expression of Art Deco '30s architecture, with its black-mirrored lounge, its graceful curving staircases, still has a very special air about it. It is also just about the last holdout from the days of the '30s and '40s when theaters everywhere offered *both* a film and stage show for one low price. The Music Hall concentrates on wholesome, family-type entertainments which can range from excellent to innocuous, but the stage show is always something special: you'll see the Rockettes (America's most famous chorus girls) and enough spectacle—stages rising and disappearing out of the pit, fireworks, curtains of rain and steam—to make you suspect it must be the Fourth of July. The theater seats 6,000 people (we told you it was the world's biggest), and there are always some 5,000 seats available on a first-come, first-served basis. Prices vary according to the day of the week and the time of day from a low of $3.25 to a top of $4. To save yourself the bother of waiting in line, you might write ahead for a reserved seat in the First Mezzanine. These cost $5 for all performances. Write to: Box Office Treasurer, Radio City Music Hall, 1260 Avenue of the Americas, New York, NY 10021.

STATUE OF LIBERTY AND ELLIS ISLAND: Let's wind up your first day's sightseeing now, with an exclamation point: a trip downtown to the Statue of Liberty, and its American Museum of Immigration. The Statue of Liberty is one sight in New York that no one, not even the most blasé, should miss. It's simple to get to: just make your way to the West Side IRT subway, take a downtown local train to South Ferry, and head for the Statue of Liberty boats; they leave on the hour from 9 until 5, with additional ferry service during July, and August, and for a fare of $1.50 for adults, 50¢ for children 11 years and under, they will deposit you, in about 20 minutes, on Liberty Island, a short distance from the statue. You'll enjoy your visit more if you come early on a weekday, since the crowds get thick in the afternoons, and particularly on weekends and holidays. (Phone for Museum information: 732-1286; for boats, 269-5755.)

Every schoolchild, of course, knows the story of the statue: of how it was given to the United States by the people of France in 1886 to commemorate the alliance of the two countries during the American Revolution; how its construction became the ruling passion of the French sculptor Auguste Bartholdi, who raised funds in France and then designed the monument (Alexandre Gustave Eiffel, who built a rather famous tower in France, did the supporting framework); and how the people of the United States, reluctant to match the one-million-franc contribution of the French people, had to be prodded into it by an intensive campaign led by the *New York World's* Joseph Pulitzer. Finally, the money was raised, and now it seems that the statue was always there, so magnificently does it blend into its site in Upper Bay, so splendidly does it typify the ideals and dreams on which the nation was built. Stepping from her chains, Liberty, a tablet commemorating the date of July 4, 1776, in her left hand, the torch of freedom held high in her right, has become the symbol, to thousands of immigrants and exiles from all over, of a new life, a new world. The story of these immigrants is eloquently told at the American Museum of Immigration, a new addition to the complex, located in the base of the statue. It's worth a look.

When you actually get to the statue, the statistics—the figure is 152 feet high, the pedestal another 150 feet, the arm 42 feet long, the head large enough for a man to stand in—become an awesome reality. There's an elevator to the top of the pedestal

Statue of Liberty

and, from there, a 12-story stairway to the top, which your kids will undoubtedly take. If you've got the energy to join them, you'll be rewarded with a magic view of the New York skyline.

Note: You won't get too close, but you'll also get a good view of the statue and the skyline from the decks of the Staten Island Ferry, another New York must that we'll tell you more about, below.

Another boat trip that you may want to make in this area, is the one to Ellis Island, the portal through which more than 12,000,000 immigrants entered the United States. Circle Line Ellis Island Ferry makes frequent spring-through-fall departures from Battery Park; fare for the 90-minute round trip is $2.50. On the island, you'll take part in a guided tour conducted by National Park Service personnel. Ellis Island is not much to look at, but it stirs poignant memories of the aspirations and disappointment of those who did—and those who did not—make it to the promised land.

Now that you've seen New York from the top, cased the biggest and the best, you deserve a rest. Plan a leisurely dinner and get yourself tickets to the best Broadway show in town.

The Second Day
(Downtown Manhattan, the World Trade Center, the South Street Seaport, the United Nations, Ford Foundation Garden, and Chinatown)

DOWNTOWN MANHATTAN: If you are interested in history— or money—or architecture—or the sea—you will have to visit Downtown Manhattan. Haunted with ghosts of the city's past, booming with construction and commerce of the present, an area rich in classical architecture and sleek, new futuristic office buildings, ringed by the sea that made its wealth possible, this oldest area of the city is so richly textured that you could spend days here without exhausting its possibilities. But even a morning's walk will give you a basic feeling of what created New York and still makes it tick. For youngsters, this area is a must. To start your explorations, take any downtown train to Wall Street (an express stop) on either the East or West Side IRT trains.

More than anything else, New York is a marketplace. Today it is the greatest one on earth. It has always been a marketplace. It was settled, back in 1626, not as a haven for political or religious freedom as most of the other colonies were, but as a fur-trading post for the Dutch West India Company. Peter Minuit, the governor of Nieuw Amsterdam, technically "bought" the island from the Manhattoes Indians for $24 worth of baubles; 22 years later the Dutch allowed the English to take possession and rename it New York without so much as a fight. But a little over a hundred years later, after a very big fight, the fledgling revolutionary government of the United States of America established its capital here and inaugurated its wartime hero, General George Washington, as its president.

The city grew with the lusty young nation: thanks to the opening of the Erie Canal, it became one of the country's major marketplaces; after the Civil War, when the canal was no longer important, its ideal deep-water harbor attracted to it the commerce of many nations. The temples of finance and commerce grew up alongside the water's edge, and this is where they still are. A modest stock exchange had already been set up—under a buttonwood tree in 1792—but it was not until the New York financiers had been able to underwrite the Civil War that Wall Street took its place as the financial power of the nation—and, indirectly, of much of the world. Residential New York grew up and moved north, but the citadel of money and power remains. And this is where you begin your downtown tour: **Wall Street.**

The best place to start your exploration is at Broadway and Wall, in the quiet calm of Trinity Church, a graceful English Gothic beauty that was built by Richard Upjohn and completed in 1846. This designated National Landmark was once the tallest building in Lower Manhattan. In its tranquil cemetery lie buried a few parishioners who once lived in this area; Robert Fulton, Alexander Hamilton, and other early leading Americans. You can visit both church and cemetery daily from 7 to 6. An Acoustiguide tour is available.

After paying your respects to these early New Yorkers (or perhaps catching a free lunchtime concert, or one of the other noontime activities), proceed down Wall Street (there really was once a wall here made of tree trunks by the Dutch settlers to protect their city from the wilderness) and stop at the corner of Wall and Nassau Streets, at the **Federal Hall National Memorial.** The place is full of ghosts: it was on this site that John Peter Zenger won the trial that established the right of freedom of the press and it was here that General Washington took the oath of office as the first president, in 1789. A statue of Washington commemorates the event. The first American Congress met here

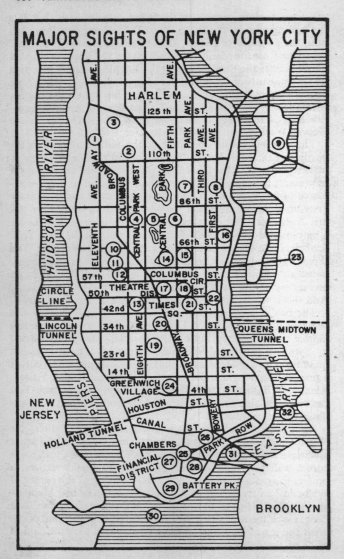

MAJOR SIGHTS OF NEW YORK CITY

KEY TO THE NUMBERED REFERENCES ON OUR MAJOR SIGHTS MAP: 1.—Grant's Tomb; 2.—Cathedral of St. John the Divine; 3.—Columbia University; 4.—Museum of Natural History and Planetarium; 5.—Shakespeare-in-the-park; 6.—Metropolitan Museum of Art; 7.—Guggenheim Museum; 8.—Gracie Mansion (Mayor's residence); 9.—Triborough bridge; 10.—Lincoln Center for the Performing Arts; 11.—Fordham Law School; 12.—The Coliseum; 13.—Madison Square Garden; 14.—Central Park Zoo; 15.—Temple Emanu-el; 16.—Cornell Medical Center; 17.—Rockefeller Center, Radio City; 18.—St. Patrick's Cathedral; 19.—Penn Station; 20.—Empire State Building; 21.—Grand Central Station; 22.—United Nations Building; 23.—Queensborough Bridge; 24.—Washington Square; 25.—City Hall; 26.—Chinatown and the Bowery; 27.—Trinity Church; 28.—Stock Exchange; 29.—Staten Island Ferry; 30.—Statue of Liberty; 31.—Brooklyn and Manhattan Bridge; 32.—Williamsburg Bridge.

and adopted the Bill of Rights. You'll occasionally find some kind of protest or demonstration being held on the steps, perhaps in response to the street plaque commemorating the Zenger trial and quoting his words: "Everyone who loves liberty ought to encourage freedom of speech." Mostly, however, office workers lounge on the steps to eat their lunch and get a bit of sunshine, quite oblivious to the history that was made on this site, or the fact that the current building (1842), first a Customs House, later a Sub-Treasury, now a museum, is considered perhaps the finest example of Greek Revival architecture in the city. Explore this Athenian gem in New York. Inside is a free museum of the Colonial and Early Federal periods, open from 9 to 4:30, Mondays through Fridays, daily June through August. Special programs—films, folksinging concerts, etc.—are often held here.

If Federal Hall is the shrine to history on Wall Street, the **New York Stock Exchange** (corner Broad and Wall) is the temple to the gods of money. Appropriately, the building is done in "Renaissance-temple" architecture. Inside, in the Great Hall of the Exchange, vast numbers of men (and four, count them, women) stockbrokers acting for clients all over the world, are buying and selling millions of dollars worth of securities in an atmosphere that, to the uninitiated, looks like a pandemonium. To understand the subtle inner workings of the whole scheme, you can take a guided tour; they are offered at frequent intervals from Monday through Friday, between 10 and 4 at 20 Broad Street. Free. The guides, naturally, are multilingual. You can also watch activity on the trading floor, see a movie and operate three-dimensional displays in the Exhibit Hall. Or, just drop in, gaze at the ticker tape, and see what's happened to your shares of General Motors while you've been away. The Exchange is the second most popular tourist attraction in New York. The public is also invited to the Visitors' Gallery of the American Stock Exchange, 78 Trinity Place, Mondays through Fridays, 9:45 to 3:30. Free.

Those who are really turned on by money and banking might continue, now, a few blocks north on Broadway to 33 Liberty Street, the site of the **Federal Reserve Bank of New York.** This formidable Renaissance palace actually has more gold than Fort Knox. To see what goes on here, take a guided tour, through the gold vault and cash and coin handling operations. Tours are given at 10, 11, 1, and 2 during banking days, and reservations must be made at least one week in advance. Family groups may include children. You may write to the Public Information Department at the bank, or phone 791-6130 to request a reservation.

Not far from here is 100 William Street, one of the more interesting examples of the new skyscraper architecture of the downtown area. It is also the site of the Lower Manhattan Ticket Center, where, every weekday between 11:30 and 5:30 one may buy half-price tickets for that night only to Broadway plays, Lincoln Center and City Center concerts, and other attractions. If you're planning on going out at night, stop in now and get your tickets.

Head back to Broadway now and walk west one block for the highlight of your downtown excursion: a less-than-a-minute elevator ride will take you zooming to the top of the **World Trade Center,** the world's almost-tallest building. Here, at the Observation Deck on the 107th floor of the South Tower (Tower Two)— more than a quarter-mile in the sky—you'll see perhaps the most spectacular view on earth. Below you is all of New York, its bridges, its monuments (now you can *see* the Empire State Building that you've just looked out of), the silent streets below, the rivers and their toy ships, and, on a clear day, a view that extends 50 miles in all directions. It's hard to say when the view is most dazzling—in morning sunlight or in evening splendor; dusk, when the lights are just beginning to come up on the darkening city, is particularly enchanting. The Observation Deck on the

107th floor is glass-enclosed; if you also go up to the promenade on the roof above the 110th floor, you'll be on the highest outdoor observation platform in the world. After you've seen your fill, have a look at the entertaining exhibit on the history of trade and a peek at the souvenir shop. Since anywhere from eight to nine thousand people visit the Observation Deck on weekends, try to plan your visit for a weekday, when there will be only a few thousand of you. It's open from 9:30 a.m. to 9:30 p.m. daily, with an admission charge of $1.70 for adults, 85¢ for children (tel. 466-7377 for information).

Now that the Observation Deck has put you in the mood for gorgeous views, you may want to see a similar view and have a drink and hors d'ouevres at the Hors D'Ouevrerie section of the stunning Windows on the World Restaurant, perched above Tower One, the North Tower of the World Trade Center (see Chapter IV for details on the City Lights Bar and the Restaurant). Or, stop for refreshment back on the ground, on the concourse level of the Trade Center, either at the Market Dining Rooms & Bar, built on the site of the old Washington Market, or at The Big Kitchen with its various food stalls (including a raw bar for seafood and a natural foods pantry), with modestly priced food for every taste. You can also have a peek at the exhibition at the United States Customhouse and even do a bit of shopping. Any children in the crowd will enjoy a visit to a branch of F.A.O. Schwarz, New York's most famous toy emporium.

Note: If you've scheduled your trip to the World Trade Center as a separate excursion, take the IRT 7th Avenue subway local to Cortland Street, or the IND AA or E train to Chambers Street. Underground parking is also available.

Return to Broadway now, and proceed south. You'll pass a branch of **John Wanamaker's,** all that remains of that once-famous New York emporium (the main building uptown was torn down some years ago) on your left, and you'll also see the Marine Midland Trust building at 140 Broadway, with Isamu Noguchi's enormous rectangular cube, precariously balanced on one corner in front of it. 140 Broadway is one of the few new buildings in the area that has made any attempt at public art or sculpture; another is 1 Chase Manhattan Plaza, where Jean Dubuffet's whimsical "mushrooms" tower skyward. This is a particularly busy area of Broadway, where you'll often see street musicians playing to the lunchtime crowds. **Bowling Green Park,** where the Dutch burghers actually used to bowl, is ahead of you (it has been restored to look the way it did a century ago with London plane trees, wooden benches, and old-time lamp posts), and so is the massive neoclassic former **Customs House,** with its imposing sculptures of Asia, America, Africa, and Europe, done by Daniel Chester French of Lincoln Memorial fame. (The building is currently being considered as a site for a multipurpose commercial and cultural center.)

Keep going, now, on the other side of the street from Bowling Green and Battery Park, until you come to the **Seamen's Church Institute,** 15 State Street, a handsome modern structure which not only serves and houses merchant seamen, but is also a favorite lunch spot for downtown office workers. You might join them, either in the cafeteria with its glass wall overlooking the shipping activities of the harbor or at the carpeted and comfortable dining room. Meals at both are very inexpensive (under $3 in the cafeteria, under $4 in the dining room), and the food is good. Note the interesting ship's bells and maritime paintings outside the cafeteria and the free-form stairways with plaques hanging in the stairwells, somehow reminiscent of a ship's mast. Rest rooms, telephones, and a gift shop downstairs all help to make this a pleasant place to break your tour.

Next door to the Seamen's Institute, at 7 State Street, is one of the few remaining examples of early Federal architecture in New York. Built by John McCoomb as a private townhouse in 1800, Watson House is noted for the colonnade that curves with the line of the Street. It is now **Our Lady of the Rosary Church,** the shrine of Saint Elizabeth Seton.

Right behind State Street is Pearl Street, and, at the corner of Pearl and Broad Street is one of New York's most famous historical houses. Built in 1709, **Fraunces Tavern** was an establishment favored by George Washington, and it became part of American history when Washington bade farewell to his troops here after the American Revolution. Upstairs is a museum of that period (open Monday to Friday, 10 to 4), and downstairs is the restaurant, where the food is still excellent, and you could have a lovely lunch, in the company of illustrious ghosts.

Now make your way to the waterfront and begin walking up South Street, once dotted with ship chandlers' stores and other establishments having to do with sailing and the sea. The old South Street and Front Street, which runs parallel to it and where, until very recently, coffee-roasting houses still processed the fragrant beans right off the ships, have been totally taken over by giant office buildings. Those who mourn the old days on the waterfront have mixed emotions about the steel-and-glass monsters, but there is no denying that some are handsome. If you're interested in architecture, have a look yourself at the soaring columns of Two New York Plaza or of **55 Water Street,** which we find the most impressive building here. It is also the site of the **Downtown Branch of the Whitney Museum of Art,** open weekdays from 11 to 3. Exhibits change every six weeks, and there is a performing art series. Closed the last two weeks in August. Phone 483-0011 for information. We especially like the plaza on its northern side (although we would prefer some grass to all that concrete) that overlooks the highway. Here one can join the local office workers eating lunch at the chairs and tables outside (or join the executive set inside at the elegant **Buttonwood Restaurant**), or just sit and watch the tugs and the whirlibirds and the harbor traffic, catch the marvelous ocean breezes, and dream a little bit about the vanished days of the tall ships, the giant clippers that came from all over the world to drop anchor at the port of New York, arching their bowsprits across South Street.

SOUTH STREET SEAPORT: To see what a very practical group of dreamers and visionaries are doing to commemorate, at least, the old days of South Street, walk a few blocks north now, and you'll soon come to the South Street Seaport Museum. The museum is a five-block center that stretches from Piers 15, 16, and 17 all the way over to Fulton Street, and it is dedicated not only to preserving New York's seaport heritage but also to encouraging city planners and builders to make the sea an intrinsic part of new construction, to create, in fact, a waterfront renaissance. Walk out on the piers, have a look at the water and the gulls swooping down, then board, if you like, some of the ships. The current fleet consists of, among others, the original *Ambrose Lightship,* which guarded the approaches to the Port of New York from 1908 on; the 376-foot barque *Peking,* one of the world's largest square-rigged sailing vessels; the *Pioneer* (a sail training vessel); the square-rigger *Wavertree;* the *Lettie G. Howard,* a Gloucester fisherman of the 1890s; and the *Major General William H. Hart,* an old city ferry built in 1925. The Seaport suggests a voluntary contribution of $1.50 for adults, 75¢ for children, for visitors: the same prices hold for going aboard the ships.

For those who have the time, there's an even more delicious

possibility: a chance to take a three-hour cruise on the 91-year-old, 102-foot-long, two-masted schooner, **Pioneer.** *Pioneer,* one of the few coasting schooners still in existence, took part in the Bicentennial Op-Sail celebration. Her destination depends on winds and tides; the passengers are limited to 25; and there is plenty of space for blankets and guitars. Those who are qualified are invited to help in sailing the ship. Bring soft-soled shoes, warm clothing, food, and beer or wine (but no liquor), and reserve as soon as you can (at least a week in advance) by phoning 766-9076. Cruises cost $12 for adults, $6 for children, and depart from the Seaport at 1 and 6 p.m., weekdays; at 10 a.m., 2, and 7 p.m., Saturdays, Sundays, and holidays. The full season runs from the end of May through Labor Day; weekend cruises only the month of May.

There's always plenty of activity going on down at the South Street Seaport, especially on weekends: chances are good that you may catch a concert of sea chanteys, attend an antique show or an art fair, watch knot-tying demonstrations, or let the kids take in a puppet show. There's usually a flea market on Sundays. Watch the papers for details.

You might also want to pay a visit to the Seaport's land attractions. Leave the kids to enjoy themselves at **The Children's Store** at 5 Fulton Street (where you can buy them a Seaport Museum T-shirt for $2), while you have a look at Museum headquarters, with its changing exhibits like "A Closer Look at Tugs" at 16 Fulton Street; at the **Book and Chart Store,** 25 Fulton Street; the **Art Gallery,** 25 Water Street; **Bowne & Co. Printers** (a re-creation of a 19th-century stationers's) at 211 Water Street; and the **Model Shop and Gallery** at 207 Water Street. Anyone who cooks will enjoy The Seaport Store with its varied housewares and gadgets for cooking and serving fish; many are 19th- or early 20th-century reproductions.

Hungry? That's easy. There's simple food right at Pier 16, but, even better, **Sloppy Louie's,** one of New York's classic seafood restaurants (see Chapter IV) is right across the street, open weekdays only. Food bars proffering a variety of tasty snacks are also found in the **Fulton Market,** diagonally across from the Seaport. After you've had your fill of wursts or health-food sandwiches, or, best of all, super-fresh steamers, fried shrimp, oysters and clams on the half shell, and a very good chowder from the **Fulton Clam Bar,** browse through the marvelous boutique area: you can shop for coffee beans and crafts, imports from Guatemala, miniature glass, and all manner of artful objects.

You may want to conclude your visit to the Seaport by stopping at the espresso sidewalk cafe, where you can relax and watch the crowds go by.

Backtrack a little bit now, and proceed a few blocks south, in the direction you came from, and you'll find yourself at the next part of your tour, the Staten Island Ferry.

If you've covered even half the places we've told you about downtown, you're probably pretty tired. The ideal way to rest your feet, recoup your energy, and catch a few more "sights" at the same time is to take a trip on the Staten Island Ferry. The cost is 25¢ for a round trip for an enthralling, hour-long excursion into the world's biggest harbor. Most of the Staten Island commuters will be sitting inside reading their papers, but do join the sightseers out on the deck, where you can view the busy harbor traffic: tugs and railroad barges, garbage scows and jaunty yachts, freighters and ocean liners on their way to Europe. En route, you'll pass close to the Statue of Liberty, and also catch glimpses of Governor's Island and of Ellis Island which, up until 1954, was the gateway to America for millions of immigrants. When the boat arrives at St. George, Staten Island, debark, walk through the terminal, and catch the next boat going back to Manhattan. This is really the best part of the trip, for now you can pretend you are coming in from Europe and catching your first sight of the fabled New York skyline looming up there ahead of you. If you have time, try a ferry ride at night, when the skyline is even more dazzling. On a hot summer night, the ferry beats air conditioning by a mile and it's practically a haven for young lovers who find riding back and forth all night the cheapest date in New York.

Pause now for a leisurely lunch (or have a snack on the ferry or in the St. George terminal) and make your way uptown to 45th Street and First Avenue, the entrance to the United Nations.

UNITED NATIONS: Downtown Manhattan is where New York history was made; the United Nations is where world history happens every day. An international enclave on the East River, bounded by 42nd Street on the south and 48th Street on the north, it is headquarters for almost 4,000 men and women from all over the world who carry on the work of the Secretariat and the General Assembly.

Just *being* at the United Nations has an excitement about it that exists nowhere else. You could have a lovely visit just walk-ing around, observing the sculptures and art works donated by the member nations (in the garden, for example, a massive sculp-ture of a Soviet worker beats a sword into a plowshare), shopping in the downstairs stores (more about these later), and observing the lively international crowd, but do take time to attend one of the General Assembly or other meetings and/or to take a guided tour. Tickets to the meetings are given out in the lobby of the General Assembly building just before they start, on a first-come, first-served basis. There is no charge. To find out in advance what meetings will be held, phone PL 4-1234 between 9:30 and 5. Once you gain admission, you can plug in your earphones and listen to the debates—sometimes quite lively—in either English or French or Chinese or Spanish or Russian—the official lan-guages of the U.N. Guided tours begin about every ten minutes, from 9:15 to 4:45, and cost $2 for adults, $1.50 for college and high school students, $1 for junior high and elementary school students (those under five are not permitted). The tours are a wonderful introduction to the history and activities of the U.N., and also give you a chance to explore the varied collections of art and sculpture. There are also tours for non-English-speaking guests.

You could easily browse away a few hours downstairs at the United Nations. Our favorite spot here is the Gift Center, where beautiful and tasteful handicrafts from many of the member nations are sold. On a recent visit, for example, we found pewter ware from Norway, beautifully painted nesting dolls from the Soviet Union, silk scarves from India, brassware from Iran, carved figures from Nigeria. The collection of ethnic dolls is enough to win the heart of any little girl on your list. Stamp buffs should stop in at the United Nations Postal Service, the only spot on the globe (besides the United Nations office in Geneva) where you can mail cards and letters bearing U.N. postage stamps; these stamps, which deal with the work of the U.N. and its agencies, are issued about five times a year. And don't neglect, during your visit to the U.N., to look for the nearby Delacorte Geyser in the East River, which spouts between the hours of 12 and 2.

If you arrive early enough, have lunch at the United Nations in the Delegates Dining Room. It's open to the public Mondays through Fridays, between 11:30 and 12 and from 2 to 2:30, on a first-come, first-served basis. Although you probably won't see any delegates (the room is reserved for them between 12 and 1), the view of the East River and the United Nations gardens is one of the best in town.

While you're in the U.N. neighborhood, it would be a shame not to cross the street and have a look at the Ford Foundation building, designed by Kevin Roche and occupying the block between 42nd and 43rd Streets. Considered one of the rare modern architectural masterpieces of New York, a structure built with humanistic concerns for its employees and its environment, it is especially notable for its splendid indoor garden—a glorious, 12-story, 160-foot-high hothouse. The noted architectural critic of the *New York Times,* Ada Louise Huxtable, called the building "a splendid, shimmering Crystal Palace" and its garden "probably one of the most romantic environments ever devised by corporate man." Don't miss a quiet few moments here. The garden is open weekdays from 9 to 5. Phone 573-5011 for information.

CHINATOWN: The final part of this sightseeing sojourn takes place at night. Head down to Chinatown, have dinner at one of the many intriguing restaurants there (see Chapter IV for suggestions), and, after you've feasted on the likes of won ton soup and moo goo gai pan and sin koo har kow, spend the next hour or so just walking around the streets. There's plenty to see here: this is hometown, U.S.A., to about 6,000 Americans of Chinese descent, and on weekends, thousands of relatives and friends who've moved elsewhere come home to visit. They pack the tiny winding alleys and streets, and so do the tourists, for this is one of the most exotic and appealing sections of the city, (If you happen to be in New York for the Chinese New Year, usually early in February, you're in for a great treat: parades in the streets, fireworks, an Oriental Fourth of July.) There is a **Chinese Museum** at 8 Mott Street (tel. WO 4-1542; open from 10 to 6 daily. Admission: 50¢ for adults, 35¢ for children on weekdays, but 75¢ and 50¢ on weekends and holidays), which the kids will like a lot. We are always quite satisfied just window-shopping, looking at exotic Chinese herbs like ginseng in the pharmacies, bamboo sprouts, thousand-year-old eggs and lily roots in the groceries. Poking around the gift shops is delightful. Many wares from the People's Republic have now made their way into what was once exclusively a Nationalist Chinese stronghold. There's a lot of good, inexpensive Orientalia here, but you can find a lot more than just fans and ivory carvings: several new gift stores have opened here recently, including some swinging pop-art and psychedelic ones. Prices are a bit lower than in midtown. Buy the kids—or yourself—a few sticks of incense, and then go back to the hotel to relax and sort out the day's impressions. Tomorrow, we promise, a gentler pace.

Note: Chinatown begins just below Canal Street, on the Lower East Side. The main street is Mott. Take either the Lexington Avenue Subway or the BMT to Canal Street and walk to Mott.

The Third Day
(A Cruise Around the Island, the Metropolitan Museum of Art, the Museum of Modern Art, Greenwich Village, and SoHo)

CIRCLE LINE: We promised we'd let you relax a bit more today, so let's spend the morning aboard a boat. You will, however, have company, for this particular vessel is the Circle Line sightseeing boat that makes a three-hour, 'round-the-island tour of Manhattan, and it is one of the most popular attractions in town and one of the best. We recommend it to those who've never seen the city and to those who've seen everything two dozen times; it's one of the best inventions for cooling off in the sultry New York summer.

The unusual thing about this trip is the perspective it gives you; the buildings that you've already seen at close range suddenly look quite different when viewed from the sea. Your orbit around the island begins at Pier 83, at the foot of West 43rd Street, takes you down into Upper Bay where you'll see the Statue of Liberty and Ellis Island, then up along the East River, as the Brooklyn Bridge, the Manhattan Bridge, and the former Brooklyn Navy Yard come into view. Up you go along the East River to view the splendor of the United Nations as seen from the sea, and further along, Gracie Mansion, the home of the mayor, comes into view. The East River merges into the Harlem River, and you go north through Hell Gate, then on into Spuyten Duyvil (the last two, former navigational hazards at the confluence of two rivers, have now been tamed), and merge into the Hudson. The giant lacework of the George Washington Bridge emerges now, and you go down the Hudson, joining slews of tiny pleasure craft, work boats, perhaps even an oil tanker or freighter coming down from the upper Hudson. To your left is Riverside Park, where thousands of New Yorkers come to cool off on a summer's day; small boys are apt to be fishing in the river, though there's nothing much to catch. You'll spot Grant's Tomb as you come down along 122nd Street. As you approach midtown, the docks of the great shipping companies—Cunard, the French Line, the Italian Line come into view. As your sightseeing yacht docks, you may be lucky enough to see a slew of tugs nudge the *QE II* or the *Maxim Gorky* into her berth!

The sightseeing boat comes equipped with both a refreshment stand and a narrator who is likely to tell some very ancient jokes; but you will emerge rested, cool, and well-informed about New York. *Parent's note:* Children about eight and over love this trip, but really young ones can get awfully wriggly; remember, it takes three hours, and you can't get off!

During the summer, trips are scheduled every 45 minutes, from 9:45 to 5, less frequently at other times of the year (the season runs from late March to mid-November), and the cost is $6 for adults, $3 for children under 12. Prices are subject to change, and may be higher by the time you read this. To reach West 43rd Street, you can take either the 42nd Street (No. 106), 49th Street, or 34th Street westbound crosstown buses; all stop within a few feet of the ticket booth. For further information, phone 563-3200.

Back on land, now, and to two of the city's great museums for the afternoon. You may, very likely, want to spend days at New York's fascinating museums (we'll give you more details later), but even if time is short, you should visit both the Metropolitan Museum of Art and the Museum of Modern Art. Since it's probably lunchtime by now, stop in at either the Metropolitan's poolside restaurant on the main floor, *very* relaxing; or the Modern's cafeteria and sculpture garden, very exciting; both are inexpensive. Then devote your afternoon to art.

METROPOLITAN MUSEUM OF ART: Long the grand dowager of the city's museums, the Metropolitan Museum of Art, Fifth Avenue at 82nd Street, is now acting like a young thing kicking up her heels. During the directorship of Thomas Hoving (1967-1978)—who, earlier, as parks commissioner, turned Central Park into a nonstop playground for swinging adults—the museum came out from its Neo-Renaissance ivory tower with revved-up contemporary shows, inviting and getting controversy, stirring the citizenry up about the functions of a great museum: repository or vital participant in community affairs.

That feeling of excitement now pervades the vast expanses of the Metropolitan which is, of course, one of the great museums of the world, a living monument to 5,000 years of man and his arts. Whether you're interested in Egyptian artifacts or Roman armor or Chinese porcelain or Renaissance or Impressionist painting, the Metropolitan is the place. You could spend weeks studying the collection of European and American paintings, a masterful group of Raphaels, Titians, El Grecos, Rembrandts, Picassos, Motherwells, Braques—enough to make the head swim. But that is only a small aspect of the whole. The Islamic galleries house one of the largest collections in the world. The collection of Far Eastern art—the jades and vases and scrolls and temple statuary of China and Japan and India are also breathtaking, as are the treasures of Near Eastern art, of Roman and Greek statuary and artifacts. In 1976, the Metropolitan began bringing its complete Egyptian collection—some 45,000 objects chronicling the daily life, history, religious beliefs, and aesthetic ideals of the civilization of Egypt, from 300,000 B.C. to A.D. 641—out of storage and into permanent display. Sixteen dramatic galleries, considered a triumph of art and scholarship, and the incredible Temple of Dendur in the new Sackler Wing are now open. The exhibit is absorbing for everyone, and the kids, especially, will love the mummies! The Metropolitan brings the world to New York, and, quite rightly, the world comes to its door (last year it counted 3,567,658 visitors—about two million more than the Statue of Liberty and the Empire State Building!). It is an SRO attraction, a major sightseeing target.

If you have time enough, you can usually take a free gallery tour, hear a lecture, or catch a film; inquire at the main desk. A tasteful gift shop sells many items of museum quality, and there's an enormous print shop on the lower level. The kids can be both entertained and instructed at the Junior Museum downstairs, with its own snackbar. The Fountain Restaurant on the main floor, named for Carl Milles's striking sculpture which stands in a pool of water, is not renowned for imaginative food, but it is certainly one of the more graceful restaurant settings in town. The Metropolitan is open Wednesdays through Saturdays from 10 to 4:45; Tuesdays until 8:45 p.m.; Sundays and holidays, from 11 to 4:45. Closed Mondays and Monday holidays. There is a "Pay What You Wish" admission charge, but you must pay something.

For recorded information, phone 535-7710; for news of concerts and lectures, 879-5512.

MUSEUM OF MODERN ART: Younger, brasher, more daring than the Metropolitan, the Museum of Modern Art, 11 West 53rd Street, has been controversial ever since it opened in 1929. The Modern's early shows—of fur-lined teacups, Dadaesque landscapes of the mind, cubism and abstractions—were considered shocking by the staid art establishment of the time; now there are painters and sculptors who actually picket the Modern, declaring it too old hat! Whichever side you're on, the Modern is a great, lively, wonderfully exciting museum which takes all of modern art and design as its province—and that includes photography, film, pottery, furniture, and architecture, as well as paintings and sculpture. As for the paintings, the "Old Masters"—the Picassos, Chagalls, Kandinskys, Mondrians, Tchelitchews—are up on the second and third floors, and a visit to this collection is surely an essential part of a trip to New York. So is a look at the splendid outdoor Sculpture Garden with its Rodins and Calders and Nevelsons and Maillols; it is one of the most special places in the city. Devotees of old and new films practically make the downstairs theater of the museum a second home: it's the place to catch an early Garbo classic, a Flaherty masterpiece, your favorite Bogart flick, recent films you might have missed at the box office, as well as the work of new filmmakers.

The Museum of Modern Art is open Mondays, Tuesdays, Fridays, Saturdays and Sundays from 11 to 6; Thursday, until 9; closed Wednesdays. Admission is free for members, $2 for adults, 75¢ for children under 16 and Senior Citizens; $1.25 for full-time students with current ID. Tuesday is "Pay What You Wish" day. Admission includes entrance to the movie. Films are shown every day except Wednesday. Because there is usually a heavy demand for tickets, it's a good bet to get there as early as possible to commandeer a reservation. For information on current exhibitions, phone 956-7070. For daily film showings, phone 956-7078.

Note: During warm weather, lunch in the Sculpture Garden is a particular delight.

Schedule the last part of this odyssey for a late afternoon and/or early evening and plan to have dinner midjourney. For this is a visit to New York's most colorful area, Greenwich Village, and you'll want to have plenty of time to savor the sights and sounds.

GREENWICH VILLAGE: Just as New York is different from the rest of America, the Village is unlike the rest of New York. Closer in feeling to the Left Bank than the East Side, it is still, despite the inroads of commercialism and high-rise apartment buildings and teeny-boppers, the American Bohemia, the place where self-expression is as necessary as bread. Its openness and ease are apparent to even the casual visitor, whether he comes to shop or stare or look at old buildings or drink espresso in the coffeehouses or listen to folk music or catch an off-Broadway play. The Village has something for everyone.

Our best advice on how to see the Village is simply to ramble. Take your time. Arm yourself with a map or not, and just Wander where fancy leads you. You might begin at Stanford White's graceful **Washington Square Arch,** Fifth Avenue at Waverly Place. Observe the statue of George Washington on the west flank done by Alexander Stirling Calder (the father of the Alexander Calder whose mobiles you saw at the Museum of Modern Art), then project yourself back into the world of 19th-century New York aristocracy as you study the elegant Greek Revival houses of Washington Square North. Henry James's novel *Washington Square* took place here, and James, Edith Wharton, William Dean Howells, Edward Hopper, and John Dos Passos have all lived on this block at one time or another. The houses look out on **Washington Square Park,** which was once a swamp, later a potter's field and hanging ground, then a public park. Today it is still a park and a mecca for Villagers, native and imported: ancient Sicilians playing chess, painters and composers from the lofts of SoHo south of the park, children and their mothers from the expensive apartment buildings, hippies, beards, panhandlers, college professors from N.Y.U. On warm Sundays, kids from everywhere flock to the fountain where an all-day, all-night impromptu folk concert takes place. If you've brought your guitar, join in.

Or walk through the park and head down MacDougal Street; there's history at every turn. This was the headquarters of Bohemia in the teens and twenties. No. 137, now a restaurant, is the site of the old **Liberal Club,** a hotbed for anarchists and free-thinkers of all stripes. A youthful Margaret Sanger preached birth control here, and it was here that Art Young, Max Eastman, John Reed, and Floyd Dell cooked up their revolutionary political magazine, the *Masses* (in the pre-World War I witch-hunts, all were put on trial for sedition, later acquitted). Next door, in what is still the **Provincetown Playhouse,** George Cram

Cook and his wife Susan Glaspell, founded the Provincetown Players; in tow they had a promising young playwright named Eugene O'Neill and a young actress from Maine, Edna St. Vincent Millay. Today the atmosphere on MacDougal Street is still flamboyant, but it is not especially artistic: the street is a collection of shops, gimmicky coffeehouses, sidewalk stands selling pizza and shish kebab, all mobbed by throngs of gum-chewing teeny-boppers who descend on the area weekend nights from everywhere (it's best to visit it during the week). Turn left on Bleecker and you'll see more restaurants, nightclubs, off-Broadway theaters, and coffeehouses where perhaps a young Joan Baez or Bob Dylan will be singing before an audience for the first time.

Or start your ramble on Seventh Avenue, at Sheridan Square. Nostalgia collectors who bemoan the tearing-down of old Village landmarks (on the site of the original Circle in the Square theater and the legendary Louie's Tavern now stands a modern apartment building, 3 Sheridan Square), will be rewarded by a walk down Seventh Avenue to Grove Street and **Marie's Crisis Cafe.** It was here that Tom Paine, a broken, defeated, old man, spent his last years; the brilliant spokesman for the American Revolution was unappreciated in his own lifetime. Continue down Seventh to Commerce Street, two blocks further south, and walk past the lovely old homes to the **Cherry Lane Theatre,** founded by Edna St. Vincent Millay. "Vincent," one of the most authentic of the Village Bohemians, made her home at 75½ Bedford Street, which is still known as the "narrowest house in the Village."

Head back to Sheridan Square now, and amble down West Fourth Street, an eclectic shopping street where **The Big Apple** turns out luscious baked goods (perfect for nibbling as you walk), and **Pottery And So Fourth** sells beautiful hand-thrown pottery by a few young craftsmen. You can also buy distinctive Village-style wedding bands, have leather sandals made to order, or pick up some ginseng, kung-fu shoes, and green tea at a Chinese craft mart, all in the same block.

Perhaps one of the Village's best shopping streets is Greenwich Avenue, which you can reach by walking north on Christopher Street from Sheridan Square. (This one block of Christopher Street alone has several charming shops, like **Gingerbread House,** a tiny treasure for little people, stocked with wonderful books and dolls and European toys and handmade rocking horses from Vermont; and **Bowl and Board** which has some of the best salad bowls in town.) Bear left around Christopher and you'll find yourself at a huge, busy center of the Village, with a big, semiopen florist shop at the corner. The street is lined with tempting shops. Note the **Rosenhouse Gallery**; **Effendi**, with its unisex boutique items from Paris, Bombay, London, and Tibet; **Nippon Craft** with tons of straw, paper, and ceramic crafts, as well as arty and useful Japanese things; the **Pottery Barn,** with its tasteful, mostly Scandinavian glass and ceramics, and excellent buys in well-known, functionally perfect dinnerware seconds like Arabia from Finland and Bennington from Vermont. Then there's Martin Proctor's **Unicorn City** at 55 Greenwich, where you can pet or purchase a mythological beastie—they come in posters, patches, pottery, pendants, and more, in a wide price range.

You can head back along Greenwich Avenue now (walking the *other* side of the street) and treat yourself to some candy kisses, homemade fudge, or chocolate-covered pretzels at **The Candy Kiss,** where rows of apothecary jars are filled with old-time penny candies—now gone up a few cents, alas. If you're hungry, stop in for a bite at **The Peacock,** an old-time Village coffeehouse a few doors away. Have some torta verde di ricotta (spinach-and-cheese pie), a big plate of anitpasto, or just some espresso or wine and pastry. If you're in the mood for pizza, **Ray's Famous,** known for the best pizza in New York, is just a few blocks up Avenue of the Americas, at 11th Street. Across the street and one block further north, at 12th Street, is **The Mad Monk,** where beautiful ceramic works are priced very modestly. Walk back south along Avenue of the Americas to Ninth Street and have a look at **Balducci's** one of the city's most exciting and best-stocked international food stores. Or just head for the big, busy corner of 8th Street and Sixth Avenue, and proceed to explore the intriguing shops as you walk along toward Fifth. And back you are at Washington Square Arch, the fountain, and the park. Sit down, relax, and contemplate the never-ending, always-absorbing Village scene.

Note: We've told you about the Village by day here: we'll explore the night scene in the Village in Chapter VIII.

SOHO: The last part of this excursion is not, admittedly, one of the "major sights" of New York, but for those who are particularly interested in art and artists and artistic shops, it might well be one of the most interesting. For New York's most vital art center is no longer Greenwich Village, or even Madison Avenue or 57th Street. About 2,000 of the city's most serious artists—as well as crafts people and dancers and filmmakers and photographers and musicians and writers—live and work in a 50-block area of rundown cast-iron commercial buildings that stretches north from Canal to Houston Streets, west from Lafayette Street to West Broadway just above Chinatown, just below the Village. This is SoHo, and a Saturday afternoon here will give you a quick look at the latest movements in contemporary art, plus a chance to shop at some delightful boutiques and break bread with the SoHo community in some neighborhood restaurants. Although the shops and galleries are open during the week as well, the area is noisily industrial during the week, and Saturday is *the* time.

If you're already in Greenwich village, you can walk to SoHo in about ten minutes; it's just south of Bleecker Street and Washington Square Village. Or, take the No. 5 Fifth Avenue bus marked West Houston Street and get off at the last stop—the corner of Houston and West Broadway. West Broadway is SoHo's main thoroughfare, so start your leisurely promenade here, stopping in at galleries and shops as fancy leads you, admiring the distinguished 19th-century palazzo commercial architecture of the buildings (most are about 100 years old). SoHo has a rich and varied street life: you might be able to pick up blankets or tops from Guatemala at low prices, buy paintings on the street, find news on a bulletin board of a lecture or happening (there are many of them going on here) that you might want to attend. A recent notice, for example, announced an evening of "Humming and other Sensory Meditations—Sound Emerging for Trans-Perceptual Experience." The most important aspect of SoHo, for us, is the feeling of aliveness and creativity in the area; it's not a commercial show (not yet, at any rate), just serious and talented people exploring new ways of expressing their own reality.

Art in SoHo tends to concentrate on works by younger artists and sculptors, and much of the work is massive (that's why the artist must work in lofts and why this small-industry neighborhood became an artists' colony). Styles vary from Minimal to Conceptual to Pop to Abstract Expressionism to Photo Realism to you-name-it: about the only thing the artists have in common is that most of them are antiestablishment. 420 West Broadway is a good place to start your explorations: here's where **Leo Castelli, John Weber, Andre Emmerich,** and **Sonnabend Gallery** all maintain showcases. Take the elevator to the top floor and walk down: the crowd is on the steps, chatting and meeting and maybe celebrity watching. Other galleries you might want to see include the pioneering **O.K. Harris Gallery, Westbroadway, Nancy Hoffman, John Gibson, Axis in Soho,** and **Razor.** Here, too are the far-out interiors and sculptures of Rudi Stern's **Let There Be Neon.** If you can't afford a commission for your place back home, maybe you can afford one of the contemporary posters, which start at $5, unframed and unmounted, at **Mark LV Frames and Poster Originals** across the street.

Roam the streets a little to find some of the other important galleries. **Paula Cooper,** an early SoHo showplace, is at 155 Wooster Street, **Louis K. Meisel,** 141 Prince Street, often mounts unusual shows, like a recent one of a wildly decorated entire stunt plane. And don't leave the area without at least a glimpse of **Makers Gallery,** a stunner of a showplace and marketplace for contemporary crafts at 124 Spring Street. Magnificent wood carvings, featherwork, pottery, macrame, quilts and much more are on display, along with many pieces of functional ceramics and glassware for under $50. Step to the rear for a refreshing drink of an "Ultimate Batido" and other fruit juices. If you're traveling heavy and can handle, say, a stained glass window from an upstate New York church for $1,500, make the acquaintance of **Urban Archeology** at 135 Spring Street, a find for collectors of architectural ornaments. To see some exquisite art works in miniature, climb one flight up to **Spring Street Enamels Gallery,** 171 Spring Street, one of the leaders in the current renaissance of this ancient and beautiful art.

For a new artistic experience, be sure to visit the **Museum of Holography** at 11 Mercer Street (one block west of Broadway and north of Canal Street, tel. 925-0526). Holography, as most people do not know, is a new form of photography that uses laser beams instead of cameras to make three-dimensional images that seem to float before the eye. It's a new art form, in its infancy: a visit here is a look at the future. The museum is open from noon to 6, Wednesdays through Sundays, until 9 Thursdays. Admission is $1.50 for adults, 75¢ for children under 12 and senior citizens.

You can get the latest copy of *Art News* and browse through beautiful art books, many from Europe and Canada, at **Jaap Rietman Art Books,** upstairs at the corner of West Broadway and Spring Streets. For what the proprietors call "the largest collection of art postcards and notecards" in the world, visit

Untitled (Harris Graphics), 159 Prince Street. Cards are 20¢ and up.

In style, taste, and imagination, some of the SoHo boutiques are an art excursion unto themselves. **Knobkerry, Third World Design and Art,** at 158 Spring Street, is laden with Javanese shadow puppets, rare 19th-century Chinese watercolors, antique and modern jewelry, pillows, paisley shawls, rugs from Iran, peasant blouses from Rumania—many beautiful things, at prices ranging from just a little to quite a lot. . . . **Small Business,** 101 Wooster Street, has handmade and ready-made children's clothes (up to age eight), animals, toys, many of them handcrocheted and knitted by local people. We can't think of a yummier new-baby present than one of their superb crib-sized patchwork quilts, from $45 to $80 . . . **Le Grand Hotel** and **Tales of Hoffman,** both under one roof at 471 West Broadway, look like a 1920s movie set, with thick carpets, old-fashioned gilt mirrors, potted palms, and Billie Holiday on the stereo. There are men's and women's far-out shoes up front, Theda Bara-type dresses in the back. . . . The cavernous, mysterious interior of **Barone,** 414 West Broadway, purposely designed to "disorient the visitor" and remove the feeling of four walls and a ceiling, does just that. Oddly enough, it's filled with non-disorienting household accessories like sponges, towels and glasses, as well as more exotic trivia like disco lashes. . . . **Pentimento,** 126 Prince Street, is the place for ruffles and laces and feather boas of half-a-century ago that look stunning on today's flappers. . . . Visit **Miso,** 416 West Broadway for very "with it" women's clothes to "wear in good health"; and **Paracelso,** 430 West Broadway, where well-heeled gypsies can stock up on colored silk dresses from Afghanistan and Japan (about $100), marvelous primitive jewelry, and heady perfumes from Arabia at $3 a bottle. . . . We love the made-to-order dresses at **Tamala w/Bagel,** a cozy little store down a few steps at 153 Prince Street. In handpainted silk or knit, they run about $150. The Bagel part of the operation is a snack counter that also sells roast beef sandwiches and such simple-yet-exotic dishes as a cream cheese with caviar sandwich for $1.25.

Food is raised to an art form at **Dean & Di Luca,** 121 Prince Street, where mounds of freshly baked breads and pastries, bins of coffee beans, stacks of dried nuts, perfect fresh fruits, a huge selection of imported cookware and kitchen gadgets complete for attention with delicious homemade pâtés, escabeche, chicken tarragon, coulibiac of salmon, and an exquisite selection of imported cheeses. A visit here is reason enough to immediately plan a picnic.

Prefer to eat right in Soho? Join the SoHoians at some of their favorites places, like self-service **Food,** at the corner of Prince and Wooster Streets, where you can get soup-and-bread luncheons, healthy heroes on wholewheat Italian bread, luscious under-$1 desserts, and mingle with local types at wooden tables. For more relaxed meals, try **Mama Siltká,** 468 West Broadway for succulent seafood dishes and local bonhommie; **The Ballroom,** 458 West Broadway, so white and pretty with its potted plants and mirrors, or at the friendly **Spring Street Natural Restaurant,** 149 Spring Street for—you guessed it—natural food. (See Chapter IV for details). If you're not really too hungry, you might settle for a loaf of crusty Italian bread from the **Vesuvio Bakery,** 160 Prince Street, or perhaps some espresso and Italian pastry at **Bruno Bakery,** 506 West Broadway, on the other side of Houston, as you head back to the Village and the end of your excursion.

Ice Skating at Rockefeller Center

Chapter VI

MORE SIGHTS AND SOUNDS OF NEW YORK

YOU'VE COMPLETED three days of sightseeing, and you're still thirsting for more. The possibilities are endless. While you certainly won't want to see *everything,* the following descriptions will give you an idea of what is available: pick and choose, according to your own time and interests. We've grouped them geographically—Midtown, Downtown, the Upper East Side, the Upper West Side, Points North and Beyond Manhattan—so you can refer to this list when you happen to be in a certain area and have time to visit, for example, just one museum. **We've marked the exhibits that are of the most interest to the small fry with an asterisk.**

Note: We haven't attempted to cover everything in New York, since this is a guide book and not an encyclopedia. Listed below are some major and minor sights of the city, chosen either for their importance or their special, if offbeat, charm.

Downtown

CITY HALL: City Hall Park at Broadway and Park Row. The mayor will be out to greet you if you're an astronaut, prime minister, or beauty queen, but you may not get to see him if you're just an ordinary mortal. You can, however, see the splendid building in which he works, a successful 19th-century blending of French Renaissance and Federal influences. Walk up the splendid marble staircase to the **Governor's Room.** It was once reserved for the use of the governor of the state when he was in New York, but now it's a museum with historic furniture (the desk George Washington used as president is here) and Trumbull portraits of George, Alexander Hamilton, and others. City

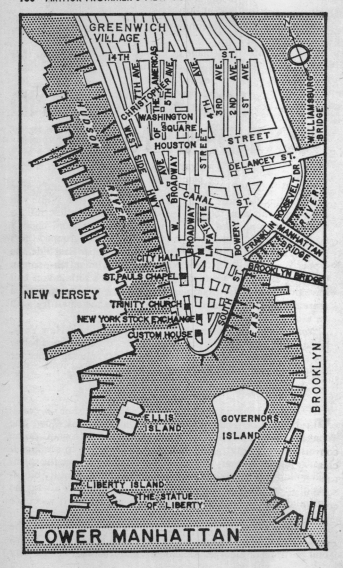

LOWER MANHATTAN

Hall welcomes individual visitors Monday to Friday, 10 to 3. Groups of more than five may troop to City Hall only by appointment.

A lot of history was made at **City Hall Park** which, in the early days of New York, was a kind of village square: political riots, hangings, police wars, and one of the first readings, in 1776, of the Declaration of Independence to a group of New York revolutionaries, all took place here.

*FIRE DEPARTMENT MUSEUM:

104 Duane Street, a bit north of the Woolworth Building. We have yet to meet the small boy who could readily be torn away from this one: three floors laden with antique fire-fighting equipment, including some splendid old engines dating back to 1820. Admission free. Open Monday to Friday, from 9 to 4, Saturday, from 9 to 1. Closed Sunday and all holidays during July and August (tel. 570-4230.).

OLD ST. PATRICK'S CATHEDRAL:

Corner of Mott and Prince Streets. Newly restored, this historic (1809) church is the predecessor of its grander sister on Fifth Avenue and 50th Street. In the cemetery outside the church is buried Pierre Toussaint, the former Haitian slave, who may one day be canonized by Rome.

WOOLWORTH BUILDING:

233 Broadway. Until the coming of the Empire State Building, this was the world's tallest: 60 stories, pretty good for 1913. It's a lovely, lacy, Gothic frou-frou. Admire.

WESTBETH:

463 West Street. You have to be an artist or a writer or musician or a dancer or a filmmaker to get an apartment in Westbeth (the former Bell Telephone Laboratories which were converted to an artist's community a few years ago). It's a vital, creative place, with art galleries, a print workshop, a theater and cabaret. For the visitor who'd like to see what makes such a community tick, Westbeth residents conduct guided tours. They cost $4, run up to two hours, and take you into artists' and craftsmen's studios as well as to the common rooms. Groups are preferred. Write to Westbeth Tours, 463 West Street, or phone 675-8174 to make an appointment.

Midtown: East Side

*CENTRAL PARK: What Tivoli is to Copenhagen or Chapultepec to Mexico City, Central Park is to New York: the great public playground. A magnificent garden in the midst of the concrete canyons, it offers city-jaded New Yorkers a breath of the country, a chance to wander along bosky landscapes, climb rocks, listen to the song of birds, and stare at the sky. It also gives them the chance to stare at each other: Frederick Law Olmstead's 19th-century greensward is one of the most popular places in town. The park offers many recreational and cultural outlets. During the summer, there's **The New York Shakespeare Festival,** plus concerts by the Metropolitan Opera, the New York Philharmonic, and many others—most of them free. The Department of Recreation also sponsors many interesting events in the park, from free tennis lessons for kids to hula-hoop contests! So many things go on in the park, in fact, that daily reports are given via a recorded tape, on the telephone. Dial 755-4100, and if you need more information on any park facility or program, call 472-1003.

*The Park for Children

For kids worn out by too much sightseeing, an hour or so in the park is the perfect antidote. First, there is the **Central Park Zoo,** Fifth Avenue at 64th Street, with an ample supply of lions, tigers, monkeys, and splashing seals in a pool, sure-fire kid pleasers. Kids also love the pony rides and the Delacorte Clock here;

Greenwich Village Art Show

the carillon chimes and carved animals dance, every half-hour. The zoo cafeteria, with its large outdoor terrace, is a good place to feed starving moppets. If you have really little ones, take them over to the adjoining **Children's Zoo,** where they can feed and pet animals, climb up Noah's Ark, and slide down Alice's rabbit hole. Then take them along to the **Carousel,** opposite 65th Street in the center of the park (a path leads here from the cafeteria). Or let them sail their model boats at Conservatory Pond near 72nd Street and Fifth, join the local youngsters flying kites, or work off some excess energy at one of the two inspired **Adventure Playgrounds;** there's one near 67th Street and Central Park West, another with an entrance at 60th Street and Seventh Avenue. Or, they can listen to stories at the charming **Hans Christian Andersen** statue, near the model boat house; the Public Library provides storytellers, usually on summer Saturdays, between 11 and 1. Most adult listeners seem as entralled as the kids.

The Park for Adults: Boaters, Bikers, Riders, Dreamers

With or without kids, don't miss taking a rowboat out on **Conservatory Lake** (72nd Street), an unexpectedly rural spot for New York. And when you've finished, join the throngs strolling around the beautiful Bethesda Fountain area, which is really the focal point of the park. The setting—with the fountain, the lake, the towers of New York in the background—is one of the most romantic in the city.

Other romantic ways to see Central Park: in a horsedrawn carriage (pick up a carriage at 59th Street and Central Park South, near the Plaza Hotel). The energetic among you can join the local jogging set, or rent a horse from the Claremont Riding Academy, 175 West 89th Street (tel. SC 4-5100; $11.50 an hour) and trot through miles of lovely bridle paths, or rent a bike from the bicycle concession near the boathouse at the 72nd Street Lake and join the throngs of New Yorkers—families, kids, boys looking for girls, girls looking for boys—who've discovered the joy of life on wheels. During the summer, the park is closed to traffic from 10 a.m. to 4 p.m. on weekdays, as well as all day on the weekends, so bikers, riders, and kids reign supreme. Tennis buffs can also find a home in Central Park; the courts at 93rd Street are insanely popular. Tennis permits cost $27.50, and they entitle you to unlimited play. There are also several bubbled courts that stay open during the winter. For information on permits and what courts are open, phone the Permit Office at

360-8204. More sedentary types can enjoy browsing through the bookstalls (New York's modest answer to the Left Bank *quais* of Paris) along the outer wall of the Park, at Fifth Avenue and 60th Street. (There are also some great little kiosks serving all sorts of international snacks.) Eventually, many of the famed booksellers of Fourth Avenue's Book Row may relocate here.

MUSEUMS, EXHIBITS, LANDMARKS: Asia House Gallery, 112 East 64th Street. Chinese Ming vessels, Indian statuary, Japanese prints—some of the most beautiful art shows in New York are seen in this exquisite gallery run by the Asia Society. Since there is no permanent collection, the gallery is usually closed between shows. Phone PL 1-4210 before you go. Open daily, 10 to 5; Thursday, until 8:30; holidays, 1 to 5. Free.

*Birthplace of Theodore Roosevelt, 28 East 20th Street. Want to see what a comfortable New York home of 1858 looked like? Trot over to the birthplace of the 26th president, and the house in which he lived until he was 15 years old. Five rooms of this lovely brownstone have been lovingly restored and are furnished the way they were when Teddy was a tot. A National Park Service site. Open from 9 to 4:30 daily from Memorial Day through Labor day, Wednesdays through Sundays the rest of the year. Admission is 50¢; children under 16 and adults over 65, free (tel. 260-1616).

Cooper-Hewitt Museum of Design and Decorative Arts, Smithsonian Institution, Fifth Avenue and 91st Street. The only division of the Smithsonian to have its headquarters outside of Washington, D.C., Cooper-Hewitt is an exquisite gem of a museum. Newly housed in the restored neo-Georgian Andrew Carnegie mansion, it contains what is acknowledged as one of the world's finest collections of design and decorative arts. Frequently changing exhibits showcase the museum's holdings in everything from porcelain, furniture, wallpaper, embroideries, jewelry, metalwork, and drawings to bird cages, pressed flowers, boxes, and Valentines. Open from 10 to 9, Tuesdays; 10 to 5, Wednesdays through Saturdays; noon to 5, Sundays; closed Mondays and major holidays. Admission is $1, senior citizens and children under 12, free.

Frick Collection, 1 East 70th Street. One of the most beautiful small museums in the world, this Fifth Avenue center, with its greenery and fountains, is an oasis. Free concerts are held here on Sunday afternoons, October through May. Phone BU 8-0700 for details. Open Tuesdays through Saturdays, 10 to 6. Sundays and minor holidays, from 1. Closed major holidays and Mondays and Tuesdays, June through August. Children under ten not admitted and those under 16 must be accompanied by an adult. Admission $1.

Guggenheim Museum, 1071 Fifth Avenue (near 88th Street). Frank Lloyd Wright's creation has both passionate defenders and detractors. It's a large, spiral ramp on which are displayed shows featuring works by established modern masters and artists currently involved in experimental approaches as well as Solomon Guggenheim's augmented collection of 20th-century art. The Justin K. Thannhauser Wing permanently displays such Impressionist and Post-Impressionist masters as Picasso, Degas, and Cezanne. Open daily, except Mondays, from 11 to 5, Tuesdays until 8. Admission: $1.50. Students with I.D. and visitors over 62, 75¢. Children under seven, free. Tuesday evenings, from 5 until 8, admission is free. Restaurant offers lunch and snacks.

The **International Center of Photography,** 1130 Fifth Avenue (94th Street), is housed in a superb Georgian building, and is New York's only museum devoted to photography. It's a mecca for photography lovers and students of the art, who are attracted by a great variety of workshops and educational programs. Changing exhibits. Open Tuesdays from 11 to 8, with free admission after 5. Wednesdays through Sundays, 11 to 5. Admission: $1 adults, 50¢ students.

Japan House, 333 East 47th Street. This stunning example of contemporary Japanese architecture, with its beautiful gallery, library, and outdoor garden is headquarters of the Japan Society. Concerts are often held on Tuesday, Wednesday, and Thursday evenings and Sundays at 2:30, and there are regular series of contemporary and classic Japanese films. Admission is $3. There are frequently special exhibits in the gallery. Even if nothing is going on, however, it's well worth having a look. The United Nations is just across the street. Open daily, 10 to 5 (tel. 832-1155).

*Jewish Museum, Fifth Avenue at 92nd Street. Felix Warburg's splendid old townhouse is the setting for this distinguished collection of Judaica—ceremonial objects, paintings, folk arts, silver, which trace the saga of the Jews through historical times, in the wanderings through many lands. A mosaic tile synagogue wall from 16th-century Persia and a painted wooden ark from Poland are among the museum's unique treasures. The museum also presents major contemporary exhibitions of painting, photography, and sculpture.

Special events include films, concerts, lectures, and children's programs. The Jewish Museum is open Monday through Thursday 12 to 5; and Sunday, 11 to 6. Closed Friday and Saturday. Closed on Jewish holidays, open on legal holidays. Admission is $1.75 for adults, $1 for children under 16 and students with ID cards (tel. 860-1888).

*Museum of Broadcasting, 1 East 53rd Street. Want to catch up on the Ed Sullivan shows of the '50s, the Jack Benny broadcasts of the '30s? You can watch Uncle Milty cavort, hear FDR's campaign speeches, and lots more at this new and enormously popular museum. Its collection includes just about everything that's ever gone out on the airwaves, and you're free to watch it or hear it at your own private console. A contribution of $1 for adults, 50¢ for children is requested. Open Tuesdays through Saturdays, from noon to 5. Next door is vest-pocket Paley Park, a cooling place to sit and snack, watch the fountain and the people, if the Museum is too crowded to get in.

Industrial Exhibits—For Free

New York houses not merely the office headquarters of some of America's largest corporations, but a number of permanent exhibitions maintained by them and shown free to the public. We particularly like Burlington Industries' **The Mill** at 1345 Avenue of the Americas (at 54th Street), which demonstrates, from a moving walkway, the making of cloth in all its fascinating steps. Especially exciting is the final section, a panorama of American history and fashion of the last 200 years, shown via 750 different color slides constantly changing on 36 screens. Young children want to "ride" this one over and over. Photography buffs should check in at the Eastman Kodak Corporation's **Kodak Gallery and Photographic Information Center** at 1133 Avenue of the Americas (near 44th Street) for advice and inspiration before training their lenses on New York.

---

*Museum of the City of New York, Fifth Avenue between 103rd and 104th Streets. For a capsule look at New York history, this is the place. You would do well to stop here, in fact, before beginning your historical tour of Downtown Manhattan. Exhibits trace the city's history from the days of the Indians to the present, through costumes, old cars, photographs, prints, ship models, fire engines, maps, furnishings, theatrical memorabilia, toys. Don't miss the fascinating Dutch Galleries, with full-scale reconstructions of Nieuw Amsterdam, or the exciting Cityrama Gallery, a multimedia exhibition which tells the story of the city from 1609 to today. Children will dote on the "Please Touch" demonstrations which are given on Saturdays, from November through April, in a reconstruction of a 17th-century Dutch home; they'll also like the puppet shows, plays, and other programs in which they can participate from November through April. And the gift shop, with many charming and inexpensive mementoes of Old New York.

A special note: During the summer months, the museum offers a series of outstanding walking tours, under the direction of distinguished historian Henry Hope Reed. The tours concentrate on architecture and social history. Areas and subjects covered have included "Town House and Private Palace" (the Upper East Side), "The World of the Astors" (the Lower East Side in its aristocratic period a hundred years ago), Downtown Manhattan, Greenwich Village, and the Columbia University neighborhoods. Reservations must be made in advance (tel. LE 4-1672), since the tours are enormously popular; the cost is about $3.

The Museum of the City of New York is open Tuesday through Saturday, 10 to 5; Sundays and holidays, 1 to 5. Free.

*Songwriter's Hall of Fame, One Times Square, Eighth Floor. This engaging small new museum, sponsored by the National Academy of Popular Music, is the place for a nostalgic journey back to the days of Tin Pan Alley. Fats Waller's piano, Victor Herbert's desk and an old-time player piano that gives out with Scott Joplin's "Maple Leaf Rag," vie for attention with an Electric Synthesizer and a Rhythmer (the kind used in making demo records), which kids can try out to their heart's content. For groups over ten, curator-folk singer Oscar Brand will provide a lively demonstration. Free. Open Mondays to Saturdays, 11 to 3 (tel. 221-1252).

Whitney Museum of American Art, 945 Madison Avenue, at 75th Street. What many consider the very best collection of modern American art is housed in Marcel Breuer's superb modernistic building, an inverted layer cake to which you gain entrance by crossing a bridge. Gertrude Vanderbilt Whitney's collection started in the Village in the '30s and is now in its third home. At least two major exhibitions are on view at all times, including selections from the permanent collection by such artists as Alexander Calder, Edward Hopper, Jasper Johns, Regi-

nald Marsh, Robert Motherwell, Louise Nevelson and Georgia
O'Keeffe. The restaurant in a sunken sculpture court offers
wines, light meals, and refreshments. Regular hours: Tuesday,
11 to 9; Wednesday to Saturday, 11 to 6; Sunday, noon to 6.
Closed Monday. Memorial Day through Labor Day: Tuesday to
Friday, 2 to 9; Saturday, 11 to 6; Sunday, noon to 6; closed
Monday. Admission: $1.50; senior citizens, children under 12
with an adult, college students with valid I.D. free; Tuesday
evenings 6 to 9 free. Admission to programs in the New American Filmmaker Series is free with your ticket; make your request
when you enter the museum.

Note: The **Whitney Downtown Museum,** a newer sister, is at
55 Water Street, in the financial district, presenting an active
exhibition program and performing arts series, organized by
students under the direction of the Whitney's Education Department. Hours: 11 to 3, Mondays through Fridays. Closed the last
two weeks in August. Admission free.

ART GALLERIES: There are probably as many art galleries on the
East Side as there are grocery stores in some other cities: perhaps
more. For art-happy New Yorkers gallery-going is a favorite
pastime, and the area of the East 70s and 80s is the new scene
of the action, although many galleries still hold forth on the older
gallery row, 57th Street. If your interest in art is more than
casual, join the crowd.

Since there is no admission fee to galleries (unless there is a
special charity benefit), you can come and go as you please.
Where you go will be determined by what you're interested in:
the moderns, the traditionalists, the Old Masters. The quickest
way to find out who's showing where is to consult the art pages
in the Entertainment Section of Sunday's *New York Times.* Some
of the big names among the galleries showing the moderns: Betty
Parsons, 24 West 57th Street; Leo Castelli, 4 East 77th Street
(also in SoHo at 420 West Broadway); Marlborough, 40 West
57th Street; Andre Emmerich, 41 East 57th Street; Fishbach, 29
West 57th Street; Tibor de Nagy, 29 West 57th Street; Saiden-
berg, 16 East 79th Street; Fulton Gallery, 799 Lexington Avenue; Martha Jackson, 521 West 57th Street; Terry Dintenfass, 50
West 57th Street; and Pace, 32 East 57th Street.

Should your taste run more to the Impressionists and French
Masters, relax at Hammer Galleries, 51 East 57th Street, or
Wally Findlay Galleries, 17 East 57th Street (which also shows

contemporary Europeans and Americans). Hirschl & Adler, 21 East 67th Street, specializes in American paintings from the 18th century to the present, as well as French and European paintings from the early 19th to the early 20th century. Old Masters? Get out your check book and head for the hallowed and haughty temples of Wildenstein, 19 East 64th Street (where you could also pick up an Impressionist, Post-Impressionist or 20th-century Master), and M. Knoedler & Co., 21 East 70th Street, which also handles Old Master paintings, 19th- and 20th-century and contemporary American and European paintings and sculpture.

AUCTION HOUSES: Scores of New Yorkers have become auction addicts. When they need to furnish an apartment, buy a painting, get a high chair for the baby, they wouldn't consider buying anything new or price tagged. For them, the game is in the bidding, the adventure in seeing who-gets-what. You can visit New York auction houses and bid for anything from sewing machines to silverware, from lamps to lorgnettes. Whether you're out for big game (or just spectator sport), the most exciting place is the **Sotheby Parke Bernet Galleries,** 980 Madison Avenue, where the cognoscenti vie for Rembrandts, pedigreed furniture, and precious jewelry. Many items, however, are not exorbitant, so don't be afraid to participate: the company notes that "the solid core of its business comprises the sale of worthy but unspectacular items." Illustrated catalogues with estimated values are published for each auction. We've known people to come up with terrific buys at **PB 84,** a branch of the gallery that

Guggenheim Museum

specializes in property of "modest value." It is located at 171 East 84th Street. For a recorded announcement of auction and exhibition schedules, phone 472-3555. **Plaza Art Galleries,** 406 East 79th Street, is also well-known for fine furniture and decorative items, a bit more within the reach of the average person. Some very good bargains in furhishings and bric-a-brac that you might want to take home with you can be found at **Tepper Galleries,** 3 West 61st Street; **Manhattan Galleries,** 1415 Third Avenue (at 80th Street); and **Lubin Galleries,** 72 East 13th Street. (The last one is in the Village.) But be warned: once you start on the auction circuit, you may never get back to Macy's. And you may end up with a Louis XVI chair that you *really* don't need. That can happen.

For news of upcoming auctions each week, check the Auction Pages of the classified section of the Sunday *New York Times.*

West Side

TOURS: *Lincoln Center for the Performing Arts, Broadway at 65th Street. Whether or not you see any performances at Lincoln Center (more details in Chapter VII on Evening Entertainment), you should take a tour of this impressive complex of theaters and concert halls. Just to see the art and sculpture on the grounds is an experience in itself: Alexander Calder's *Le Guichet* in front of the Library and Museum of Performing Arts; Richard Lippold's *Orpheus and Apollo* in Avery Fisher Hall; Henry Moore's gigantic *Reclining Figure* in the reflecting pool in front of the Vivian Beaumont Theatre; Marc Chagall's lilting paintings for the Metropolitan Opera House. The buildings themselves—the Metropolitan Opera House, the New York State Theatre, the Vivian Beaumont Theatre, Avery Fisher Hall, the Juilliard School—have been both criticized and praised: take a look and reach your own conclusions. You'll probably see all the buildings and may even get to watch rehearsals of some of the famed companies, like the New York City Ballet or the New York City Opera Company. But if you have your heart set on seeing the interiors of the theaters, do *not* come on a Saturday or Sunday afternoon; that's matinee time, and the doors are closed to tour takers. Tours are given between 10:30 and 5 daily, last an hour, and cost $2.95 for adults, $1.95 for children, $2.50 for students. Telephone: TR 4-4010.

LIBRARIES: *The Library and Museum of the Performing Arts,** at Lincoln Center, 111 Amsterdam Avenue (entrance at 65th Street). A branch of the Public Library and of Lincoln Center, the Library and Museum of the Performing Arts, is an entity unto itself, and one of the liveliest places in town. Everything is dedicated to the performing arts here and you can do a lot more than just borrow a book. You can sit down in a comfortable chair and listen to a recording of an opera or a musical (while studying the score at the same time), see excellent exhibits, catch concerts, plays, dance performances every night (more details in Chapter VII on Entertainment), take the children to free story hours, puppet shows, concerts, dance presentations, films, in the Heckscher Oval. Best of all, it's all for free. A wonderful place. Hours: Monday and Thursday from 10 to 8, Tuesday and Wednesday from 10 to 6, Friday and Saturday from 12 to 6. Closed Sunday.

MUSEUMS: *The American Museum of Natural History,** Central Park West at 79th Street. One of the great scientific museums of the world, the American Museum brings the natural history of man and animals to vivid life for visitors of all ages. There's always something special going on here, as dance, music, and crafts from all over the world are shown in live programs at the People Center. And then there are those perennial crowd-pleasers (especially kid-pleasers) like the reconstructed section of Meteorites, Minerals, and Gems; through the Hall of Man in Africa, the Hall of Mexico and Central America; the amazing Hall of Reptiles and Amphibians; and the Hall of Ocean Life, with its 94-foot whale suspended from the ceiling; or any of the other 31 halls. You could spend days, no, weeks here, enjoying the ethnological and anthropological collections, attending slide and gallery talks, watching free movies and special programs (many for children), taking a tape-recorded tour of the building or seeing the animals in their natural habitats. School-age children will enjoy the Natural Science Center for Young People.

A big favorite with children six to 16 is the newly opened **Discovery Room,** in which 25 children at a time, each accompanied by an adult, play with learning games in a box—"Feel and Guess," "Reflections", "Skull and Mirror," and the like—for a variety of human and scientific experiences. Modeled after a similar room at the Smithsonian in Washington, the Discovery Room admits visitors on a first-come, first-served basis. Best to get tickets (free) at the Information Desk on the main floor when you enter. There's an inexpensive but crowded cafeteria in the basement and two wonderful gift shops, one just for children; take home an ancient Chinese puppet, beautiful Indian jewelry, or a colorful book of birds. The museum is open every day of the year except Christmas and Thanksgiving, from 10 to 4:45, Monday through Saturday; Wednesdays to 9; from 11 to 5, Sundays and holidays. There is a discretionary admission fee. Telephone: TR 3-4225.

*The American Museum—Hayden Planetarium, 81st Street at Central Park West. This is one of the most exciting shows in town—for children, for adults, for anyone who ponders the mystery of man and the stars, of the great drama of outer space. Through the magic of the Zeiss projector, the dome of the auditorium turns into the night sky, the heavens open, and the show is on. The programs change every month or two: you might see, for example, "Sunrise at Stonehenge," "Captives of the Planets," "100 Times Around the Sun," "Adventure of a Light Beam," or "Laserium." The programs are given several times during the afternoon and evening, with an admission fee of $2.35, for adults, $1.35 for children and students with IDs. Included in this price is admission to the Guggenheim Space Theater, where Henry Fonda and the late Cyril Ritchard, among others, tell the story of astronomy from its very beginnings to the Space Age. A phone call to "Dial-A-Satellite," 873-0404, will give you the schedule for the day as well as reports on what planets will be visible in the night sky over New York. *Note:* The Planetarium "discourages" attendance by children under five.

Museum of Contemporary Crafts, 29 West 53rd Street. This showcase for the American Crafts Council is one of the most imaginative small museums in the city: changing exhibits on such unlikely subjects as "Bread" or "Doors" or "The Great American Foot" can be absorbing. Objects in metal, clay, glass and fiber are treated as works of art. Open Tuesdays through Saturdays, 11 to 6; Sundays, 1 to 6. Adults, $1, children under 14, 25¢, senior citizens, 25¢. Good for older children. Telephone: 977-8989

The New York Historical Society, 170 Central Park West, at 77th Street. Like to pore over 18th-century newspapers or see the original drawings of Audubon's *Birds of America*? This distinguished collection devoted to New York City, New York State, and American history is the place. Open Tuesdays through Fridays, 11 to 5; Saturdays, 10 to 5; Sundays 1 to 5.

GOTHIC NEW YORK: Cathedral of St. John the Divine, Amsterdam Avenue and 112th Street. The world's largest Gothic cathedral is right here in New York, and its interior is an awesome masterpiece of religious architecture that must be seen and experienced. The entire St. John complex includes a lovely little park and a beautiful biblical garden, plus an especially appealing gift shop. The Cathedral Museum of Religious Art contains important Medieval and Renaissance paintings and tapestries (including the Mortlake tapestries designed by Raphael), plus contemporary religious art. Take one of the tours given daily at 11 and 2, or on Sunday after the 11 o'clock service, or just walk in, any day from 7 until 6. A recorded tour is available at the craft shop.

Riverside Church, 490 Riverside Drive (between 120th and 122nd Streets). From the observation deck in the imposing Gothic tower of Riverside Church, one can get one of the best views of the New York skyline, the George Washington Bridge, and the surrounding Upper Manhattan area. Admission is 25¢. Tower open 11 to 3. On the way up (by elevator), you can also stop to view, or maybe hear a concert (every Saturday at noon, plus Sundays at 2) played on the Laura Spelman Rockefeller Memorial Carillon, the largest tuned bell in the world and 73 others. The church itself, inspired by the cathedral of Chartres, with its stained-glass windows (duplicates of those at Chartres) is a great beauty. Visitors are welcomed daily from 9:30 to 5, and Sunday services are held at 10:45. Both Riverside Church and the Cathedral of St. John the Divine function as centers for the entire community, and there are many cultural, social, and artistic events frequently going on at both.

*OCEAN LINERS: Want to pretend you're off on a gala cruise? It's easy. To go aboard the great liners that dock in the Hudson, simply check the Shipping News page of the *New York Times* to find out when the ship you choose will be departing. Present yourself an hour or two before sailing time, just as if you were seeing somebody off. Call the steamship company in advance as some have special security measures. You are expected to make a small donation to a seamen's charity fund, and the run of the ship is yours. A natural for kids.

Special: New York on a Culture Bus

One of the easiest and least expensive ways to see the sights is to take the **Culture Bus Loop 1,** a new and very popular service of the Metropolitan Transport Authority. **It runs on Saturdays, Sundays, and holidays only.** Here's how it works: you board the Culture Bus at any of 22 stops along a 17-mile route, pay a $1.25 exact fare, receive a free guide book, and are then entitled to get on and off the bus at will, picking up the next one as you continue on your route. Culture Bus Loop 1, which runs from 10 to 6, makes a wide loop: up the West Side from Pennsylvania Station to 155th Street and Broadway (the Audubon Terrace Museums), down to Fifth Avenue, 34th Street (the Empire State Building), over to the United Nations, Rockefeller Center, and Central Park, etc. Tickets, available at any bus stop, may also be purchased at Grand Central Terminal, Pennsylvania Station, Port Authority Bus Terminal, Times Square, Rockefeller Center, or Columbus Circle. For a map of all the bus stops—which you will recognize en route by the symbol M41 enclosed in a laurel wreath—stop in at the New York Convention and Visitors Bureau, 90 East 42nd Street, or phone the MTA at AU 6-2000, and one will be mailed to you. Two extra bonuses: Your $1.25 ticket also allows you transfer privileges to several crosstown busses, at no extra fare, and, entitles you to discounts at various reataurants and sightseeing attractions along your route.

After you've completed the Manhattan Culture Bus tour, you might be game for Culture Bus II, which goes to Brooklyn (stopping en route in lower Manhattan, Chinatown, the financial district, and the Lower East Side).

Points North

MUSEUMS: *Audubon Terrace Museums, 155th Street and Broadway. Somehow, few visitors know about the lovely little museums on upper Broadway, but they are well worth a short trip, especially if you have the youngsters with you. From midtown, it's about a 20-minute subway ride by either the IND 8th Avenue local train (Washington Heights) to 155th Street or the IRT Broadway local (242nd Street) to 157th Street. The No. 4 or the No. 5 Fifth Avenue bus (or the Culture Bus on weekends) will also take you there, but it will take closer to an hour: get off at 155th Street.

A visit to the small, exquisite **Hispanic Society of America** is like an instant trip back in time to the days of Old Spain. Outside is a statue of Don Quixote; inside, in the old-world building with its cobbled floors and skylight, is a collection of arts and artifacts —paintings, furniture, jewelry, laces, ivories—that trace the history of Spain from the days of the Moors to the present. Do not miss the outstanding collection of paintings: Goya's *Duchess of Alba* is here, as well as important works by El Greco and Velasquez. Open Tuesday through Saturday, 10 to 4:30; Sundays, 1 to 4. Free (tel. WA 6-2234).

*The Museum of the American Indian, Broadway at 155th Street. A must for laymen, serious scholars of Indian culture, and just about anyone in between, this is an utterly absorbing spot. The largest Indian museum in the world, it concentrates on the tribes of North, Central, and South America, and displays its materials in an arresting manner. You can study the masks of the Iroquois False Face Society, examine rare specimens from the Southeast like polychrome Chitimacha baskets and Alibamu beaded belts, observe the huge doorposts and totem poles of the tribes of the Northwest. Do stop in at the exciting Museum Shop where you can buy authentic, Indian-made products—no tourist junk here—like Kachina dolls, masks, beadwork, pottery, and weaving to take back home with you. A marvelous museum, and, of course, we don't have to tell you that, with the burgeoning interest in Indian culture, young people and children will find this place fascinating. Open Tuesday through Sunday, 1 to 5. Admission: adults $1, students and senior citizens, 50¢. On Tuesdays, general admission is 25¢.

The Cloisters, Fort Tryon Park. One of the high points of New York, artistically and geographically. The Cloisters is a bit of medieval Europe transplanted to a cliff overlooking the Hudson. The Metropolitan Museum of Art, of which this is the medieval department, has brought intact from Europe a twelfth-century chapter house, parts of five cloisters from medieval monasteries, a Romanesque chapel, and a 12th-century Spanish apse. Smaller treasures include rare tapestries like the 15th-century *Hunt of the Unicorn,* paintings, frescoes, stained glass, precious metals. All is set in tranquil gardens overlooking the Hudson and piped-in madrigals can usually be heard over the loud (or soft) speaker. Since this extraordinary collection is one of the most popular in the city, especially in fine weather, try to schedule your visit during the week, rather than on a crowded Saturday or Sunday afternoon. The Madison Avenue Bus No. 4, marked "Fort Tryon Park—The Cloisters" takes about an hour from midtown;

quicker, but less scenic, is the Eighth Avenue Subway A train to 190th Street (Overlook Terrace), which then connects with the No. 4 bus. Open Tuesdays through Saturdays from 10 to 4:45; Sundays and holidays, from 1 to 4:45: Sundays, May through September, from 12 to 4:45. Closed on holidays that fall on Monday (tel. 923-3700). Pay-what-you wish admission.

HISTORIC HOUSE: Morris-Jumel Mansion, in Roger Morris Park at West 160th Street and Jumel Terrace, just east of St. Nicholas Avenue. Built in 1765 by Roger Morris, this Georgian mansion was headquarters for General George Washington in 1776. Aaron Burr was married here in 1833. Open Tuesday through Sunday, 10 to 4; 50¢ (tel. WA 3-8008). Luncheon served to groups by appointment. To reach Morris-Jumel Mansion, take the IND Subway AA or train to West 163rd Street. Sit in the last car of the train and you will get out at St. Nicholas Avenue, very near the Mansion. You can also get there via bus nos. 2, 2A, 3, 100, or 101.

Beyond Manhattan

BROOKLYN: *Brooklyn Museum, Eastern Parkway. One of the best reasons for leaving Manhattan is to see the Brooklyn Museum, among the best museums in the country. It has superb collections of Egyptian, Oriental, American, and European art, as well as a fine primitive collection, 25 period rooms, and a Fashion Theater. There are new Japanese and Korean galleries. The Frieda Schiff Warburg Sculpture Garden is a repository for some of the architectural relics of the city: bits and pieces of the old Steeplechase Amusement Park in Coney Island and the Pennsylvania Station that was torn down to make way for the new Madison Square Garden, as well as the scene of changing exhibits. Don't miss a visit to the Gallery Shop, with its wonderful handicrafts from Mexico, Japan, South America, Scandinavia, all of it authentic, beautifully made, and well-priced. The kids can stock up here on slews of inexpensive presents to bring their friends back home. The IRT Broadway-Seventh Avenue Express brings you to the museum's door at the Eastern Parkway-Brooklyn Museum Station. Open Wednesdays through Saturdays, 10 to 5; Sundays, 12 to 5; holidays, 1 to 5 (tel. 638-5000.) Admission free.

Brooklyn Botanic Garden, 1000 Washington Avenue. Next

door to the Brooklyn Museum, and a major destination in its own right, the Brooklyn Botanic Garden is a glorious 50 acres' worth of flowers, trees, exotic plants. If you are in town in May, make a pilgrimage here to see the flowering of the cherry trees; they are even more beautiful than the ones in Washington, D.C. (Phone the garden at 622-4433 to check on blossoming time.) The Japanese mood also prevails in the traditional Japanese Garden with its pretty bridges crossing a pond, and in the austere Ryoanji Temple Stone Garden, modeled after a Zen garden in Kyoto. You can browse through the greenhouses with their exotic tropical plants and be convinced you are light-years away from Brooklyn. The Garden is open most of every day, but since hours change with the seasons, call, again, 622-4433 for exact times. General admission is free, but on Saturdays, Sundays, and holidays you'll pay 10¢ to get into the greenhouses and 25¢ admission to the Ryoanji Temple Stone Garden. Closed Mondays except holidays.

*Brooklyn Children's Museum, 145 Brooklyn Avenue (between Eastern Parkway and Atlantic Avenue). This is one museum that children will want to return to over and over; here they can do things with the Museum's objects instead of just looking at them. BCM made "participation" its key principle at its beginning 78 years ago as the world's first children's museum. It recently replaced its two old Victorian mansions with a new $5 million building for children. The semi-underground structure is an architectural tour de force, a flexible five-level, learning-looking-growing environment, with its own windmill, greenhouse, steam engine, running water stream, workshops, and children's library. Natural science, technology, cultural his-

Staten Island Ferry

tory, arts, and humanities are explored in unified exhibitions and programs. No one—from kids climbing through transparent plastic hexagons looming skyward to enthralled grownups—will want to leave. Admission is free. Open six days, closed Tuesdays. For hours and activities, phone 735-4432.

*Coney Island. Don't say we didn't warn you: New York's most popular beach is very crowded on a hot summer day, and the water is sometimes polluted. (Personally, we would opt for an air-conditioned movie.) But, if you must, take either the West End or Sea Beach Express train on the BMT subway, and get off at Stillwell Avenue. You can swim, sunbathe (if you can find a spot of unoccupied sand), try the amusements, eat hot dogs and popcorn and candied apples. Kiddies will love it all, and you should take them (whether or not you go to the beach), to the **New York Aquarium,** West 8th Street and Surf Avenue, to ogle whales and penguins and sharks and seals and other finny characters. There are sea lion and dolphin shows daily. There's a pleasant rooftop cafeteria with outdoor tables. The Aquarium is open daily from 10 to 5 all year long. Admission: $2 for adults, 75¢ for children two to 12 (tel. 266-8500).

*Bronx Zoo, Bronx Park. For many years, the Bronx Zoo, one of the biggest (252 acres, 3,000 animals) and the best zoos in the world, has been a prime visitor's magnet, and now it's better than ever. Traditional zoo cages are on their way out and, instead, natural habitats and moated exhibits like the African Plains and Lion Island are coming into the foreground. The newest of these features is Wild Asia, which offers a guided twenty-minute safari, via monorail (the Bengali Express) through 46 densely forested acres where the elephants, tigers, et al, roam free ($1 for adults, 50¢ for children 12 and under). Don't miss the architecturally exciting exhibits in the World of Birds, a $4 million, volcano-like exhibit building, complete with waterfalls, thunder, and other special effects in which visitors walk through rain forests and into jungles while birds swoop around their heads. A big one for the kids! Take the moppets to the "Children's Zoo," to pet tame animals. They'll also love a ride in the **Skyfari,** a four-seater cable car. The zoo opens every day at 10 and closes anywhere between 4:30 and 5:30, depending on the time of year. Admission is free on Tuesday, Wednesday, and Thursday, but on other days, you must pay $1.50 for adults, 75¢ for children six to 12. Express bus service is available from midtown Manhattan to the zoo and the New York Botanical Garden (see ahead). The fare is $1.50 each way (exact amount required): phone 881-

1000 for schedules. Or, take the IRT Lexington Avenue subway, the no. 5 Dyre Avenue Express train to East Tremont Avenue. On the West Side IRT, take the 241st Street-White Plains Road express train no. 2. There's plenty of space to park, and the fee is $2, Friday through Monday, and $2.50, Tuesday through Thursday (tel. 933-1759).

New York Botanical Garden, Bronx Park. Greenhouses, gardens, seasonal plantings, and an air of peace and quiet make this the place for a lovely respite from city tensions. See the Hemlock Forest, largely unchanged since the days of the Indians in Manhattan; the magnificent gardens of rhododendron, daffodils, azaleas, chrysanthemums. Newly restored to its turn-of-the-century elegance is the Crystal Palace, a 90-foot domed landmark Conservatory (covering one acre of gardens under glass and similar to London's Kew Botanical Garden), with its coconut palms, jungle plantings, waterfall, desert area, and animal-shaped topiaries. It is open six days a week, closed Mondays; admission is $1.50 adults, 75¢ senior citizens and children. Stop in at the gift shop for unusual objets d'art and plants, have lunch at the romantic Snuff Mill Restaurant; it's on a terrace overlooking the Bronx River, which looks positively rural at this point. Open daily, from 10 to dusk. Free. Take the IND subway, 6th Avenue D train (Concourse-205th Street) to Bedford Park Boulevard, and walk east eight blocks to the garden. Or, take the Pelham Parkway Express from midtown (tel. 931-9250), see above.

CITY PLANNERS TOURS: New York City has its problems, but is also has some strikingly innovative solutions to those problems. **Planners New York Tours,** sponsored by Hunter College's Graduate Program in Urban Planning, conducts tours that explore contemporary urban problem-solving in three areas: Central Manhattan, where the tour focuses on loft conversion in SoHo and car-free, dog-free Roosevelt Island; Brooklyn, for a look at the Brownstone Revival Area and the highly acclaimed, community-run Bedford Stuyvesant Restoration Project; and East Harlem-Bronx, to view Co-Op City, the largest housing complex in the nation, "sweat equity" projects, and urban homesteading in the Bronx. Each tour is led by a professional urban planner. Three hours spent on one of these tours will give you an in-depth look at the city of the caliber that few New Yorkers ever get. Tickets are $8 per person, $5 for students and senior citizens. Make reservations, in advance, please, by writing:

"Planners New York Tours," Hunter College C.U.N.Y. Graduate Program in Urban Planning, 790 Madison Avenue, New York, NY 10021 (tel. 734-1366).

---

*A New York Odyssey

An ideal first thing to do when you arrive in the city would be to take yourself to **The New York Experience.** When you emerge, the city will be an old friend. This thrilling armchair tour of New York past and New York present is done with wit, taste, and a great sense of excitement—thanks to a 180-degree screen, 45 projectors, 16 film screens, 68 special effects and an ultra-quadraphonic sound system. The whole family will love the show and the adjacent Antique Amusement Arcade, where you can have your picture taken dressed in old-time clothes, sip refreshments at soda tables and chairs, or perhaps get a complete reading from "Princess Doraldina" for 25¢. Now in its sixth year, The New York Experience is one of New York's leading tourist attractions. Showings daily every hour on the hour from late morning until early evening. At the New York Experience Theater, McGraw-Hill Building, Lower Plaza, at Rockefeller Center (49th Street and Avenue of the Americas). Adults: $2.90; children under 12, $1.50 (tel. 869-0345).

ARCHITECTURAL TOURS: A highly enjoyable way to learn about the architecture, history, culture, and future planning possibilities of the city is to join one of the tours given every Sunday at 2, from May through October, by the Municipal Art Society. The lively three-hour walking tours, among the city's most popular, cost $3. Six tours are available every Sunday. And every Tuesday at 12:30 p.m. they offer a free walking tour of Grand Central Terminal. Tour participants get to walk in the catwalks of the grand windows facing Vanderbilt Avenue, visit the mysterious whispering gallery, and learn about the Terminal's colorful history. For departure information, phone 586-4761.

Classical America, a group dedicated to helping people learn about and enjoy New York's heritage of classical architecture, sponsors a fascinating series of Sunday walking tours "for people who don't like walking." Join them in surveying "Classical Broadway: The Broadway Theatre as a Work of Art," or "The Classical Courthouse" downtown or "Classical Brooklyn." Nonmembers pay $3. Send a postcard to Classical America,

10-41 Fifty-First Avenue, Long Island City, New York, NY 11101, and they'll send you a schedule. (tel. EM 1-0171).

Watch the papers for news of other walking tours: many interesting ones are held by various groups in warm weather.

. . . AND OTHERS: Dedicated theater goers will love **Backstage on Broadway's** tours: they take you behind the scenes at a Broadway show, to meet the people—the stage managers, directors, lighting designers, etc.—who make the magic happen. Excellent for older children. Tours cost $3.75 for adults, $2.75 for students. Backstage on Broadway is at 228 West 47th Street, (tel. 575-8065). . . . **Holidays in New York,** 152 West 58th Street, arranges tours of unusual artistic and cultural merit: behind the scenes to the top wholesale fashion houses, tours of Jewish landmarks, and visits to artists' and dancers' studios. There are special tours for retired persons, students, and children, too (tel. 765-2515). . . . Voluble **Lou Singer,** a self-taught historian who must know more about Brooklyn than anybody, conducts absorbing tours focusing on Revolutionary and architectural Brooklyn, via bus or private car. You'll see the private parlors of restored Victorian brownstones, the masterful last landscape by Louis Comfort Tiffany, Stanford White's "Prison Ship Martyrs' Monument," and much more. Unusual lunch stops are arranged. Singer, who teaches at Brooklyn College, will arrange special trips, to ethnic neighborhoods and elsewhere, for special interests. Costs should run about $10 per person. A worthwhile and enjoyable excursion (tel. 875-9084).

George Washington Bridge

Chapter VII

THE BEST ENTERTAINMENT VALUES IN NEW YORK

BY NOW, you've cased the town, you've dined and wined your way around the city, climbed to the top of the Statue of Liberty and explored the caverns underneath Rockefeller Center. But now it's time to put away the sightseeing maps, tuck whatever kiddies you may have into bed and step out for an evening on the town. You didn't come all this way just to sit in your hotel room and watch your color television set. You want to see plays and movies, go to concerts and operas and night clubs. But all that takes a bit of doing—and it's not just a matter of money. Too often, getting tickets to something in New York seems a matter of adding insult to injury. It's bad enough spending $40 for a pair of seats to a hit Broadway musical (especially when you want to see four of them) and $50 for the Metropolitan Opera, but how to get the tickets in the first place? There is no need to despair. Provided you know the ropes, you *can* get tickets, you can see a lot more entertainment than you had even planned, and you won't have to break the budget to do it.

New York City is, of course, the entertainment capital of the nation, and it is here that you will catch not only Broadway theater and New York opera, but outstanding musical, dance, and theater groups from all over the world, everything from the Bolshoi Ballet to the Coldstream Guards to the Comédie Française. But that's just the beginning of the story. Since the city has literally thousands of young actors and musicians and dancers and other performers here studying or working their ways up the ladder, there are vast numbers of inexpensive entertainments to showcase these talents. Many are free; some charge modest admissions. In addition, there are innumerable lectures, poetry readings, off-beat entertainments that beckon the visitor. If you want to wander off the beaten track, you can have your horoscope forecast, go on an "encounter" weekend, do asanas with the yogis or meditate with the Zen masters. All that is required is some pocket money and your own ardent interest in exploring the new and adventurous. First though, some inside tips on one of the most subtle of the New York arts: Getting Theater Tickets.

THE RULES OF THE THEATER-TICKET GAME: The very name "Broadway" has become synonymous with the American theater, and whether you're a "tired businessman" or ardent avant gardist, you will want to attend at least a few plays while you're in New York. But you will have two problems: first, getting seats; second, getting seats that you can afford. There are four general rules for dealing with this sticky wicket.

1. Do your homework. As soon as you know you are coming to New York—even if it's months ahead of the date—write to the theater box-offices for the tickets you want. This is especially important for a hit musical, which is often sold out months in advance. (To find out what will be playing, consult the Entertainment Section of the Sunday *New York Times,* which is sold everywhere.) That way, you will be assured not only of a seat, but of a seat at box-office prices. If you wait until you get into town, you will probably have to resort to a ticket broker's services (they have branches in almost every hotel in the city), and then you must pay a commission, of at least $1.75, on every seat. And you will have a hard time getting seats for the hits. *Note:* It usually works better to send your own mail-order requests from, say, Kalamazoo or San Diego, than to have your cousin in New York go to the box-office for you. Theater ticket-sellers usually make a special effort to fulfill requests from out-of-town customers.

2. Avoid the weekend scene. Most New Yorkers work during the week, so they save their theater-going for weekends, and it's then that the prices are highest. Happily, you're here on vacation, and you can go during the week or to a Wednesday matinee when prices are lower. If you attend a musical on a Saturday night, for example, you'll have to pay from $8 to $20 or more for a seat. During the week, the range is from $8 to $18.50. On

Wednesday matinees, two or three dollars lower (prices vary from show to show). Prices for "straight" or nonmusical plays are slightly lower. *Motto:* Skip the music, head for a matinee, and see more shows for the money.

3. Pick the previews. Not so long ago, it was *de rigueur* for Broadway shows to try out in either New Haven or Boston or Philadelphia before proceeding to New York for the hoped-for opening-night triumph. All of that got too expensive and too complicated and so, in the last few years, the trend has been more and more to substituting New York "previews" for out-of-town tryouts. Philadelphia's loss is the New York theater-goers' gain, for you can often realize considerable savings on a preview ticket, even for musicals. There will be some changes before opening night, of course, when the shows are "set," and you are taking a chance since you have no reviews to guide you. But if, for example, it's a play that's been imported after a long and well-reviewed run in England, or has top stars, or is the work of an important playwright, you're not risking too much. So be your own critic. Preview dates are listed along with the regular ads in the *New York Times, New York Magazine,* the *New Yorker,* and in *Cue Magazine,* all good sources of detailed theater information.

4. If you don't mind waiting in line, the easiest way to get tickets for a show is to join the queue over at **TKTS (Times Square Theater Center)**, at Broadway and 47th Street. Half-price theater tickets are made available for the day of performance only, beginning at 3 p.m. for evening shows, at noon for matinees. Naturally, these are for shows that haven't sold out, so don't expect to get into the big hits this way. The Center is open from 3 to 8 daily, from 12 to 2 on Wednesday, Saturday, and Sunday (matinee days). There is a service charge of $1 for tickets priced over $10, of 50¢ on those under $10. There's a similar center downtown, at the Galleria, 100 William Street, in the financial district. Both centers, by the way, also sell tickets to Lincoln Center, opera, ballet, and concert attractions, as well as to Broadway and Off-Broadway.

5. Take the "twofers." When a show gets close to the end of its run—say it's been running for three years, and the house is not completely sold every night—it often goes on "twofers." This means that, by presenting a slip at the box-office, you are entitled to buy two seats for the price of one, on certain nights of the week. You're running little risk here, since any show lasting long enough to go on "twofers" has some merit: you will probably not, however, see the original cast. "Twofers" are available at many places: at most hotel desks, at restaurant cashier's booths, and almost always at the offices of the Visitors and Convention Bureau, 90 East 42nd Street.

But let's suppose you just decided to come to New York last week, nothing you want is either previewing or twofering, and you've just got to see the biggest hit in town. You *could* try the box office right before curtain-time (someone may be trying to return tickets), but don't count on that. You could, if you have the right connections, wangle a pair from "scalpers" for about $50. But we don't recommend that. Your best bet for a musical is to hie yourself to one of the ticket brokers. The best seats in the house are usually commandeered by them, and for their $2 commission, they may or may not get you into the show of your dreams, but they will get you into something. You can often get a ticket for a nonmusical by just going to the box office a day or two before the performance.

Note: An easy way to get theater tickets is via **Ticketron,** a computer ticket service with convenient locations at major traffic areas. Service charge per ticket is $1. You can find a Ticketron at Macy's and at the Yankee ticket booth at Grand Central Station, on the mezzanine level, open to 5 (they also handle all major sporting events). For information on other Ticketron locations, phone 977-9020.

MAKING THE OPERA SCENE: Up until very recently, it was even harder to get tickets for the Metropolitan Opera Company at Lincoln Center than it was for Broadway. But now that the novelty of the new house has worn off a bit, the situation has eased, and it is likely that you will be able to pick something up for most performances, even though most of the Metropolitan's seats are taken by subscribers. The best way to do it is via mail order, as far in advance as possible. To find out what and when, write to the Met for a schedule of performances, and enclose a stamped, self-addressed envelope. The address: Metropolitan Opera Mail Order Department, Lincoln Center, New York, NY 10023. An even neater trick is to persuade a friend who lives in the city to get to the box office on a Monday morning seven weeks ahead of a scheduled performance to pick up a ticket (or phone 580-9830).

Failing all else, present yourself to a ticket broker or to the Metropolitan box office as soon as you arrive in town. Unless it's a *very* popular production, you will almost always be able to get a seat, although usually one in the orchestra at about $25 to $30. With a little more advance notice, you may be able to get a lower-priced seat; they start at $7 in Family Circle. The only way to really save money is to stand; standee's places are sold for $3 in Family Circle, $4 in the orchestra; they go on sale one week ahead of time. Usually, however, something will be found for you at the box-office.

Happily, it's not quite as difficult to get seats for the **New York City Opera Company,** which also has a superb company, but slightly less cachet. This is home base for Beverly Sills. Mail orders a few weeks in advance will usually do the trick. Otherwise, try a ticket broker or the box office: it's also at Lincoln Center, at the New York State Theatre. Prices go from $3 to $20.

Bargains in Entertainment

Once you forsake the realms of the Broadway theater and the top musical companies, it becomes relatively simple to plan an evening out. Reservations can be taken care of by a simple phone call to the box office. Off-Broadway theaters are, unhappily, not as cheap as they used to be (when a show gets rave notices, some producers have a deplorable habit of raising the prices, sometimes to Broadway—or higher—levels; an extreme example of this is the $25 top for "Oh! Calcutta!", which got terrible notices, but created a sensation as the dirtiest show in town. Then it moved to Broadway, other shows got even dirtier, and the top ticket went down to $17! But typically, prices run from $7 to $12.50 Off-Broadway, sometimes less. At most of the other events we describe here, admission will either be free, by contribution, or by paying a small admission charge, from $2 to $4. Best of all, you'll be catching some of the most exciting events in the city, where new ideas are being explored, new talents being perfected, new—and sometimes radical—innovations being made in the performing arts. To wit:

Theater

OFF-BROADWAY: New York theater-goers have been going "off-Broadway" for about fifty years now, ever since the Provincetown Playhouse set up shop on MacDougal Street to show the works of a young playwright named Eugene O'Neill. Off-Broadway went into high gear, however, in the '50s and '60s, the golden years of Circle in the Square, the Theatre de Lys, and the Cherry Lane Theatre. It was at places like this that Geraldine Page rose to stardom, that Edward Albee tried out his first works, and that names like Ionesco and Beckett and Bertolt Brecht and Kurt Weill (his *Threepenny Opera* ran here for seven years) became household words. The longest-running show, on Broadway or off, is Tom Jones's and Harvey Schmidt's *The Fantasticks,* now going into its 18th year! It's at the Sullivan Street Playhouse.

Off-Broadway can still afford to be more daring than uptown theater, mainly because there is much less financial risk involved in mounting a production. The houses are much smaller than the Broadway ones (they are often converted factories, or church basements, or cellars); and the actors and technicians receive much less than a Broadway wage scale. This freedom sometimes leads to great artistic successes, to brilliant revivals of the classics, and sometimes to the merely inept and mediocre (there is, however, no shortage of the latter on Broadway, either).

Happily, it is much easier to get a ticket to an off-Broadway production than to a Broadway one. Check the listings in the *Times, New York* or *Cue* magazines, or the *New Yorker,* phone the theater, and pick up your reservation about an hour before curtain time. Since many theaters are in the East or West Village (although some are in the West 40s and East 50s), you can pick up your tickets first, have dinner in the neighborhood, and be in time for the curtain. The uptown Wednesday-Saturday matinee bit is usually waived in favor of a matinee Sunday at 3, and two

Times Square

performances on Saturday nights: at 7 and 10 p.m. Many off-Broadway playhouses will honor student ID cards.

OFF-OFF-BROADWAY: As off-Broadway aspires to become Broadway, so OOB hopes to make it to the "big time" of off-Broadway. Fledgling playwrights, directors, actors come together in small theaters, cafes, churches, school auditoriums, to do their thing; sometimes it's beautiful, sometimes unspeakable. The more professional—and at least more sane—productions will usually be put on by theater schools and repertory groups like the Manhattan Theater Club, La Mama, etc. and the Actors & Directors Lab.

The brightest news in the OOB scene in many a year has been the creation of **42nd Street Theatre Row:** the transformation of the once seedy block between 9th and 10th Avenues into a sparkling new theater neighborhood, complete with eight theaters (including the Harold Clurman Theatre, Playwrights Horizons, and the Black Theatre Alliance), more a-building, and new quality attractions opening constantly. Tickets here will range from $2.50 to $5, with the average around $3. Admission to most other OOB productions is free, but a small contribution, usually $2.50 to $3, is often asked. The most extensive OOB listings—and sometimes reviews—are found in the *Village Voice.*

For news of productions at 42nd Street Theatre Row and at a number of other OOB theaters, phone Ticket Central at 279-4200. You can also make phone reservations, using major credit cards.

THE BARD—SUMMER AND WINTER: The **New York Shakespeare Festival** can be counted on all summer long for high-quality productions of the Bard, in a delightful outdoor setting in Central Park. To get tickets for the free performances (every night during July and August), present yourself at the Delacorte Theatre at 6:15. One ticket is given to each patron. Seats are reserved, and you can be seated between 7:15 and 7:45. So, take yourself off to dinner in a West Side restaurant nearby or, better yet, join the picnickers on the grass. The Delacorte can be approached from either 81st Street and Central Park West or 79th Street and Fifth Avenue.

During the winter, producer Joseph Papp and the other presiding lights of the Shakespeare Festival get into the "now" mood themselves. They run the **Public Theatre,** 425 Lafayette

Street, and let new playwrights have their fling. At this writing, there were some seven theaters under the Public Theatre roof and the complex presents perhaps the most vital and compelling theatrical experiment in New York today. It was at the Public Theatre that *A Chorus Line, That Championship Season* and *No Place To Be Somebody* got their start. At every performance, one-fourth of all seats (including those for the biggest hits) is saved for Quiktix, available at $3 and $4 instead of the usual $6 and $8. Be on line at 6 for evening performances, 1 for matinees.

REPERTORY COMPANIES: Repertory companies, long a fond dream for the American commercial theater, are finally becoming reality. In addition to the New York Shakespeare Festival, several other repertory companies can be counted upon for quality new productions and significant revivals. Look for excellent productions at less-than-usual prices at any of the following: **Circle in the Square,** uptown and downtown; **Chelsea Theatre Company** and **The American Place Theatre,** uptown; the **Circle Repertory Theater,** downtown; **WPA Theatre,** way downtown, on the Bowery; and the **SoHo Repertory Theater** in SoHo.

Equity Library Theatre presents solid, highly professional (all the performers are members of the actor's union) revivals of classics like *Twelfth Night* and musicals like *Follies.* The season runs from the middle of October through the middle of May. Tickets are free (but you'll probably want to make a contribution) and can be reserved by calling MO 3-2028. Performances are held at the Master's Institute, 103rd Street and Riverside Drive, Tuesday through Sunday evenings, with matinees on Saturday and Sunday.

The Library & Museum of the Performing Arts, 111 Amsterdam Avenue (65th Street), the New York Public Library at Lincoln Center. Since this unique and splendid institution believes in bringing the performing arts to *life* (as well as providing books, records, manuscripts, research materials about them), it runs a *free* winter series in its auditorium of concerts, dance programs, *and* plays. Recent theatrical events have included the Equity Informals (Equity Library Theatre players trying out new ideas); the Commedia dell' Arte, and the Stage Directors and Choreographers Workshop. Performances are held at 4 p.m. weekdays and 2:30 on Saturday, from September through June. Tickets are handed out a few hours before performance time, and the small auditorium fills up quickly, especially for dance events. Note, too, that there are frequent programs for children.

To find out what's going on, pick up a list of the New York Public Library's bulletin *Events,* published bi-monthly, and available at any library branch (Central Circulation is at 42nd Street and Fifth Avenue). Or, phone the Library & Museum of the Performing Arts at 799-2200.

Television

You say you've always wanted to be on television—even in the audience? Here's your chance. Tickets to many television shows filmed or taped in New York are free and are available at the offices of the Visitors and Convention Bureau, 90 East 42nd Street; pick them up as early in the morning as possible. They are also available at many hotel desks, restaurants, other places where tourists gather. For the most important shows, you should write in advance to the networks involved, or go directly to their studios on the day of the program, again, as early as possible. The addresses: Ticket Division, Columbia Broadcasting System, 524 West 57th Street; Ticket Division, National Broadcasting Company, 30 Rockefeller Plaza; Ticket Division, American Broadcasting Company, 1330 Avenue of the Americas. CBS also maintains an on-the-spot "box-office" at the Ed Sullivan Theatre, Broadway at 53rd Street. And NBC offers guided tours through its studios.

Music

There is never a dearth of musical activity in New York. You can hear the lofty New York Philharmonic or a neighborhood symphony, the world's greatest soloists at Carnegie Hall or Avery Fisher Hall or an aspiring young pianist at a local music school in dozens of musical events every week. While the very top music events are expensive, most are not, even at such prestigious halls as Town Hall and Judson Hall. And there are many, many concerts that charge $2 or $3 or are free. For week-by-week details on the inexpensive music scene, the *Village Voice* is your best source of information. It is available at newsstands throughout the city.

OPERA: If the Met is the number one opera company in town, the New York City Opera the second, then the third might well be the **Amato Opera Theatre,** a professional company in its own

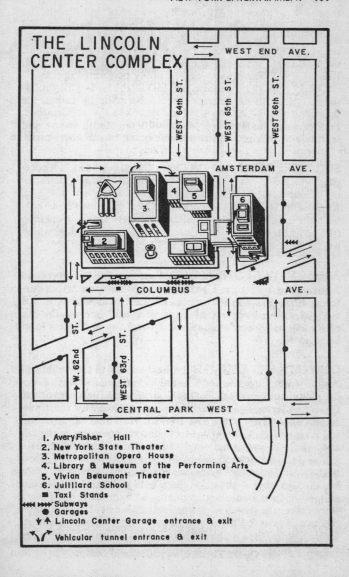

THE LINCOLN
CENTER COMPLEX

WEST END AVE.

WEST 64th ST.
WEST 65th ST.
WEST 66th ST.

AMSTERDAM AVE.

COLUMBUS AVE.

ST.
W. 62nd
WEST 63rd ST.

CENTRAL PARK WEST

1. Avery Fisher Hall
2. New York State Theater
3. Metropolitan Opera House
4. Library & Museum of the Performing Arts
5. Vivian Beaumont Theater
6. Juilliard School
■ Taxi Stands
◄◄◄ ►►► Subways
● Garages
↓ ↑ Lincoln Center Garage entrance & exit
↘↗ Vehicular tunnel entrance & exit

theater downtown, at 319 Bowery, corner of 2nd Street. The Amato has been a New York standby for over 20 years now, and scores of its "graduates" have gone on to sing at the Metropolitan and the New York City Opera. They give full productions, not workshops, of the classic repertory—Verdi, Puccini, Mozart, Rossini and Donizetti—as well as rarely performed operas.

The $5 price ($3 for senior citizens) is unheard-of for professional opera! Phone reservations can be made by calling the theater at CA 8-8200 up until a day before the performance. Performances are given weekends over a ten month season, and in July and August, Amato is out singing in suburban parks.

STILL MORE OPERA: The **Bel Canto Opera** is a fine small company which uses the Madison Avenue Baptist Church, performing classical operas—like *Medea* and *Lakme*—every weekend. Admission: $4, $2 for students and senior citizens. Phone 889-6366 for details. And the **Lighthouse Singers Opera Workshop** (the performers are all blind!) is another one to remember, which has an annual production early in June.

AND SOME LIGHT OPERA: Should your taste run to Gilbert and Sullivan, don't miss the **Light Opera of Manhattan,** which performs at the Eastside Playhouse, 334 East 74th Street (tel. LE 5-6310). They are considered the finest of performers in the city of *Ruddigore, Pirates of Penzance, Iolanthe,* et al. Tickets from $4.50 to $8.

CONCERTS AND RECITALS: To hear artists of the calibre of Andre Watts, Eugeneia and Pinchas Zukerman, and Ruth Laredo, plus chamber groups like the Guarneri and Cleveland String Quartets playing in intimate surroundings, head for the **Kaufmann Concert Hall of the YM-YWHA,** 92nd Street and Lexington Avenue (tel. 427-6000). Most concerts are given in the fall and winter months, and single admission is from $4 to $10.

The **Juilliard School,** one of the best performing art schools in the world, schedules more than 200 performances from October through May to showcase the talents—and they are considerable—of their students. (Sometimes a major artist like Joseph Fuchs takes the stage.) Major orchestra concerts take place Friday evenings at 8:30. Performances by the Juilliard American Opera Center, the Drama Division, and the Dance Division are scattered throughout the week in the school's four theaters and concert halls at Lincoln Center, Broadway at 66th Street. Almost all performances are free, except that contributions to scholarship funds are required for the opera and dance events. No tickets are required for the numerous student recitals, and available tickets for the Friday-night orchestra programs can be had three days in advance from the Juilliard Concert Office. Complete details about all Juilliard events can be had by phoning 799-5000, ext. 235. *Note:* Every Wednesday during the school year a free performance is given at 1 p.m. in Alice Tully Hall. These may range from orchestra and solo performances to choral, dance, and opera scenes. No tickets are necessary.

The **Library & Museum of the Performing Arts** at Lincoln Center is also very involved in the music scene. Showcases for young concert artists are held in the auditorium several times a week. Other branches of the **New York Public Library** hold frequent concerts, too. You might, for example, catch a classical guitar trio doing Paganini at the Hudson Park Branch Library in the Village, 10 Seventh Avenue, or a violin-piano duo at the Donnell Library in midtown, 20 West 53rd Street (which also is the scene of many other events), or an ensemble group at the Countee Cullen Library in Harlem, 104 West 136th Street. Check the *Events* calendar of the New York Public Library, free at all branches.

The **Brooklyn Academy of Music,** the oldest performing arts center in the United States, consists of three theaters: the 2,200-seat Opera House, the 1,100-seat, newly renovated, more intimate Playhouse, plus the experimental Lepercq Space. BAM is the New York home of the Royal Shakespeare Company and the Pennsylvania Ballet. Recent productions have included appearances by the Abbey Theater of Dublin, the Royal Shakespeare Company, Twyla Tharp and dancers, the Cleveland Quartet. The season runs from September to May and offers programs in drama, music, dance, film, even country music. Ticket prices range from $2.50 to $12. For program information, call 636-4100.

Music in the Museums

What could be lovelier than hearing a major concert artist give a Sunday afternoon recital, free, in the splendid setting of the **Frick Collection?** Phone them at BU 8-0700 for details on getting tickets. Or listening to live concerts or recorded music on certain Sundays in the medieval splendors of **The Cloisters** (part of the Metropolitan Museum of Art, but located uptown in Fort Tryon Park; tel. 923-3700 for ticket information). These are only a few of the many fine musical offerings in New York's major museums. Check the papers for news of frequent concerts, too, at the **Metropolitan Museum of Art**, the **Museum of the City of New York**, the New York Historical Society, the **Nicholas Roerich Museum**, and the **Brooklyn Museum.**

Music in the Churches

Some of the finest music in New York is heard in the city's churches—and it's all free. For example, during the fall and winter season, **St. Bartholomew's**, Park Avenue at 51st Street, noted for its mixed choir, presents a series of outstanding concerts every Sunday at 4. . . . At the **Riverside Church**, Riverside Drive at 122nd Street, a Service of Music is held occasionally on Sunday afternoons at 2:30 which includes organ recitals, orchestra, choral, and solo work by some of the world's top artists. Every Saturday throughout the year (and on Sundays at 2 p.m. as well), there is a carillon concert at 12 noon. . . . Sunday evenings from November to May are given over to choral concerts and sometimes to organ recitals at the **Church of the Ascension**, Fifth Avenue at 10th Street. . . . **St. Peter's Lutheran Church**, in its stunning new home at the CitiCorp Center, 54th Street and Lexington Avenue, offers "St. Peter's on the Terrace" every Wednesday night at 5:15 during summer months. Rooftop concerts of jazz, Dixieland, folk, or classical music are followed by discussions and a $2 buffet meal prepared by church members. St. Peter's Jazz Vespers at 5 on Sundays are a vital part of the city's cultural fabric. Listings can be found in the *New York Times* (tel. 753-4669).

A Little Street Music

Street musicians abound in New York. Soloists and chamber music groups, instrumentalists and vocalists, everyone from youngsters playing steel drums to violin students working their way through Juilliard. A good place to catch them is in the CitiCorp Center Market Atrium at 54th Street and Lexington Avenue, where they entertain lunchtime and after-work crowds on a fairly regular summer schedule. Good weather also brings them out to Fifth Avenue and 42nd Street, in front of the New York Public Library and in front of the Metropolitan Museum of Art, Fifth Avenue at 83rd Street, among other spots. A few coins in the hat is the usual price of appreciation.

Films

The top New York movie houses *are* expensive: most of them now charge admissions of $4 to $5. The best movie bargain in town is undoubtedly the one at **Radio City Music Hall,** described in our chapter on sightseeing, where tickets range from $3.25 to $4, and where your price of admission includes a gala stage show as well as the film. Theaters showing revivals of top American and foreign films charge much less: from about $1.50 to $3. Note the **Thalia** at Broadway and 95th Street, the **Regency** at Broadway and 67th Street, the **Carnegie Hall Cinema** at Seventh Avenue and 57th Street and its downtown affiliate, the **Bleecker Street Cinema** (Bleecker at LaGuardia in the Village) for especially imaginative programming. Films are included in the price of admission at the **Museum of Modern Art,** where you might catch up with Myrna Loy or Norma Shearer or the early Marx Brothers and at the **Whitney Museum's** "New American Filmmakers Series," featuring works by creative newcomers. **The Anthology Film Archives,** 80 Wooster Street (tel. 226-0010), screens a steady flow of modern film classics and avant-garde films and video (Bresson, Buñuel, Dreyer), mostly for serious viewers (program notes, rather than subtitles are available). Admission is $2, and shows are held at 7 and 9, weekdays; 8 and 10, weekends; 2:30, Saturday matinee.

For lighter fare, try **Theater St. Marks,** 80 St. Mark's Place, which screens oldies from the '30s and '40s. Branches of the **New York Public Library** present free films. In the midtown area, **Donnell Library,** 20 West 53rd Street, is the busiest, with everything from a Film Program for Preschool Children to a Film at Noon Program and evening performances of short subjects.

THE MUSEUMS: These are mostly daytime events, but short films of high quality are presented at the **Metropolitan Museum of Art,** Fifth Avenue and 82nd Street (tel. 879-5500); **The New York Historical Society,** Central Park West at 77th Street (tel. TR 3-1300); and the **American Museum of Natural History,** Central Park West at 77th Street (tel. TR 3-4225), with especially good films for the whole family. Free.

MISCELLANY: Free or low-cost films are presented at New York University's **Loeb Student Center,** 566 LaGuardia Place, in the Village, offering many free and low-cost programs in film, theater, dance, and art as well as music. Phone 598-2022 or 598-3757 for information. Check the *Village Voice,* which will direct you to the newest and most experimental "underground" cinema.

Dance

The top dance programs in New York will usually be held at Lincoln Center: at the New York State Theatre, where the highly acclaimed **New York City Ballet** makes its home; at the Metropolitan Opera House, home base for the splendid **American Ballet Theatre,** and host to many visiting foreign troupes; at the New York City Center, home to the exciting **Joffrey Ballet** and also to the **Alvin Ailey Dance Company,** as well as to numerous visiting groups. Both the Lincoln Center halls, City Center, and the Broadway theaters frequently play host to visiting modern-dance and folk-dance groups from overseas for short seasons: you may be lucky enough to catch the **Royal Ballet** of London or our own **Martha Graham** company if you're here during the winter: the **National Ballet of Canada** often performs during the summer. Carnegie Hall and Felt Forum often get into the dance scene, too, hosting the likes of the National Dance Company of Senegal or the Soviet Georgian Dancers. The Kaufmann Auditorium of the YM-YWHA has been a prestigious haven for modern dance for many years, and is now the official home of the **José Limon Dance Company.** And the Brooklyn Academy of Music has lately presented such top names as **Merce Cunningham** and **Paul Taylor.** New York's dance offerings are among the greatest in the world. Prices are about the same for these events as for Broadway plays. There is also plenty of free and low-cost dance of high quality. For a start, you might try the following.

Cooper Union, 7th Street and Third Avenue (tel. AL 4-6300). From October to March in the Great Hall of Cooper Union, programs in the performing arts are given every Friday night at 8. Dance performances may include anything from Olatunji and his African dancers to a Flamenco Fiesta. Admission is free, no reservations necessary. Just come early: the 900 seats get filled up quickly. Doors open at 7:30. To get a schedule of programs, write to Cooper Union Forum, Cooper Square, New York, N.Y.

The **Cubiculo,** 414 West 51st Street, is up to its ears in all kinds of experimental performances—theater and poetry—as well as dance. Performances of all these groups will be listed as they occur, in the *Village Voice,* or call 265-2138 for information. Admission is $2.50 to $3.50.

New York Offbeat
Entertainment for When the Spirit Moves You

Now here's some news for the esoteric set. If your idea of fun is casting horoscopes, chanting mantras, listening to talk on psychic phenomena, or learning to meditate with the yogis and the Zen masters, you've come to the right place. Spiritual, semi-spiritual, and occult groups have lately been flourishing in our town to such an extent that, if not for the lack of palm trees, you might think it was Southern California. Herewith, a brief sampling, for those moments when you want to explore the world within.

YOGA: One of New York's reigning gurus, the genuine article, is Swami Satchitananda of the **Integral Yoga Institute,** an Indian teacher whom almost everybody describes as "beautiful." The swami occasionally lectures in New York (call 929-0585 for details), but even if he's not in town, there will be plenty going on at the Institute's two centers (there is one uptown at 500 West End Avenue, at 84th Street; and in Greenwich Village at 227 West 13th Street): weekly programs in chanting and meditation and daily classes in Hatha Yoga, those relaxing-yet-energizing exercises that make you feel so marvelous. Should you want to spend a morning or an evening brushing up on your asanas, you are welcome to come by for a class. Bring a leotard or shorts. Admission is by contribution, minimum $2.00. (The downtown branch also runs a health-food store.)

Another place where you can come for an open class, maybe learn the headstand or the lotus, is the **Sivananada Yoga Vedanta Center,** 243 West 24th Street (tel. 255-4560). Classes cost $2.50. Visiting yogis frequently lecture here. Should you happen to be spending the winter in New York and need some respite from the cold, check with them about charter flights to their sunny yoga retreat on Paradise Island, in Nassau, Bahamas ($25 a day, all-inclusive). They also run a yoga ranch in the nearby Catskill Mountains; good for swimming or skiing (only $12.50 a day, all-inclusive).

Meditation and practical psychology are taught by Gurudev

Chitrabhanu, the popular Jain leader, Fridays at 8 p.m. at the **Meditation International Center,** 120 East 86th Street (tel. 722-7474). Also yoga classes and weekend retreats. . . . Those who were turned on by Swami Muktananda when he visited this country recently can join the local devotees in daily meditation and chanting at the very beautiful, very Indian **Siddha Yoga Dham** of New York, 324 West 86th Street (tel. 873-8030). Evening programs begin at 7 and supper is served at 6. . . . The "chaotic meditation" taught by Bhagwan Shree Rajneesh takes place most days of the week ($3) at Wismar Studio, 101 Fifth Avenue (at 17th Street). They also have weekend workshops and intensives. The current location is temporary; for news of a permanent center, phone 662-6699. . . . TM in New York? Of course. you You can hear a lecture on transcendental meditation Thursday at 7 or Wednesday at noon at 277 West End Avenue (tel. 362-1070).

You can spend an enlightening weekend in the country, courtesy of the **Yoga Society of New York,** which runs Ananda Ashram in Monroe, New York (an hour's bus ride from the city). Ananda is a beautiful, 60-acre country estate with its own lake, sauna and massage facilities, vegetarian food, and a wide-ranging program involving yoga and other self-awareness disciplines. Costs are moderate. Phone 914/783-1084 for details. The same group offers classes in Hatha Yoga and Indian dance at its city headquarters, 152 West 42nd Street, Suite 510 (tel. 840-7417). Contribution is $2.50.

Swami Rama, of the Himalyan Foundation, known for his work with the Menninger Clinic on changing physiological states, has a new center in New York: it is **East West Books** at 78 Fifth Avenue (14th Street). Besides an extensive collection of books on spiritual subjects, it offers frequent classes in hatha yoga, and often presents holistic health and other new age seminars (tel. 243-5994).

KABBALAH AND ARICA: If you'd like to study the secrets of the Kabbalah, Rabbi Joseph Gelberman is the man to see. He gives frequent weekend seminars on Kabbalah, and his home base is The New Light Temple. For information, phone 866-3795.

The **New York Arica Center** is a teaching center for Arica Institute's training programs and short courses which offer scientific methods for the development of an individual's fullest capacities. Free open house introductions, presenting samplings of current Arica programs, are held every Tuesday and Thursday evening beginning at 7 at 24 West 57th Street. (tel. 489-7430).

BUDDHISM, TIBETAN AND ZEN: New York has a huge number of Buddhist meditators. The place to learn about Zen is the **New York Zendo,** a magnificent and authentic temple at 223 East 67th Street (tel. UN 1-3333), which admits the public once a week, on Thursday nights from 6:15 to 9 for *zazen*—zen sitting. Instruction is given to newcomers, but be sure to get there before 7, since there is often a crowd, and once the doors are closed they will not be opened again. A small contribution is requested. If it's the Zen spirit and aesthetic that moves you, then do find out if you can see any of the special programs given by the **Buddhist Academy,** 332 Riverside, at 105th Street (tel. RI 9-8719). Affiliated with the Buddhist Church, this intriguing group gives classes in judo, kendo (Japanese fencing), and the art of archery. It also has special programs open to the general public: in November, there is a Bazaar in which demonstrations of ikebana (flower-arranging), the Japanese tea ceremony, and the self-defense arts are given and authentic Japanese food is served; in June, there is the annual recital of Japanese classical dances; and in July, the most exciting event of the year, the Bon Dances. These ancient and beautiful Japanese religious dances celebrate the arrival in paradise of one's ancestors. They are held on the Riverside Dancing Mall at 105th Street, and are performed by hundreds of men, women, and tiny children in colorful kimonos. Should you care to attend the Buddhist Church, services get underway every Sunday morning at 11. Check the local papers or phone for information.

A leading center for Tibetan Buddhism in New York is **Dharmadhatu Meditation Center,** 49 East 21st Street (tel. 673-7340). Programs open to the public begin at 7 p.m. on Tuesday and Thursday and include meditation followed by a tape by Chongyam Trungpa, Rinpoche, a high-ranking lama who is the group's teacher. The public can also come to all-day meditation on Sundays.

MISCELLANY: The East/West Center for Holistic Health, 275 Madison Avenue, offers some of the most exciting programs in town, with a series of low-cost lectures, films, and workshops exploring the integration of body, mind, and spirit. Speakers of the caliber of Dr. Elizabeth Kubler-Ross are presented (tel. 689-1321). . . . Local headquarters for the popular **Movement of Spiritual Inner Awareness (MSIA)** are at 365 Canal Street (tel. 925-6136). Monday night meetings present recorded video tapes by MSIA founder John-Roger. . . . To explore the ancient Huna wisdom secrets of the Hawaiians, get in touch with dynamic, island-bred Tanao Sands Kumalae of the **Self Center Foundation**, 3 East 65th Street, for news of open house meetings and seminars on self-development (tel. 744-2150). . . . The **Silva Mind Control Center**, 6 East 39th Street, promises to teach you how to get in and out of Alpha states and beyond, in a four-day intensive training course that graduates swear by (tel. 684-6477). Free introductory lectures every Wednesday at 8. . . . Lectures and classes on a wide variety of New Age topics are given at **Lindisfarne**, 49 West 20th Street (tel. 929-2722), where you might hear William Irwin Thompson speak on "Mythology, Sexuality, and Human Evolution," or Jerze Grotowski, founder of the Polish Lab Theatre, discuss his methodology.

THE STARS ARE FAVORABLE: Hung up on astrology? So, it seems, are half the people in New York. The **New York Astrology Center**, 127 Madison Avenue at 31st Street, runs frequent lectures and classes and also has one of the largest collection of astrology books in the world, as well as books on Eastern medicine, palmistry and yoga. Phone 679-5676 for news of current happenings. Uptown, **Mason's Bookshop**, 789 Lexington Avenue (61st-62nd Street), run by Zoltan Mason, astrologer and teacher, is small, but has everything one could possibly want in the occult sciences.

Note: For news of weekly events in astrology, yoga, and other spiritual matters, check listings and ads in *The Village Voice* or in *The New Sun* (available in health food stores), which runs an extensive New York calendar; and watch the notices at **Weiser's Book Store**, 740 Broadway (at Waverly Place), which has probably the most extensive collection of occult books in the country; you could easily spend several incarnations here, reading everything from *The Egyptian Book of The Dead* to *Transcendental Magic.* An utterly absorbing place, even if just to look and browse. Uptown, two of the best places for books of this sort are the **Gotham Book Mart** at 41 West 47th Street (better known, perhaps for its superb collection of in and out-of-print books in belles-lettres).

Chapter VIII

NEW YORK AFTER DARK

ALTHOUGH THEY KEEP saying that New York nightlife ain't what it used to be back in the days of the posh supper clubs and the big-name entertainers, the town is still very much alive after dark; the New York night scene is enjoying a renaissance. Venerable landmarks like the original El Morocco, the Persian Room, and the Latin Quarter may have passed from the scene, along with many a lesser luminary, but there are new versions of the Stork Club and the Copa on hand, and a raft of new watering spots that keep the town swinging until late, late and then some. Most of the old stereotype nightclubs, the kind you used to see in B movies, are gone. For a long time now the trend has been toward smaller places sans formalities, programmed entertainment, snooty maître d's at the velvet ropes, and dressing to the nines. The trend is also away from the "name" entertainers —country music is big, so is jazz and folk, and cabaret and comedy are on the rise again. Discos are very big at the moment, but they come and go, and today's darling is tomorrow's memory.

In general, you should know that, barring Miami Beach, New York is the "latest" town in the country. Bars and lounges are permitted to stay open and serve liquor until 4 a.m. every night except Saturday, when the early-morning curfew is 3 a.m. Informality is the mode of dress—come-as-you-will—allowed everywhere, except in the top rooms where coats and ties are *de rigueur* for the men. Nowadays, with Women's Lib in the ascendant, ladies solo or in tandem can count on being welcomed everywhere. Even McSorley's Ale House, 15 East Seventh Street, that erstwhile century-old sanctuary for males, was "liberated" a few summers ago. (Caution: Any distaffers inclined toward a visit to this East Village outpost should be advised that separate plumbing facilities have not been installed for the ladies.) Drinks average $2 or more in the fancier places, somewhat less elsewhere. Even in the neighborhood pubs, the days of the 25¢ glass of beer are no more: plan to spend 75¢ and up.

How much will it all cost? Here, the latitude is enormous, and the choice is yours. You could easily spend $70 or more (for a couple, including tips) as you dine, dance, and watch the big names in entertainment. Or you can go pub crawling with the natives and spend about $12 for two. *Tips:* Many places have lower-priced or no covers or minimums during the week; weekend prices soar everywhere. Also, a drink or two at the bar can often be your price of admission to some of the best entertainment in town. Note that we have given charges only where they are fixed; otherwise, a phone call will keep you abreast of the current prices. Most covers and admissions will vary with the performer, the time of year, and the state of business. Except in the neighborhood pubs and the singles bars, reservations are imperative: for the major clubs, it might be wise to phone a day in advance.

The Major Nightclubs

The days of the high-stepping chorus lines are back at, of all places, the **Rainbow Grill**, on the 65th floor of the RCA Building at 30 Rockefeller Plaza. This is the entertainment arm of its older sister, the Rainbow Room (which specializes in dining and dancing; see Restaurants, Chapter IV), and its views of the city are just as spectacular. Indoors, the view is of leggy chorines in a smartly paced revue, and of all manner of spectacle, aided and abetted by a smoke machine, electronic fireworks, and a dazzling lighting system. Two shows nightly at 9:15 and 11:30 (no show Sunday), with disco dancing in between, and after the last show. There's a $7 cover charge during the week, $8 on weekends. A la carte entrees range from $9.95 to $13.95. Reservation: PL 7-8970. Note to the budget-minded: the views of the city are all yours for the price of a drink in the South Lounge, which opens at 5 p.m. Reservations: PL 7-8970.

The romantic traditions of Spain and Latin America are wrapped up in one *muy simpatico* package at the venerable **Chateau Madrid**, in the Hotel Lexington, Lexington Avenue and 48th Street. The main salon, the Alameda Room, usually concentrates on full-scale revues, offers dining from an extensive menu of American, Spanish, and Latin American dishes, and two bands for dancing. And the clientele is serious about their dancing; you'll see them executing some of the snappiest cha-

cha-chas, rhumbas, and mambos being done anywhere. (Cover charge, $2; minimum, Tuesday through Thursday, $10; Friday, Saturday, and Sunday, $11 per show. A la carte entrees, $7.25 and up.) The intimate **Flamenco Room** offers a continuous mini-revue starting at 9:30 nightly with flamenco dancers, singers, and guitarists. (Two-drink minimum daily, three on weekends.) There is also a neat, dimly lit cocktail lounge, open daily from 5, called El Conquistador. And matinee dancing only, every Sunday from 4 to 8 p.m. (A $6 entrance fee entitles you to two drinks.) Closed Monday. Reservations: 752-8080.

Reno Sweeney, 126 West 13th Street. An elegant hotel club could be anywhere in the world, but Reno Sweeney's, one of the best cabarets in town, could only be in New York. It's a very contemporary '70s interpretation of what New York nightlife felt like back in the '30s when it was riding high. It's campy, hip, and attracts everyone from Andy Warhol superstars to Madison Avenue vested types to the kids in Levis. You might catch anyone from Blossom Dearie to a talented young folk-singer like Mirabai to somebody you didn't even know could sing—like Geraldine Fitzgerald. There are two shows each night, at 9 and 11:30, with a dinner seating one hour in advance of each show. The covers ($5 to $6) and minimums vary with each performer: call the club for specific information (tel. 681-0900).

For an elegant time trip back to the '30s and '40s, head for the **Stork Club**, a new version of the august night spot, recently opened at 112 Central Park South. Plush decor and surroundings, a celebrity crowd and very good French and American cuisine (à la carte from $9.50 to $15.50) set the scene for the cheek-to-cheek dancing to the gentle strains of bands like Peter Duchin or Irving Field. The most danceable Sunday brunch in town is held from 1 to 4. Minimum is $7.50. Reservations advised for weekends: 581-7080.

COMEDIANS AND CABARETS: The stand-up nightclub comic, long considered a casualty of television and changing time, is back again in New York. One of the best places to find him is at **Dangerfield's**, 1118 First Avenue, near 61st Street. As the name might imply, Dangerfield's signifies Rodney, the comic who "don't get no respect." Seating is on low divans to simulate living-room atmosphere. The very funny boniface actually does show—usually twice nightly—to do his persecution numbers. His paranoiac agonizing is preceded by a song recital from rotating young hopefuls. The $7 minimum can be worked off with simple supper-type items like barbecued spare ribs and prime sirloin steak, as well as by booze. There's also a $5 cover charge Mondays through Saturdays (tel. 593-1650).

The **Monkey Bar** in the Elysee Hotel, 60 East 54th Street, is well into its fourth decade now. Heretofore it has always been considered quite naughty but in the light of the new permissiveness, that reputation may have paled somewhat. But more or less continuous hilarity is still the order of the night from 9:30 on, with three acts incessantly bouncing off one another. Sunday to Thursday minimum, $6; Friday to Saturday, $7.50 (tel. PL 3-1066).

Undiscovered comics—and other entertainers—are always on hand, waiting to be discovered at two very popular clubs: Bud Friedman's **Improvisation**, 358 West 44th Street (tel. 765-8268), and **Catch a Rising Star**, 1487 First Avenue, near 77th Street (tel. 794-1906). Both give the performers a chance to hone their acts before a live audience, which will usually include talent scouts, agents, and others who can help a young talent along. Join the crowd, and you may get to hear them even before Johnny Carson does. At the Improv, shows get underway at 9:30 Sundays through Thursdays, when there's a $2 cover and a $4 liquor minimum. Fridays and Saturdays, showtime is 8:30 and 12, and the tabs go up to $3 and $5. At Catch A Rising Star, shows begin at 9:30 and go on more or less continuously until 2:30 or 3 a.m. Sundays through Thursdays, when there's a $2 cover plus a two-drink minimum; all drinks are $2.50. Unscreened auditions take place Mondays. On Fridays and Saturdays, it's 9:30 and 1 for the show, plus $3 cover and the two-drink minimum. Food is optional and extra at both.

Besides being one of the coziest restaurants in town, with its Art Deco touches, antique furniture and good food at moderate prices, **Once Upon A Stove**, Third Avenue at 24th Street (tel. 683-0044) also has the picture-pretty Valentine Room upstairs, where the song's the thing. Every Friday and Saturday, the singing waiters and waitresses do their show at 9 and 11, and there's a trio for dancing as well. Cover is $4, two-drink minimum. Tuesdays, Wednesdays, and Thursdays, song stylists perform. Depending on the act, it's a $3, $4, or $5 cover plus the two-drink minimum.

Everybody agrees that one of the nicest small cabarets in town is **The Ballroom**, 458 West Broadway, down in SoHo. The Ballroom has that rather remarkable combination of good food (see

Restaurants, Chapter IV) and good entertainment, all in a low-keyed, SoHoian atmosphere. The Ballroom is known both for launching bright new performers and for presenting leading American songwriters doing their own numbers (like Sheldon Harnick or Weber and Rice of *Jesus Christ, Superstar*). Show-time is 8:30 and 10:30 every day. Tuesdays through Thursdays there's a $4 cover, plus a $4 minimum; Fridays and Saturdays, it's a $6 cover, $5 minimum; and Sundays and Mondays, Show-case nights, it's $3 cover and $4 minimum. Reservations: 473-9367 or 673-9121.

Look for cabaret theater of a high level at the **Public Theatre Cabaret** (part of the New York Shakespeare Festival Public Theatre at 425 Lafayette Street; tel. 677-6350; $8 or $9 admission), and at the Cabaret Room of the **Manhattan Theatre Club**, 321 East 73rd Street (tel. 472-0600), where admission is usually $3 or $4 plus a two-drink minimum.

SPECIAL EFFECTS: If atmosphere's the thing, the loveliest room in New York is **La Chansonnette**, 890 Second Avenue, near 47th Street. It's a blue gem fashioned in Paris, small, smart, and soignée. Its chatelaine is the hyper-vitaminized Rita Dimitri, who perches on the flower-garlanded baby grand à la Helen Morgan to belt out her joyous, round-the-world arias. Her ac-complice at the piano—and foil in some sexy badinage—is hubby Stanley Brillant, himself an urban folk-balladeer-guitarist man of parts. Excellent French kitchen. Weeknight minimums of $5; $6 on weekends; plus a $2.50 cover charge during the week; $3 on weekends (tel. PL 2-7320). . . . One of New York's most charm-ing old brownstones, the home of actor John Drew way back when, is the setting for the **37th Street Hideaway**, 32 West 37th Street. Examine the antiques while you dine, dance on the small parquet floor, or just listen to music and watch the show. No cover or minimum (tel. 947-8940). . . . It's hard to imagine a more deliciously *dolce-vita* club than **Roma Di Notte**, 137 East 55th Street, where you can dine in a private cave, dance on the marble floor to the soft strains of the togaed musicians. The food is good and there is no cover or minimum. Music from 7:30 p.m. to 1:30 a.m., except Sundays (tel. 832-1128). . . . **Mitchell's Place** at the top of the Beekman Tower, 49th Street and First Avenue (tel. 689-5227), has breathtaking views along with songs and music and "Deli-in-the-Sky." No cover, no minimum. . . . The most romantic spot in town for drinks and music? That could well be the City Lights Bar and the adjoining Hors d'Oeuvrerie restaurant at **Windows on the World,** atop the World Trade Center. There's continuous music from 4:30 until very late every day, either for dancing or listening (Tea Dancing on Sundays from 4 on), marvelous international hors d'oeuvres for nibbling and a billion city lights for backdrop.

THAT MIDDLE EAST MADNESS: Much simpler than a trip to the Middle East is a short hop across town to that area on Eighth Avenue between 27th and 30th Streets known to aficionados of Greek dancing and tummy twirling as the Belly Belt. There are perhaps half a dozen niteries of Greek-Arabian-Egyptian cast here, where the local Middle-East population, plus any outsider who's discovered the area, go to hear the music, drink the ouzo, and, of course, watch the girls go through their gravity-defying gyrations. Some of the girls come from Turkey and Egypt, some straight out of Brooklyn (the Middle Eastern section of Brooklyn, that is). At any rate, they're all good, and the show is worth the seeing. Among the best clubs: **Egyptian Gardens, Britania,** and **Ali Baba.** (There's also an Ali Baba East at 400 East 59th Street.) Since they are all virtually next door to one another, cruise the area and choose the one that seems most inviting. On weekdays, there is usually no minimum; the average $4 to $5 minimum on weekend nights can be easily worked off by a couple of drinks (the liquor is better than the food at most of these places). And since Middle Easterners, remember, are night people, go late: after 11 p.m.

The craze for Mediterranean nightlife has lately been spreading to some other areas of our town. Grandest of the offerings is a lush Egyptian caravanserai, **Club Ibis,** 151 East 50th Street, where tented banquettes, golden palms, and murals of the pyramids set the scene for sword dancers, whirling dervishes, and Las Vegas dancers in a spectuacular show. Shows at 9:45 and 12:30 nightly (on Saturdays at 8:45, 11:30, and 1:30), with either a complete dinner (no cover) at $18.50 or à la carte, $7.50 cover. Reservations: 753-3884. . . . Greenwich Village fairly bursts with the Middle Eastern mood. One of the best of the clubs down here is **El Avram,** 80 Grove Street, where Avram himself sings, belly dancers gyrate, and an Israeli-Mediterranean show provides pleasant accompaniment to the Kosher Israeli-Mediterranean food. There's a $5 minimum Tuesdays to Sundays, and a cover charge ($3) only on Saturday nights. Closed Mondays and Fridays (tel. 243-9661 or 243-0602).

INTERNATIONAL POTPOURRI: No need to fly down to Rio, now that **Cachaca,** a stunning new south-of-the-border supper club has opened at 403 East 62nd Street. The throbbing jazz sambas of Brazil are only part of the excitement here. Show times are 11 and 1, with a minimum of $12 and a music charge of $5. Reservations: tel. 688-8501. . . . Palm trees and hula maidens bound at **Hawaii Kai** (tel. PL 7-0900), Broadway and 50th Street, where the whole family can have an evening of good, schmaltzy fun, South seas style: leis, hula dancers, audience participation. No minimum or cover, but a $1.50 music charge. The first show starts at 8 during the week, at 9 on weekends. Complete dinners are $7.50 to $11.95, also à la carte. There's music for dancing, too. . . . Friday and Saturday evenings are the time for an evening in Indonesia, courtesy of **Ramayana,** an authentic Indonesian restaurant club at 123 West 52nd Street (tel. 581-1170), sponsored by the Indonesian government. Dancers from Bali and Sumatra perform at 8:30 and 10:30, and afterwards, there's dancing—American style. Order à la carte or have the rijstaffel dinner at $15. Cover charge is $2.50.

THE DISCO CRAZE: Saturday Night Fever has gripped New York. Every week, or so it seems, a new disco opens, or a venerable old institution (like the famed Roseland Ballroom) adds a disco. Boogie is the name of the game everywhere in the Big Apple from **Studio 54's** playpen for celebrities over on West 54th Street to literally hundreds of clubs all over the city and suburbs whose patrons share a passion for ear-shattering noise, mind-boggling light shows, and sardine-tin crowds. You should know that nobody who is anybody arrives until very late (from 11 p.m. on), that discos do not admit all comers (it all depends upon the whim of the management) and that the door fee can be very high (up to $20 per person); those who have memberships ($150 to $250) have a slightly better chance of getting in and save a few dollars at the door. While disco clubs come and go with alarming rapidity and many are too special (for gays, blacks), faddy, or ephemeral to bear listing here (best check the local papers and magazines when you arrive), the following, in all likelihood, will still be doing business. Reservations are recommended everywhere.

Celebrities line up at the velvet ropes outside **Studio 54,** 254 West 54th Street (tel. 489-7677) and beg (yes, beg) owner Steve Rubell to let them in. Some less famous folk also make it in to this hottest of all the discos, ablaze with neon sun, fake flames, and dazzling lightpoles, but don't count on it; your chances of being allowed in go up with the bizarreness of your costume (a couple sprayed head to toe in silver recently turned up on the dance floor and in the papers). Admission for nonmembers is $9 and $10. . . . Then there's **Xenon,** a close competitor of Studio 54, at 125 West 43rd Street (tel. 221-2690), where those who get inside the door can watch the $90,000 descending spaceship ("The Mothership") as they dance to a $100,000 sound system. Again, outrageous costumes are the order of the night. $12 admission. . . . It might be a bit easier to gain access to **New York, New York,** 33 West 52nd Street (tel. 245-2400), a living theater with its laser lights and smoke machine that periodically engulfs the dancers waist-high in fog. $8 and $10 admission for nonmembers. . . . **2001 Odyssey,** another far-out adventure, manifests at the Statler Hilton Hotel's Penn Top Ballroom (Seventh Avenue at 33rd Street, tel. PE 6-5000) on Friday and Saturday nights only, $8 admission. . . . **Sybil's,** a sophisticated disco spot at the New York Hilton, 101 West 53rd Street (tel. 977-9898) also offers classy dining along with the disco beat. $5 and $8 admission.

Remember the **Copacabana,** New York's legendary glamor nightclub of the '40s? It's reopened at the same old stand, 10 East 60th Street (tel. 755-6010), and now it's the downstairs disco, Friday and Saturday night from 10 p.m. to 4 a.m., that brings the crowds, rather than the Copa girls of old. Upstairs, cabaret shows every night. Your $10 minimum includes two drinks. Over 21, jackets required. . . . **Shepheard's** that Egyptian enclave at **Loews Drake Hotel,** Park Avenue and 57th Street, still glitters, but it is really only a demi-disco now. Besides recorded music for dancing, there are shows spotlighting newish pop groups at 9, 11:30, and 1:15. The decor is a show unto itself with its black and gold reclining sphinxes by each tented booth, the gold leaves covering the center of the ceiling, the pretty people. There's a French-American menu, a music charge of $6 weekdays, $8 weekends and a $25 dinner—cum music package. The scene can be surveyed handily from the high-traffic bar. . . . Unless you're a member in good standing of the Beautiful People, you won't know a soul at **Régine's,** 502 Park Avenue at 59th Street, (tel. 826-0990). This international night spot with mirrors reflecting the subdued lighting is very dressy, very "in," and the food is outrageously overpriced for what it is. $10 is the cover charge. Reservations. . . . Also very dressy, and very "in," is **Hippopotamus**, 405 East 62nd Street (tel. 486-1566), with an English clubby atmosphere, very good food, backgammon, and disco music until 4 a.m. $12 minimum. Jackets required for the men. . . . Disco à la française? Allez vite au **Cocu Discotheque Francaise**, 152 East 55th Street (tel. 371-1559). This French place has a stainless steel dance floor, disco from 10 p.m. to 4 a.m. Wednesday through Saturday, and sandwiches available. On weekends, there's a $6, two-drink minimum. . . . The closest thing you'll get to dancing in the streets is an evening at **Wednesday's**, 210 East 86th Street (tel. 535-8500), an underground street festival. This subterranean spot recreates the ambience of a lively European thoroughfare: sidewalk cafes, wine and cheese shops, bistros, gas lights, and even trees! A disc jockey presides over the stereo set, the atmosphere is casual, and the menu features everything from steak to hamburgers. Cover charge is $3.50 on Fridays, $4 on Saturdays, $1 Sundays, $2 Wednesdays. Free entrance Tuesdays. Closed Mondays. . . . Even **Roseland**, 239 West 52nd Street (tel. 247-0200) that mecca for ballroom dancers (see below), has gotten into the disco act, with midnight disco Wednesdays, Saturdays, and Sundays, $5 admission.

MORE DANCING—AND JUST LISTENING: Trude Heller's, down in the Village at the corner of Avenue of the Americas and Ninth Street (tel. 254-8346), was never really a discotheque at all. The music was always live—and still is. Trude's arrived on the heels of the famed Peppermint Lounge and through the years has evolved into something of an institution. It's a major tourist magnet—and everybody in the world has been there at least once. There's a $3 cover plus a two-drink minimum, depending on the act. Suggestion for keeping the tab down: take your stand around the bar. You can see all, join the dance-floor activities, and get by for the price of a couple of drinks. Showtime is 10:30 and 12:30 nightly.

Sidling up to a piano bar may be your thing. If so, seek out **Jilly's**, 256 West 52nd Street, Sinatra's wee-hours hang-out when he's in town. It has an excellent combo and saloon singers going from 9:30 to legal closing time; no minimum, no cover.

Member of the Bobby Short Fan Club—and they include some of the fanciest people of three continents—can swoon nightly over several sets of their man's music at the **Cafe Carlyle**, in the Hotel Carlyle, 76th and Madison. There's dinner and drinks plus a $10 cover after 9:30. At the **Bemelmans Bar** of the same hotel you can often catch jazz stylists like Marion McPartland. $3 cover at tables. Closed Sunday and Monday (tel. 744-1600). . . . George Feyer, a singing pianist-parodist who is something of a cult himself, can be found in the **Rembrandt Room** of the Stanhope Hotel, 81st Street and Fifth Avenue. Dinner, plus a $3 cover. No music Sunday and Monday (tel. BU 8-5800). . . . Opera buffs are hereby directed to the Village, to that hearty perennial, **Asti's**, 13 East 12th Street, or to the slightly less hoary **Bianchi and Margherita**, 186 West 4th Street. In both places, dinner runs from $10 to around $14, and nearly everyone—waiters, bartenders, bus boys, even the customers—usually feels an aria coming on.

Two New York landmarks are offering their share of music to listen to. **The Front Row**, the 15th floor cocktail lounge at No. 1 Times Square (formerly the Times Building) offers a splendid view of nighttime New York, the sophisticated song stylings of singer-pianist Martin St. Lawrence and reasonably priced drinks with no cover or minimum. From about 7 on, Tuesdays through Saturdays. Dancing, too. . . . People still meet **Under The Clock** at the Biltmore Hotel, the latter being the name of the famed bar of F. Scott Fitzgerald days. It's still there, and a pianist singer performs Mondays through Fridays from 7 on.

For those hankering after a nice old-fashioned ballroom fling, there's half-century-old **Roseland**, 239 West 52nd Street, with a dance floor approximately the size of the Gobi Desert. Two live bands alternate Wednesdays and Fridays from 5:30; Thursdays, Saturdays, and Sundays from 2:30; and there's midnight disco Wednesdays, Saturdays, and Sundays. Matinee admission is $4, evenings $5.

THE JAZZ REVIVAL: Jazz went through some lean years in New York, but now it's back, bigger and better than ever. So big has the jazz revival become, in fact, that a Jazzline (tel. 421-3592 to find out who is playing where) has been established and is flourishing mightily. On the club scene, much of the action is downtown. The **Village Vanguard**, 178 Seventh Avenue, at 11th Street (tel. 989-9011), has been around almost forever with some of the best jazz there is. Both the giants (like Sonny Rollins and Bill Evans) and newcomers are showcased nightly except Sunday, starting at 10 p.m. Every Monday, Thad Jones leads an 18-piece jazz orchestra. . . . **The Top of the Village Gate,** prestigious jazz address at Bleecker and Thompson (tel. 982-9292), serves natural foods, seafood, and chicken by Hisae, along with the cool sounds. Open nightly. The Village Gate, downstairs, presents cabaret on the order of "The Incredible World of Magic and Illusion," nightly except Mondays. . . . **Hopper's** a good restaurant-cafe at Sixth Avenue at 11th Street, is a stylish new Jazz address in the Village, with performers of the rank of George Shearing and Milt Jackson on tap. All is quiet on Sundays. . . . The crowds don't mind going way west to Tenth Avenue and 17th Street to **West Boondock** at #14 (tel. 924-9723), where the relaxed, sawdust atmosphere and moderate prices for the boss soul food (among the best in New York) compete with the good and easy, top jazz. . . . **Sweet Basil,** at 88 Seventh Avenue South, at Bleecker Street, is one of the newest Village jazz clubs, strong on talent. . . . At University Place, on the other side of Fifth Avenue, are two jazz-restaurants worth a listening: **The Cookery,** University Place at 8th Street, goes in for fancy jazz piano stylings; piano plus bass is the usual combo at **Bradley's,** University Place at 11th Street. Both are also known for commendable, medium-priced kitchens. . . . SoHo's neatest jazz spot is **W.P.A.,** 152 Spring Street (tel. 226-3444), with decor right out of the '30s, sounds from the contemporary '70s. Closed Mondays.

Jimmy Ryan's, 154 West 54th Street (tel. 664-9700), has long been the city's midtown headquarters for New Orleans jazz. Seven nights, no cover, no minimum. . . . A similar reputation for the best of Dixieland belongs to **Eddie Condon's,** 144 West 54th Street (tel. 265-8277), which also serves steaks, ribs, and burgers all the way until 3 a.m. . . . You can mix with the Columbia University kids and other enthusiastic jazz buffs at the **West End Cafe,** Broadway at 113th Street (tel. 666-8750), a very informal place for a mini jazz festival with legendary names from the swing era. . . . Over on the East Side, a chic crowd hangs out at **Sibi,** the upstairs jazz room of Club Ibis, 151 East 50th Street (tel. 753-3429). Performers like Bobby Cole bring in their fans, while downstairs, it's a Las Vegas-type revue. . . . Storyville, a famous jazz name of old, has metamorphosed into **Storytowne,** 41 East 58th Street, and presents top jazz names, with occasional cabaret shows. . . . There's always plenty of action at **Gregory's,** First Avenue at 63rd Street (tel. 371-2220), where a bevy of jazz masters hold forth. . . . **Red Blazer Too,** 1576 Third Avenue (88th to 89th Streets; tel. 876-0440) is making news by offering a different jazz band every night, good food, no cover, $3.50 drink minimum weeknights, $5 weekends. . . . **Michael's Pub,** 211 East 55th Street (758-2272), an English pubby type of place that everybody seems to like, has an eclectic entertainment policy—everyone from Mort Sahl to balladeers. They're big on jazz, too, with Woody Allen's New Orleans Funeral & Ragtime Band checking in whenever the comedian is in town.

Most jazz clubs charge minimums of $3 to $6 and/or a one-or two-drink minimum, but it all depends on the performer. And with the jazz renaissance in full swing, new clubs are opening all the time. Check the listings in the magazines, also in the *Village Voice* or call Jazzline to see just what's happening while you're here.

FOLK AND ROCK: Out of the folk and acid rock of the late '60s seems to have come a new melding of musical styles and appreciation, and New York's musical showcases reflect this trend. There are few all-rock or all-folk stages or even artists left. And folk and rock are no longer the province of the Village alone. They have made their way uptown to larger quarters and have even taken over the prestigious halls of high culture.

One of the most popular of these, **Carnegie Hall,** has hosted stars as popular and diverse as Jerry Jeff Walker, Fairport Convention, and the Nitty Gritty Dirt Band. And **Avery Fisher Hall,** which usually hosts the New York Philharmonic, has seen the like of the Electric Light Orchestra, Dory Previn, and Weather Report. Labelle has played the **Metropolitan Opera House. Madison Square Garden** and its neighboring **Felt Forum** are popular concert halls and once provided a stage for Sly Stone's well-publicized wedding. Check, too, the movie theaters to see who's playing when you arrive. Already **Radio City Music Hall** has played host to Todd Rundgren, the Jefferson Starship, and David Bowie, and the **Apollo** to Ike and Tina Turner. Others are and will be following their leads. Legitimate theaters, too, are getting into the act. When Bette Midler played the **Palace** a few years back, she sold out for almost three straight weeks. The **Minskoff** is now becoming more of a music hall than a Broadway theater.

In the summertime, Central Park resounds with the **Schaefer Summer Festival** in the Wollman Skating Rink and year-round the Palladium Theatre at 14th Street and Third Avenue is a pacesetter of folk and rock entertainment, with everyone from

Renaissance to John Sebastian to the New Riders of the Purple Sage making the scene.

Although it's considered the preeminent rock club in the city —some say in the country—the huge, always-packed **Bottom Line,** 15 West 4th Street (tel. 228-7880), does not limit its acts strictly to rock—you might catch folk singers, jazz artists (of the stature of Don Shirley), even classical performers. Blues singer and jazz pianist Mose Allison is one of the frequent performers here. The crowd is young, the food ordinary. Admission is usually $5 to $6, depending on the performer.

Back in the days when it was known as The Bitter End, **The Other End,** 149 Bleecker Street (tel. 673-7030), launched such. superstars as Peter, Paul, and Mary. Still going strong, this is a smaller room, where you might even catch the likes of Bob Dylan for $5 admission, $2.50 minimum. . . . You'll see lots of bright new faces at **Home,** 91st Street and Second Avenue, usually folk singers and small bands. They also have natural food in addition to steak and booze. **Max's Kansas City,** Park Avenue South at 17th Street (tel. 777-7870), may be showing folk performers of the stature of Oscar Brand, or underground rock disc jockeys like Wayne County, along with the rest of their mixed musical bag. Catch **Mr. William Shakespeare's Pub,** at the corner of MacDougal and Eighth Streets (tel. SP 7-2540), for aspiring new talent.

FREEBIES: During the warm weather, you can often hear some of the top club performers in the city doing their thing for free. It all takes place at the atrium patio of the **Citicorp Center,** at Lexington Avenue, between 53rd and 54th Streets. Bringing in snacks or not to munch on, you sit at tables and watch the show. Usually from 6 to 8; check the papers for details.

THE SOUNDS OF COUNTRY: Strange as it may seem to out-of-towners, the newest "in" thing in urbane, sophisticated New York at the current moment is country music. When Charlie Rich and Merle Haggard played the Felt Forum a few years back, the reception was overwhelming. Country music clubs have come and gone, but one that seems destined to remain forever is the very popular **O'Lunney's,** 915 Second Avenue, between 48th and 49th Streets (tel. 751-5470). It's a warm, woodsy, very Western place: on one wall is a mural of a country boy with a guitar walking to the city—a prophecy? You can dine on moderately priced, basic American fare while listening to all the greats. Monday is talent night, Sunday from 8 on is given over to bluegrass, and the rest of the week, from 9 on, it's sincere, soulful Country Western—the kind you'd expect to hear in Nashville rather than New York. There's a $3 food or drink minimum at the tables (none in the bar area), plus a $2 entertainment charge. Open every day except Christmas.

Another big country music mecca, home to leading touring country artists, is the **Lone Star Cafe**, Fifth Avenue at 13th Street (tel. 242-1664), where they serve Lone Star Beer, celebrate Texas Independence Day, and have a full Texas-American menu (try the chili and the Texas stuffed peppers!). Despite its plush trappings—a marble staircase, lots of mirrors, brass, and mahogany—and its size—it seats 300 people on two levels, has upstairs and downstairs bars and two bands—the Lone Star Cafe has an intimate, casual air. Up on the big stage, under the golden horseshoe, you might catch Billy Swan, Crystal Gale, or Grammy winner Larry Gatlin, plus other big names of country and western music. The music charge varies between $3 and $5, plus a two-drink minimum during the show.

PUB CRAWLING ALL AROUND TOWN: 'Tis pleasant in the cool of evening to drop into a warm and/or atmospheric public house and slake the thirst with a brew, a drop of the grape, or a belt of the grain. In New York no one need go thirsty. At most places, mixed drinks will average $1.50 to $2.

Almost all visitors to Fun City find themselves at a Broadway theater on at least one evening. Say you want just a nightcap afterward and would like to stay somewhere in the area. The most obvious suggestion is **Sardi's**, 235 West 44th Street. A contingent of authentic Broadway personalities can be depended upon to arrive around 11:30 and the supreme vantage point for checking all comings and goings is the bar, just inside the entrance. Fine for an after-theater supper, too (see Chapter IV, Restaurants). On Eighth Avenue near 44th Street is **Downey's**, often called "the poor man's Sardi's." But here, too, certifiable showfolk—usually the younger, on-the-way-up variety—put in an appearance. Or there's the **Blue Bar** in the Algonquin Hotel (on 44th, between Fifth and Sixth Avenues), which may be the petitest, chummiest lounge in Manhattan and where you'll surely be privy to every conversation. Here, too, celebrities, often itinerant actors or authors from Britain, materialize.

In full view of the Lincoln Center complex are the **Ginger Man,** 51 West 64th Street, a charming watering hole with period-piece fixtures; and its brother enterprise, **O'Neals' Baloon,** 48 West 63rd Street, easily recognizable by the theater lights on the canopy. Both have sidewalk cafes and are popular after-concert places.

Bookish types touring the Village will want to knock back an "arf 'n arf" at the **White Horse Tavern,** at the corner of Hudson and 11th Streets, where Dylan Thomas dwelt and drank himself to death, and where such American literary lights as Norman Mailer, Louis Auchincloss, and Calder Willingham used to be regulars in the backroom. . . . They should also have a look at **Mr. William Shakespeare's Pub,** at the corner of MacDougal and Eighth Streets. . . . The **Lion's Head** at 59 Christopher Street, just off Sheridan Square, attracts younger writers, newspaper men (columnist Pete Hamill's favorite pump), and folk singers (notably the Clancy Brothers). . . . Theater folk have found a new Greenwich Village home at cozy **Gottlieb's,** 343 Bleecker Street fine for drinks and dinner.

The Gramercy Park neighborhood has at least three attractive dispensaries: **Max's Kansas City,** 213 Park Avenue South, whose downstairs caters to artists, writers and friends, upstairs remains the launching pad for talented new performers; **Pete's Tavern,** the oldest original bar in New York City, at 18th Street and Irving Place, a 113-year-old shrine, habituated by O. Henry (who lived across the street) and commemorated by him in one of his stories; and **Molly Malone's Pub,** Third Avenue near 22nd Street, a white-plaster, shingle-roofed Irish pub which exudes all those endearing Irish charms and draws unto it congenial, youngish souls from the high-risers around the lovely park.

Fifteen blocks or so north on Third is **Kitty Hawk's,** near 37th Street, a mini-museum of aviation memorabilia appropriately situated close to the East Side Terminal. Patronage is about equally divided between airline personnel and young dwellers in the Murray Hill neighborhood. Another 18 blocks due north on Third, at 55th Street, you come to **Clarke's** (only the noncognoscenti persist in calling it—incorrectly—P. J. Clarke's). This is truly a landmark and one which began its life as a workingman's saloon—and still looks the part. Now *tout le monde* turns up there. (Jackie Onassis digs the hamburgers the most.) The time to go is late (well after midnight), in time to catch the celebrity flow that sweeps in many a famous face, looking a little worse perhaps for the wear. That old booze picture starring Ray Mil-

Eating and Meeting at the Singles' Bars

The singles' bars movement which hit New York in the mid-'60s is still going strong. It swings primarily along First Avenue—known to habitués as "The Strip"—all the way from 60th Street up through the 70s. There you'll find mingling, mixing, eyeing, spying, and just plain good ole fun. And even if you don't find the one of your dreams, you're sure to fill your stomach cause there's food aplenty and the price is right. **Friday's**, at 63rd Street, was perhaps the first of the bunch and is the grandaddy of several other night spots around town (**Tuesday's**, Third Avenue near 17th Street; **Wednesday's**, 210 East 86th Street; and **Thursday's**, 58th Street near Avenue of the Americas). It's got low lighting, a crowded bar, booths, semioutdoor seating, good drinks, and some of the solidest food around. The burgers—many varieties, each $2.95—are thick and done as you like. The spare ribs, $5.45, have a delicious sauce. Almost everything else (except the steak, $9.50) is under $6.50.

Across the street is **Adam's Apple**, near 61st Street, now in its seventh year. Much larger than Friday's, it has two dining rooms, a bar area and two suspended dance floors. It's been opulently revamped with lush, live foliage and tropical lighting. Food is à la carte, $2.75 to $9.75.

Mugg's, up near 63rd Street, has a menu similar to Friday's, with prices around $5 to $6. **Noah's Ark**, at 65th Street, offers slightly more diversified fare. **Mr. Laff's**, near 64th Street, has drinks, disco dancing, and music but no food.

Maxwell's Plum, at the 64th Street corner, is the finest and classiest of the lot and draws an older, well-heeled crowd. Glittery with Tiffany lamps and Art Deco frills, it has an enormous, diversified menu, with diversified prices—most of which are slightly higher than elsewhere on The Strip. Late night dinner dancing, too.

If you're willing to consider The Strip more a state of mind than of geography, **Thursday's**, 57 West 58th Street, is definitely part of the action. Here, too, the food is very good, and the prices reasonable, from $3.55 for the likes of hamburgers and omelets, on up to $11.50 for steak. The crowd reconvenes on Sunday morning for great big brunches, sometimes all-you-can-eat—usually champagne or Bloody Marys, omelets, eggs Benedict, and the like—for about $6.95.

land *(The Lost Weekend)* was filmed here, by the by. . . . Still another six blocks north on the same avenue (at 61st) is a century-old saloon which now goes under the name of **Daly's Dandelion.** You'll recognize it by the sidewalk cafe which sports columns from a Vermont country porch. It is owned by Skitch Henderson. . . . The **Autopub,** below the General Motors Building on Fifth Avenue and 59th Street, has done wonders with the motorcar motif. Try the Pit or the Drive-in Theatre with its loveseats and showings of old feature-length movies, or the Eldorado Room, where you can draw the curtains behind your table and have total privacy.

In the East 60s and 70s, the big action is the singles' bars (see box). Arrive at East 86th Street, and you're in the heart of Yorkville, where the German-Viennese flavor is still strong, despite the French restaurants, rock clubs, and other more recent forms of divertissement that have moved on to the street. Join the folks doing polkas, drinking beer, and listening to the oom-pah-pah bands at the **Lorelei,** 233 East 86th Street, if you like. . . . **Barney Google's,** 225 East 86th Street, has a grillwork that gives it a New Orleans look; inside you'll find a convivial bar, dancing, rock bands, an occasional star performer like Tiny Tim or Buddy Rich. **Elaine's** Second Avenue between 88th and 89th Streets, is indubitably the most "in" joint on the East Side, and the people at the next table could well be Leonard Bernstein, Truman Capote, George Plimpton, or one of that there crowd. The likes of us might enjoy walking next door to **Dresner's Other,** a neighborhood restaurant where the welcome is warm, and nobodies will not be seated in Siberia. In fact, its glassed-in sidewalk cafe is a fine vantage point for watching the somebodies on their way to Elaine's.

Many of the pubby-type hangouts serve mind-boggling (and inexpensive) Sunday brunches.

Chapter IX

SECRETS OF THE NEW YORK SHOPPING WORLD

WE KNOW quite a lot of people—and not all of them women —who come to New York for only one reason: to go shopping. Not for them the excitement of Broadway, the dazzle of the nightclubs, the adventures into the exotic world off the beaten path. For them, the greatest show in town begins right on Fifth Avenue. One woman we know flies in regularly from Detroit, checks into her hotel, grabs a cab, and heads immediately for Saks. "Then," she says, "I know I'm in New York."

What our friend senses, of course, is the fact that New York is one of the great fashion capitals of the world, a city where *Women's Wear Daily* sits on the best coffee tables, where the fashion business provides a living, a *raison d'être* or, at the very least, a subject of conversation for thousands of people. As a result of this high-keyed fashion consciousness, the New York woman, regardless of her income, is one of the best, most individually dressed women in the world. Close at hand she has the great department and specialty stores like B. Altman, Lord & Taylor, Saks Fifth Avenue, Bonwit Teller, Bergdorf Goodman, Bloomingdale's, Macy's, and Gimbels. She also has hundreds and hundreds of small boutiques and shops where she can buy anything from a Paris evening gown whose price tag runs into four figures to a Mickey Mouse T-shirt for $3. She can suit her flights of fancy with a pair of Italian boots, a silken sari from India, a peasant dress from Morocco, or a poncho from Mexico. She can rummage through old capes and costumes in the Village, or pick the cream of the Puccis at SFA. It's a wide-open, swinging scene, and one that any woman (or man, for that matter, since men's boutiques are proliferating almost as widely as women's) with an ounce of fashion curiosity will find absorbing.

To help you find your way through the maze-like shopping

world of New York, we're going to divide this section into three parts. First, we'll briefly skim the highlights of the New York department, specialty, and jewelry stores, but we won't stop to dwell on them, since any edition of the daily paper will tell you more than you need to know about all of them. Second, we'll give you an extensive rundown of the best bargains in town, in and out of the department stores, and swinging as far afield as those great bargain meccas of the Bronx, Brooklyn, and Manhattan's Lower East Side. Third, we'll take you on a tour in search of serendipity—to some of the charming, offbeat, one-of-a-kind shops that have helped make New York one of the great shopping bazaars on the planet. So, wallet packed, credit cards at the ready, let's begin.

The Department and Specialty Stores

If you've been following our sightseeing suggestions, you've probably already been to **Macy's**, 34th Street and Herald Square, which, as the world's largest department store, has it all, from elegant boutiques like The Little Shop to The Cellar, a street of gourmet shops in the basement. Selections in every department are vast and always of good quality. Across the street is **Gimbels**, another friendly giant (check its basement for occasional close-outs from its more elegant sister store, Saks Fifth Avenue), and both could keep you busy for weeks. Walk east along 34th Street now until you get to **Ohrbach's**, one of New York's great bargain stores (about which more later). At 34th and Fifth is prestigious **B. Altman & Co.**, an oldie with a young contemporary reputation, emphasizing top designers in women's, men's and children's fashion, unique gifts and china, Oriental objects, gourmet delicacies, rare books and autographs, and the refreshing Charleston Garden for breakfast, lunch, tea, and Thursday dinner. Proceed up to 38th Street and Fifth, and there's 150-year-old **Lord & Taylor**, with its shimmering new street floor, the swinging Young New Yorker shop, beautiful antique furniture, many lovely, lovely things for every member of the family. Its Bird Cage is a busy lunch- and tea-time aviary. The next big stop is at 50th Street and Fifth and that, of course, is **Saks Fifth Avenue**—a name long synonymous with fashion elegance. Here's where you can indulge yourself in a Revillon fur, revel in a whole shop of Louis Vuitton luggage and accessories, and shop the top French and American designers' collections in their own boutiques. Twice a year, in January and June, Saks runs store-wide clearances, and everyone in town shows up for the bargains. **Bonwit Teller** looms up at 56th and Fifth Avenue with a breathtaking new environment for such Bonwit specialties as Hermes, Boehm porcelains, an international roster of designer clothing, exclusive Turnbull & Asser menswear from England, plus a new Missoni Boutique, and an Orsini's Caffee for coffee and pastries, Italian style. **Bergdorf Goodman,** at 57th and Fifth, and **Henri Bendel,** just west of Fifth, present the ultimate in fine clothing and accessories. Both are filled with charming little boutiques and all sorts of nooks and corners for precious goodies.

Head east to Lexington Avenue and 59th Street now (and if you have children with you, you'll undoubtedly have to make a stop at the corner of Fifth and 58th at **F.A.O. Schwarz,** America's most famous toy store), to **Bloomingdale's.** Bloomies, as it is affectionately known to the chic sophisticates who practically make it a second home, has a series of nifty boutiques on the second and third floors, all dedicated to the young, plus a marvelous bakery/gourmet department on the first floor, plus scads of moderately priced merchandise on the basement level. Uptown, at 86th Street and Lexington Avenue (a short subway ride from Bloomingdale's), is the area's newest and northernmost department store, and that's **Gimbels East,** more sophisticated than its downtown sister, with good values in every category, and, again, a very good bakery/gourmet section.

Jewelry and Gifts

New York is the diamond center of the country, and if you're convinced that diamonds (or even pearls) are a girl's best friend, you should have a look at some of the town's outstanding jewelry shops. Start at the top with the splendor of **Tiffany's** (which surprises with inexpensive gift items in addition to the likes of emerald brooches and diamond necklaces) and **Cartier,** Fifth at 52nd Street, where you can find old Cartier designs of the '20s and '30s as well as today's classic jewelry, plus Paris-designed watches, jewelry, and small leather goods at "young prices" in the Les Must de Cartier boutique. A stroll along 47th Street, between Fifth and Sixth Avenues, where diamonds are being traded on street corners, polished in workrooms and sold in a number of small jewelry stores, puts you right in the heart of the jewelry world. To catch the village jewelry scene, walk on West Fourth Street between Sixth and Seventh Avenues; here and elsewhere in the Village you'll find any number of small shops selling avant-garde rings, pins, brooches, that are both beautiful and/or way out.

The Best of the Bargains

But we promised to let you in on some special secrets of the New York shopping world, on the essential information which will tell you where to pick up an $85 dress for $35, a mink coat for $1,000, or a great pair of pants for $12—or where to get designer's originals for one-third the price in the salons. So let's move on now to **Ohrbach's,** 5 West 34th Street, where the biggest selection of high-fashion, bargain-priced women's clothing is to be found. The only trouble is that those millions of other shoppers are pushing and shoving and poring over the counters in a mad scramble for the same dresses, handbags, gloves, sweaters, lingerie, etc., that you are. There is also a good men's department, and lovely, imported children's clothing at below-usual prices. *Tip:* Come early in the morning before the crowds get thick, and avoid the lunch hours, 12 to 2, like the plague.

On you go, to **Alexander's,** Lexington Avenue at 58th Street, where the values are good in every department, but especially outstanding in knitwear and sweaters. We once coveted, but did not buy, a $44 Paris-imported sweater set in an uptown boutique: the next week, there it was in Alexander's, priced at $24! Furs and cashmeres are other good buys here, and so are children's toys and games.

Besides offering substantial discounts on name-brand sportswear and streetwear with a young look, **The Emotional Outlet,** whose main store is at 91 Seventh Avenue, corner of 16th Street, happens to be one of the nicest, friendliest stores in town. Coffee and cookies or wine, or cream cheese and bagels (on Sunday), are offered as soon as you come in, and while it's nice to munch and watch the tube here, it's even more fun to get out and scout the racks. Unless you specifically ask for help, no salesperson will interfere with your bliss as you wander through racks and racks of suits ($75 to $200), shirts ($13 to $40), pants ($19 to $50), dresses ($25 to $150)—all marked at approximately 20% to 40% off what you saw them for in the specialty stores. Another 5% discount is given if you pay by cash. Once you get into the dressing room (with as many garments as you like), the salespeople really go to work for you, bringing in things that they think you'll want to try on. Anyone who's shopped the off-price stores and has had to dress and run and dress and run again knows that this is indeed rare. Besides clothes, there are French and Italian imported shoes, and handbags, too, at discounts of up to 40% Customers range from late teens to early fifties, since the store carries both Junior and Contemporary sizes. There are two more Emotional Outlets—at 435 East 86th Street (near Gracie Mansion, the mayor's residence), and at 250 East 51st Street, near Second Avenue. The 16th Street store, however, is our best recommendation for family shopping, since Barney's, that gigantic men's emporium (see below), is just across the street.

If French designer's clothing is what you covet, *allez vite* to **Azriel Altman,** Fifth Avenue near 25th Street (tel. 889-0782). Altman has taken over the premises of a former bank, and now its assets range from French embroidered jeans in what used to be the vault, to cachet names like Ted Lapidus, Pierre Balmain, Bernard Danae of Paris, and Cacharel scattered throughout. Prices are not inexpensive (most dresses run from $60 and up), but the finest suits, coats, raincoats, leather coats, precious silks, are all 25% to 30% less here than elsewhere. Imported shirts and sportswear for men, too. There's another A. Altman at 182 Orchard Street on the Lower East Side.

Shoppers' Bus

If you're planning on doing a lot of shopping in one day, a **Midtown Shopper's Bus Ticket** will come in handy. For $1, you can take as many rides as you like within the area between 32nd and 59th Streets and Third and Eighth Avenues. The ticket is good Monday through Friday between 9:30 and 4:30, Thursday evening from 6:30 to 10 p.m., and Saturday from 9:30 to 6:30. Buy your ticket—exact fare, please—on any bus within the area.

Designer's originals at undesigning prices—that's what you'll find at **Bolton's,** uptown at 1180 Madison (near 86th Street), also on the East Side at 225 East 57th Street, on the West Side at 53 West 23rd Street, Broadway near 81st Street, and in the Village at 45 East 8th Street. Clothes can get *très elegant* here and rather expensive: up to $200 and more for dresses and suits. But there are modestly priced racks, too, where dresses average $25 to $60. And you're paying about two-thirds of what they would cost elsewhere. Top manufacturers are represented here, and everything is in excellent taste.

Although there are some slight irregulars (and they are so marked), there's nothing damaged about the goods at **Damages,** 130 East 85th Street (tel. 628-6040); it's just that Mr. Martin Damages owns the store. It's a pipe-rack type place, and you can browse among high-quality women's sportswear at prices that look to be 40% to 50% lower than regular stores. Pants and jeans from Paris, with that special French cut, are among the big favorites in imported sportswear here.

Call **S. & W. Famous Designers Apparel** "off Seventh Avenue," if you will. It features name brands from the Seventh Avenue houses, at very low prices. Some of the items are "as is," so look carefully, but the values are extraordinary. Ogle the suedes and leathers, sports clothes, beautiful coats at 283 Seventh Avenue (26th Street). A friend of ours recently purchased no less than *two* all-wool winter coats here for $180! If you still have any money left, round the corner to 165 West 26th Street for the dresses, sportswear, ultra-suedes, suits, and evening clothes. Handbags, too. Closed Saturday, open Sunday through Friday (tel. 924-6656).

CANAL STREET: You'll get more than you bargained for at **The City Dump,** 323 Canal Street, which, despite its name, has no official connections. And there's nothing dumpy about the merchandise here—it's all brand-name goods which the owners have bought at auctions or closeouts or as overruns, and which they sell at less than dealer's cost. No telling what you'll find on any particular visit, but it more than pays to look. We've found $250 Gruen watches here for $59, $30 Pony sneakers for $7.95, an $80 Nordic cookware set for $30, a $12 name-brand perfume for $2.95, and scads of good buys in camping and sporting goods, hardware, pet supplies, kitchenware and china, toys, designer sheets and comforters, stationery supplies, party goods—to name just a few. It's open seven days a week, and weekends are a particularly good time to shop here and browse Canal Street; this is one of the city's biggest bargain, surplus, outlet marts, where you can pick up anything from steel shelving at **Tunnel Machinery** (no. 353) to diamond solitaires at **Manny Winick** (no. 167) to surplus military togs at **Canal Jean Company** (no. 304). Canal Street is just north of Chinatown and south of SoHo, so there are plenty of good places to eat within a few blocks. The IRT Broadway-Seventh Avenue or Lexington Avenue locals, the

A and AA trains on the IND, and the N train of the BMT all have stops on Canal Street.

THE LOWER EAST SIDE: You could spend a week shopping the Lower East Side and we could write a book just telling you about the bargains here, in these narrow, tenemented streets where New York's immigrant Jewish colony once flourished. Many of the shopkeepers live uptown or in the wealthy suburbs now, and so do most of the customers. But they still keep coming down here for marvelous bargains in just about everything, and now, with inflation rampant, business is brisker than ever. We'll simply point you in the direction of a few of our favorites and let you take it from there. Remember to bring plenty of cash, wear good walking shoes, be prepared for inconvenient or nonexistent fitting rooms, and a strict no-return policy. Try to come during the week, since most places are closed Saturday, and Sunday is total insanity. Take the F train (Queens line) on the IND subway or the Q, M, or J trains of the BMT to Delancey and Essex Streets, or the D train (Sixth Avenue line) on the IND subway to Grand Street; you should be there in about 20 minutes from midtown Manhattan.

Let's start with women's clothing: our favorite places are **Fishkin's**, at 314 Grand Street and also at 63 Orchard Street (which also carries shoes and handbags); **Sylvia's Best of New York**, 78 Orchard; **Forman's**, 82 Orchard; **M. Friedlich**, 196 Orchard, and **A. Altman**, 182 Orchard (see above). All have top-name designer and imported dresses, suits, tops, pants, coats, etc., at remarkable prices. Men can be well outfitted at **Haar & Knoebel**, 49 Orchard Street, and at **Charlie's Place**, 61 Orchard; they can pick up designer's shirts at, of all places, **Ezra Cohen**, 307 Grand Street, who is best known for buys in designer linens, towels, bedspreads, etc., as is **Harris Levy**, 278 Grand, which has been selling to New York's finest families for many a long year. (Harris Levy is also a direct importer of fine bed and table linens and features a complete bath shop). You'll be dazzled by the array of beautiful handbags at **Fine & Klein**, 119 Orchard Street, and there is another good supply at **Bargain Basement**, 143 Orchard. Pick up your couturier underwear at **Sidney's Undergarments**, 97 Orchard, and see the nice people at **D & A Merchandise Company**, 22 Orchard, for all kinds of lingerie and underwear for everybody in the family.

Buy the kids their new wardrobes at **Rice and Breskin**, 323

Almost Wholesale on Seventh Avenue

Gaining access to New York's famed wholesale houses, unless you have a connection, is not so easy. But we've discovered something that we like even better: shopping at the showrooms of the jobbers and exporters who are the middlemen of Seventh Avenue. Besides carrying a vast array of merchandise from many manufacturers, they welcome retail customers, provide fitting rooms (nonexistent in wholesale houses), courteous service (you are usually not allowed to browse), and exceptional merchandise at prices that may range from as little as 20% to as much as 50% or 60% of what you would have to pay retail. Usually, it's cash only, and no returns.

Start your Seventh Avenue expedition at **Abe J. Geller,** on the Fifth Floor of 491 Seventh Avenue (37th Street). You'll be dazzled by racks and racks of stunning clothes, all with the top designer's labels still in them! Expect to spend from $39.75 to $169.75 for most of the dresses, from $59.75 to $199.75 and up for coats and suits. Mr. Geller claims that prices are 40% to 60% lower than they are in the fancy stores. Open weekdays from 10 to 5:30; Saturdays, until 3:30 (tel. 736-8077).

You may have to wait a little while to be waited on at **Ms., Miss Or Mrs.,** on the eighth floor of 462 Seventh Avenue (35th Street), but we can assure you that it will be worth every minute. MMM represents close to 350 of the top-name manufacturers on Seventh Avenue, and their merchandise if first quality, available as soon as or even before the stores have it. The gamut runs from name brand sportswear to all-wool coats, fake furs and fur-lined coats, raincoats, and imported tweeds to an extensive selection of designer dresses in fabrics such as ultra-suede, silk, and crepe-de-chine—all in all, a vast and exciting collection, priced from $25 up to $500. Their markup is very low, your savings are phenomenal (40% to 50%—and more at the time of seasonal closeouts). They ask that you phone them at 736-0557 first, and tell them you read about them in this book. Open weekdays from 9:30 to 6; Thursdays to 8; Saturdays to 4. Closed Saturdays in July and August. Diagonally opposite Macy's.

Despite its name, **National Ladies Specialty Corporation,** on the second floor of 470 Seventh Avenue (35th Street) is not just for the ladies. Sure, they have scads of dresses, from $24.75 to $89.75; coats and raincoats from $39.25 to $179.75 (with fur trim); plenty of pants suits, $24.75 to $85 for women, but they also have a complete men's haberdashery. Designer handbags and accessories and brand-name lingerie, too. Free alterations on items over $35.75 add even more to the 20% to 40% savings on all merchandise. Open weekdays from 9 to 6; Saturdays, until 4 (tel. 695-1350).

Grand Street, and shoe-shop at **Nathan Rosen,** 142 Orchard (for men), or the front part of **Fishkin's,** 314 Grand Street (for women), or **Lasky Brothers,** 85 Orchard (for kids). Pick up some knitting or crocheting supplies—and get some free instruction if you want it—at booming **Bell Yarn Company,** 75 Essex Street, and some fine fabrics from **Samuel Beckenstein,** at 130 Orchard.

There's nothing like shopping to whet the appetite—and tire the feet—so have a rest and enjoy either a dairy meal at **Ratner's,** 138 Delancey Street, where the pastries are mind-boggling, or a meat one at **Katz's Delicatessen,** 205 East Houston Street, where the corned beef and hot pastrami are legendary. It would be unthinkable to come home from the Lower East Side without "a little something for later"—perhaps pickles or sour tomatoes right from the open-air barrels at **Guss's Pickle Products,** 42 Hester Street, or a knish or a kugel from **Yonah Schimmel's Knishery,** 137 East Houston Street, or some lox or caviar or pistachio nuts from **Russ & Daughters,** 179 East Houston Street, which happens to be one of the city's most prestigious appetizing stores. Taste, shop, enjoy!

BARGAINS IN THE BRONX AND BROOKLYN: A number of very well-dressed women we know confide that there is only one secret to their success: Loehmann's. **Charles C. Loehmann,** who has stores in the Bronx and in Brooklyn (and now in many suburban cities quite far afield), is the granddaddy of the design-ers-clothes-at-pipe-racks-prices stores (they've been in business over 50 years). The surroundings are pleasant but bare, the place is mobbed, and there is nothing at all elegant: except the clothes. Lovely dresses, suits, coats, gowns, at just about half to two-thirds of what you'd pay in the big stores in Manhattan. Some-times the savings are even more extraordinary: we once bought a pair of summer slacks here for $6, and saw them downtown the next day for $22. There are racks of $20 dresses, good value for the money, but the best buys are in the $40 to $80 range; and then there are three-figures designer's originals which, still, are about half what you'd pay in the master's salon. A trip to Loeh-mann's takes time, but we always find it eminently worthwhile, since we invariably come back with three dresses, two skirts, a pair of slacks, a few sweaters, maybe a bathing suit or two (name brands of $30 suits are usually $15). *Directions* for the big-game, big trek: The Bronx store is at 9 West Fordham Road (tel. CY 5-4100). Take the IRT Lexington Avenue subway (the Woodlawn Avenue Express train) to Fordham Road; Loehmann's is right on the corner. The Brooklyn store is at 19 Duryea Place at Beverly Road, off Flatbush Avenue (tel. IN 9-9800). The BMT Brighton line will take you to Beverly Road. Hours in the Bronx are from 10 to 9:30 p.m., Mondays through Saturdays. Hours in Brooklyn are from 10 to 5:30, six days; open Wednesdays until 9:30.

It will take you about a half hour from midtown to get out to **Aaron's Fifth Avenue**, 627 Fifth Avenue in Brooklyn, but you'll be ecstatic once you arrive. The racks are dotted with first quality merchandise from such top domestic and imported designers as Cacharel, Liz Claiborne, Harvey Bernard, Evan Picone, Anne Klein, and Kasper, just to mention a few. And since the prices are anywhere from one-third to 50% off retail, you'll undoubtedly come home with arms laden. You may also luck into a fantastic fur purchase at Aaron's; we once coveted, but did not buy, a $1690 nutria coat here, only to see it the very next week at an uptown department store for $3400! There are also designer's handbags at the same remarkable savings. Aaron's is known for its helpful, non-pushy service by salespeople who've stayed with the store for many years—as do most of its customers. Take any BMT express to DeKalb Avenue, then switch to the RR local and get off at Prospect Avenue; Aaron's is one block away. Open weekdays from 9 to 6, Thursdays until 9 (tel. 768-8710).

SOMETHING FOR THE MEN: With the price of men's suits rising astronomically, many of the better-heeled men in town have left their usual haberdashers and are now shopping the outlet stores. There are many such stores advertised, but not all deliver first quality: some simply buy last year's or unpopular styles. The ones that we mention here (husband-tested) carry fine clothing and prices of about 30% to 40% lower than elsewhere. Most levy a slight charge for alterations. The decor is pipe rack, but service is usually good—and you can't beat the prices. Our favorites include **Syms**, 45 Park Place, in the financial district (tel. 791-1199); **Mern's**, Madison Avenue at 54th Street (tel. 371-9175), and also at 75 Church Street, and **Harry Rothman**, 111 Fifth Avenue at 18th Street (tel. 777-7400), whose customer roster reads like Brooks Brothers. **Saint Laurie, Ltd.**, 86 Fifth Avenue (14th Street) is a very special operation; they have been manufacturing classic men's clothing since 1913, and it is sold at some of the finest stores in the country at nearly double the prices offered at their factory showrooms. Just for the record, even though it's not a discount operation, **Barney's**, Seventh Avenue at 17th Street (tel. 929-9000), is the biggest men's clothing store in town, has scads of specialized departments under one roof (for everything from boy's chubby to international designers to the Madison Avenue look), provides consistently good value, and even has a cafe for lunch and snacks.

In Search of Serendipity

Those three ancient kings who went in search of serendipity— looking for something rare, undiscovered, exceptional—would have had a splendid time shopping in New York. The unusual shop, the one-of-a-kind discovery, abounds here. Below, we'll tell you about some of our personal favorites off the beaten path, uptown and downtown, where you might pick up the perfect gift for your friends back home—or for yourself.

ANTIQUES: Hung up on patchwork quilts? **American Hurrah Antiques**, 316 East 70th Street, has the largest collection of antique American quilts in the world, most made between 1830 and 1930 in New York and Pennsylvania (many Amish quilts). Prices range from $100 to $500, but there are many between $150 and $200. Since they do a lot of business with European dealers and collectors and are familiar with European bed sizes, they can advise Europeans precisely which quilts will be suitable. Also beautiful: folk art and Americana like hooked rugs, paintings, pottery, handmade antique ship figureheads, 19th-century daguerrotypes, and much more.

A campy, funky collection of '30s, '40s, and turn-of-the-century *objets* is the stock in trade at **Carol Alderman Antiques**, 353 Third Avenue (26th Street). You might find anything from antique clothes and furs to mirrors, candlesticks, mannequin parts, and a vast collection of jewelry, from Woolworth's to Art Deco. Ms. Alderman also boasts the largest collection of stained-glass panels in New York. A great fun stop for incurable collectors, with many good bargains.

Want to do all your antique hunting under one roof? The **Manhattan Arts & Antiques Center**, 1050 Second Avenue at 56th Street, is a handsome, enclosed mall where some 85 collectors have gathered their wares. The range goes from country furniture and Art Nouveau to rare Chinese porcelains, from African masks to temple hangings from Tibet. Collect a print or a Persian carpet, a music box or an Old Master, depending on what the budget will bear. Open daily from 10:30 to 6:30; Sunday, from 12 to 6 (tel. 355-4400). Convenient parking.

BOOKS: Curious about Oriental philosophy or acupuncture or herbal remedies or flying saucers or parapsychology? Get on your magic carpet and fly down to **Samuel Weiser,** 740 Broadway, near 8th Street, which is the largest, most internationally respected occult, philosophical, and metaphysical bookshop in the country, possibly in the world. Its carefully selected stock of half a million volumes (including secondhand and rare tomes, some dating back as far as the 17th century), attracts countless scholars, collectors, scientists, philosophers, and just plain interested people. Or, steer the carpet towards the **Naseralishah Bookshop** at 240 West 72nd Street, not far from the Lincoln Center area, which boasts a slightly smaller, but similarly absorbing eclectic collection.

Barnes & Noble, at the corner of 18th Street and Fifth Avenue, has what is perhaps the largest collection of books in the country, displayed in a highly-browsable fashion. If you can't find what you want here, chances are it's just not findable. Directly across the street is its Sales Annex, a veritable supermarket of books. Since prices seem cheaper here than they are at regular supermarkets, you'll probably come home with bagsful of books —everything from best-sellers to children's books to publisher's overstock to encyclopedias—for about 50% off. Sunday afternoon at the Sales Annex is a great New York pastime. The uptown Barnes & Noble Sales Annex, at 48th Street and Fifth Avenue, is another must for bargain-hunting bibliophiles.

CANDLES: Candles that look like Christmas ribbons or fruits or green jade sculpture, candles that exude marvelous scents as they burn—these and many more unusual candles can be found at **Will-O'-the-Wick,** 1138 Lexington Avenue at 79th Street. We especially like the kind of candles that can burn and/or glow indefinitely, since they can be replaced with votive candles. Prices range from $2 to $25 (tel. 535-1558).

CERAMICS: Two Village addresses should be noted by those who love handthrown and handbuilt ceramics—at very reasonable prices. The first, **The Mad Monk,** at 500 Avenue of the Americas and 12th Street, represents the work of over 50 upstate and New England potters; their handsome teapots, casseroles, ornamental mirrors, jars, pitchers, candlestick holders, planters, and the like, range mostly from $4 to $20, but very special pieces can go as high as $3,000. The markup is low here, and the genial Mr. Monk who presides over the store has also gathered together a fine collection of books on East-West philosophy, which he sells at a discount of 20% off. Emerging, perhaps, with a whimsical butter dish and/or a book on Buddhist meditation, make your way on to Richard Rappaport's **Studio Workshop**, on the eighth floor of 3 West 18th Street. Here you can watch the potters at work, order things made (this is one of the few places that will do dinnerware to order), or buy some of their lovely creations—casseroles, goblets, bowls, decorative pieces—on the spot. Prices range mostly from $3 to $50. There are some extraordinary works here. If all this has whetted your appetite for the crafts life, Richard will teach you how to throw a pot on the wheel yourself—for free. The studio is always open, but phone Richard first at 242-9615.

CHILDREN'S FAVORITES: Looking for some very special clothes and other pretties for children? **Chocolate Soup**, 249 East 77th Street (tel. 861-2210), is a honey of a store, laden with beautiful items like traditional handmade patchwork quilts from the Amish country (average price is $75), toys and dolls all handmade with artistry and love. French painted denim skirts and hand-smocked Liberty of London dresses ($40 to $45) are the big items here. Infants to size 14. . . . French underwear, Italian sunglasses, patchwork baby buntings and Appalachian handworked clothing are just some of the many pretties to be found at **Stone Free Kids**, 142 West 72nd Street, along with the most wonderful rag dolls and stuffed animals. Prices are modest at this West Side boutique. . . . The flavor is British at the East Side version of this store **Stone Free Junior** at 1086 Madison Avenue (82nd Street), what with the all-wool camel coats, cashmere sweaters, Liberty dresses, and hacking jackets. Everything is in 100% cotton, wool, or all-natural fabrics.

COLLECTOR'S ITEMS: **Collector's Cabinet**, 153 East 57th Street is more like a natural history museum than a shop. "The treasures of Mother Earth" are here in lavish abundance, waiting to be collected: framed sea life, pearled shells, framed butterflies (the largest collection in the world) and wildflowers, coral, fossils, ostrich eggs, piranhas, giant sea horses, as well as gems and minerals in the rough. Note the exceptional lines of miniature animal sculptures and the fine collection of bonsai. Prices go from 25¢ to several thousand dollars, but most objects are in the $2 to $10 range. Perfect for children.

HEARTS: Helena and Jonathan Stuart have been collecting hearts for over 12 years, and the result is **Only Hearts,** a love of a little shop at 281 Columbus Avenue (73rd Street), where everything is in the shape of—or has something to do with— hearts. Whether you fancy a rainbow heart pin at 50¢ or a one-of-a-kind handmade, heart-shaped antique fabric bag at $70, there is something here you'll have to have: perhaps a heart-shaped toothbrush holder or cookie mold or comb or even hand-painted ankle socks with hearts. Only Hearts also happens to be in the heart of the Columbus Avenue shopping-dining area (a kind of miniature Greenwich Village), next door to three popular sidewalk cafes—Anita's Chile Parlor, Indian Oven, and Cafe Carob—and across the street from **Design Observations,** 286 Columbus, with tasteful and unusual European and American home accessories. The exciting shopping continues uptown for several blocks. Not far from the Lincoln Center complex, this area is well worth a special trip.

HERBS, SPICES, AND SOAPS: Kiehl's Pharmacy, 109 Third Avenue (13th Street), has been known since 1851 for one of the largest selections of herbs (and their own herbal products) in the country—for herbs to ward off a spell or ward off a cold, for exotic potions, homeopathic remedies, their own perfumes (be sure to sample the musk oil), as well as beautifully natural and luxurious bath and facial preparations. They have every kind of herbal tea imaginable. Alas, they no longer carry leeches (the demand for blood-letting has died down), but they stock every modern as well as time-tested remedy available. When you can find frankincense and myrrh, ginseng and pennyroyal and rasp-berry leaves (helpful in childbirth), and penicillin and vitamins all under one roof, you have to be at Kiehl's.

The oldest perfumers and chemists in the United States, **Cas-well-Massey,** Lexington Avenue and 48th Street, in business for 225 years, still carries the same colognes that were favorites with George and Martha Washington and the Marquis de Lafayette! Sarah Bernhardt used their cucumber cold cream (and so can you), and you can also pick and choose from the largest collection of imported soaps in the world. There's also imported shaving equipment, pomanders, potpourri, cough drops and lozenges from England and France. A wondrous nostalgic place full of things you can't get elsewhere. Write for their fanciful catalogue: $1.

Cambridge Chemists, 702 Madison Avenue, near 63rd Street, is the kind of place that makes visiting Europeans feel they're right at home. Here's where one can buy pure and natural products by Cyclax of London (they are the only U.S. agents for these beauty products used by Queen Elizabeth), Floris of London, Innoxa and Culpepper of England, Roc and Vichy of France, and a variety of other toiletries, cosmetics, and treatment preparations from England, France, Switzerland, and Germany. Although the Rockefellers and other local folk of that ilk are their customers, everyone is treated with old-fashioned courtesy. A wooden shaving bowl, a natural clove pomander in a bed of potpourri, a perfume vaporizer, or a crystal atomizer are a few unique gift possibilities here.

INTERNATIONAL GIFTS: Noto, 245 West 72nd Street, is a friendly little boutique, jam-packed with folk treasures from around the globe, and all reasonably priced. Note the very large collection of jewelry from around the world—Afghanistan, Turkey, Africa, Israel, India—as well as authentic mummy beads (discovered in digs in Egypt), beautiful American Indian jewelry, and some unusual pieces made by local craftsmen using antique stones, $10 to $50. Baskets from many countries and wall hangings aplenty from the Far East and South America suggest the international mix. And be sure to see the shop's own fanciful creations: wooden-like reproductions of Notre Dame gargoyles, Art Deco and Mediterranean mirrors, and carved heads from Spain, all under $20. The price range here goes up to $200, but there are many under-$10 gift items. Stop by on a Sunday, from noon to 6, when browsers are welcomed with wine and cheese.

MINERALS: There is an enormous stock of gems and minerals at **Astro-Minerals, Ltd.,** at 155 East 34th Street, both to look at (in exhibits in the natural history gallery) and to wear: necklaces, from $95 to several hundred dollars, rings, pendants, brooches. Amethyst rock crystal is their specialty, but they also have many jade and tiger's eye carvings, plus malachite, amber, crystal, ivories, turquoise, carnelians, and even beggar beads imported from the East.

PAPER PRETTIES: For lots of charming little presents, especially for children, **The Paper House**, Madison Avenue at 64th Street and 80th Street, 18 Greenwich Avenue, and 1370 Third Avenue, is a discovery. You'll find piñatas from Mexico, children's favors, books, toys, masks, fantasy creatures, miniature chairs and sofas, paper houses, lanterns, teddy bears on little wicker chairs, glittery swans in bright colors—as a start.

PATCHWORK: **Domino Patchwork,** in a cheery Greenwich Village loft on the ninth floor of 333 Avenue of the Americas (at West Fourth Street), turns out beautiful works of patchwork, quilting and applique and sells them to the public at about one-third less than the prices they command at specialty stores around the country. Everything from scarves and skirts and clutch bags to window shades and bedspreads and hammocks is available here, at prices from $6.50 up to about $300. Especially enchanting are the patchwork baby quilts ($40 to $60), beautiful enough to hang on the wall, as are the full-sized quilts as well. Anything can be custom-made, including a do-it-yourself kit that brings your savings up to around 50%. Call first for an appointment: 989-7254.

SCIENCE FICTION: Step inside the black-and-silver spaceship known as the **Science-Fiction Shop,** 56 Eighth Avenue (Horatio Street), and explore two thousand science-fiction titles, including out-of-print as well as hard-to-find classics. Posters, games, puzzles, cards, jewelry, anything with an extraterrestrial motif can be found here. Send for a free catalog.

SWEET TREATS: It's only fair to warn you that a visit to a **Treat Boutique** (at Seventh Avenue and 54th Street or at 200 East 86th Street) can be addictive: to the most luscious hand-dipped chocolates (how about chocolate-covered strawberries for a start?), the finest and freshest nuts from around the world, honey-glazed or beautifully plain dried fruits, the creamiest fudge studded with nuts, and a rafter of old-time penny candies like jawbreakers and Mexican hats and chocolate babies. The likes of such goodies are not inexpensive ($7 to $10 for a pound of chocolates), but a little goes a long, long way. Be sure to sample the Ambrosia, a toothsome mixture of dried apricots, pineapple, and papaya, plus whole cashews, walnuts, almonds, etc., $2.39 the half-pound. Gift packages to order, sent anywhere.

UNICORNS: "Now I believe there are unicorns," said William Shakespeare in *The Tempest,* and you will agree with him when you walk into **Unicorn City** at 55 Greenwich Avenue. Here, assembled under one roof, are all the crafty unicorns in captivity, captured in silver and gold pendants, pillows and T-shirts, wallets, picnic bags, posters, and more. Pick up a sterling-silver unicorn pendant, $25, as a good-luck symbol, get a bean-bag unicorn for the kids to play with, or have a lifesized unicorn that will watch over your garden sent home for $450.

Washington Square

Chapter X

EXCURSIONS IN THE NEW YORK AREA

TO MOST PEOPLE, New York is the classic megalopolis, whose pavements stretch out into infinity. But just beyond New York's suburban sprawl—sometimes within it—lies a rich collection of historic mansions, natural wonders, and recreational areas of unquestioned beauty. No visit to New York is really complete without a look at the charming countryside that surrounds the city—especially to the north in rural, unspoilt New York State.

This chapter concerns itself with some of the most popular excursions from the city—popular with New Yorkers as well as visitors—and divides them into two major categories. First, we'll deal with those destinations close in to town, places on Long Island, in the lower Hudson River Valley, and in the nearby parts of Connecticut and New Jersey. Every one of our suggestions is easy to reach by car in under two hours. And if you don't have a car, we'll give you hints on how to get there by train or bus. Then we have some trips for the more ambitious, expeditions into the forested regions of New York State (whose precincts are relatively unknown to New York City dwellers). The excursions further afield climax with one of the earth's great natural wonders, Niagara Falls.

But now, to specifics:

One-Day Excursions

LONG ISLAND: Our first destinations lie on Long Island, favorite of Walt Whitman, the rich 19th-century industrialists (who built many palatial mansions here), and latter-day target of housing developers. Two boroughs of New York City—Queens and

Brooklyn—actually are on the westernmost tip of Long Island. Beyond the city limits stretch housing developments, interspersed with posh residential suburbs, until finally it all thins out into random potato farms, elegant beach villages (like Southampton, East Hampton, etc.), small towns, and finally Montauk Point. The eastern reaches of "the island," as it's called by natives, are particularly popular in the summertime, when many New Yorkers open up (or rent) beach houses. The Hamptons, Quogue, Montauk, and the like are really suited for longer vacations, but for a splendid beach within 30 miles of the swelter of Times Square, head for—

Jones Beach

Four miles of powdery white sand fronting on the south (Atlantic) shore of Long Island make this—in the opinion of most New Yorkers—the city's best nearby beach. So many people share this high opinion of Jones Beach that it's very difficult to get out there on a summer weekend, unless you leave very early in the morning. During the week, however, when everyone's at work, it's another story. Then you can skip the inevitable weekend traffic jams and clogged parking lots, and comfortably enjoy the many facilities. First and foremost is the beach itself—wide and white, backed by low dunes and a grassy bay, and echoing with the low thunder of surf. Since Jones Beach is a State Park, there's quite a bit of handsome landscaping behind the beach, also picnic areas, big modern bathhouses, swimming pools, a solarium, moderately priced cafeteria, courts for paddle tennis, even the Jones Beach Marine Theatre, which presents family-type spectaculars in a big outdoor amphitheater.

You can get to Jones Beach by taking the Long Island Expressway to Exit 38, then the Northern State Parkway to the Meadowbrook Parkway exit. Follow the Meadowbrook Parkway south to the beach. If you aren't driving, you can take a Gray Line bus from the Port Authority Terminal at 41st Street and Eighth Avenue (almost continual departures during July and August), or a Long Island Railroad train from Penn Station. And remember—go during the week if you can.

Sagamore Hill

This rambling, shingle-Victorian house was the home of the colorful Teddy Roosevelt. During his presidency it was the "summer White House," and while its location three miles east of the hamlet of Oyster Bay in the Village of Cove Neck is no longer remote as it once was, the house and grounds retain the flavor of oldtime Long Island. The mansion itself has a sort of regal informality to it. Everything is of splendid proportions, and decorations include large mounted hunting trophies. The Old Orchard Museum has TR's papers and mementos of his years in Washington and New York. This is undoubtedly one of the most historic—as well as aesthetic—spots on Long Island, and has been, for good reason, designated a national monument.

You can reach Sagamore Hill by taking the Long Island Expressway to exit 41N, then following the signs north on Route 106 to and through the hamlet of Oyster Bay. The estate lies beyond the hamlet, on Cove Neck Road. Alternately, you can take a regular Long Island Railroad train to Oyster Bay, then a cab from the station. Open daily, 9 to 5; from 9 to 6, July to Labor Day. Admission is 50¢; for those under 16, free. Information can be obtained from the National Park Service (516/922-4447), which administers the park.

Vanderbilt Museum and Planetarium

This magnificent estate, some 45 miles from the city, was built by William K. Vanderbilt II. The ornate furnishings and gorgeous informal gardens give us another glimpse of the grand life that used to be lived (and sometimes still is) by the millionaires of Long Island's north shore. Located just east of Huntington, in Centerport, the Vanderbilt Museum (Eagle's Nest) makes an ideal day's outing. After wandering through the opulent old mansion, you can visit the Natural History Museum, stocked with ship models, rare and beautiful shells, marine specimens, stuffed animals, and fascinating curios that Mr. Vanderbilt—himself a great adventurer—brought back from the far corners of the world. The museum is open from May through October, from 10 to 4, Tuesdays through Saturdays; from 12 to 5, Sundays and holidays. Admission: $1; senior citizens, 75¢; children under 12, 50¢.

While you're here, you should also visit the beautiful new planetarium, with programs presented daily except Mondays throughout the year. Phone for showtimes. Admission is $1.50, $1 for those seven to 12; under sevens are *not admitted,* except to the children's program, every Saturday at 11 a.m., 75¢.

Best way to get there is via the Long Island Expressway to exit 51 northbound, or take Northern State Parkway northbound to exit 42. Follow the signs to Centerport, then Little Neck Road. The museum is open May through October, daily except Monday.

HUDSON RIVER VALLEY: The next few attractions lie in the southern reaches of New York's mighty Hudson River Valley. Blinded by the glass and brick canyon walls of Manhattan, New Yorkers sometimes don't even notice the majestic river that flanks our city. But a relatively short distance to the north, the pavements and skyscrapers soon disappear, giving way to romantic forest-covered mountains, sheer cliffs, and peaceful villages nestled by the riverside. An occasional mountaintop castle, perhaps built in the late 19th century by a prosperous city dweller, sometimes gives the valley an almost European look.

The Sleepy Hollow Restorations and Windows by Chagall and Matisse

Sunnyside, Van Cortlandt Manor, and Philipsburg Manor comprise three of the most historic and legendary sites on the Hudson River. Sunnyside was the Hudson River retreat of author Washington Irving, who immortalized the region with the story of Ichabod Crane and his encounter with the Headless Horseman. The unique house, which Irving designed according to his whims and fancies, where he lived until his death in 1859, stands as it did then, in a peaceful location by the shady riverbank. Guides in 19th-century costumes take visitors through Sunnyside in Tarrytown, restored with Irving's furniture, possessions, and library. After your visit you can picnic amid the estate's woods and lawns overlooking the Hudson. And any children with you will love watching the graceful swans in the pond on the grounds.

Van Cortlandt Manor lies a bit to the north in the village of Croton-on-Hudson. The house dates from the 17th century, and was originally part of a Dutch estate that comprised most of what is now Westchester County. The Van Cortlandt family backed the patriot cause in the American Revolution and also played major roles in New York politics. Today the Manor is considered one of the best period restorations in the United States, appearing as it did during the Revolutionary War period, when it was headquarters for the 86,000-acre manorial estate. In addition to the Manor House, filled with family treasures from early America, the property includes restored Ferry House buildings and delightful picnic areas shaded by centuries-old trees.

The third restoration is Philipsburg Manor in North Tarrytown. Water again provides power to operate the Manor's gristmill as in the early 1700s. Then Philipsburg was an important industrial-trading site and also northern headquarters for the 90,000-acre land holding of a powerful Dutch-American family, the Philipses. The two-story stone Manor House was begun in 1683 and contains furnishings of the early 18th century. Philipsburg also has a 200-foot-long oak-timbered dam that ponds up the Pocantico River to operate the mill, plus a large 18th-century barn filled with farm and handcrafts implements of the period.

All three properties are open daily year-round from 10 to 5, and are closed Thanksgiving, Christmas, and New Year's Day. Admission is $2.25 per adult to each property and $1.50 for children six to 14, and senior citizens. Children under six are admitted free. Two-property tickets, good for a month, are $4 and $2.50, respectively, and three-property tickets, good for a year, are $5.75 and $3.75.

The most scenic route to Sunnyside and Philipsburg Manor is via the West Side Drive, which turns into the Saw Mill River Parkway, to Ashford Avenue. Go left on Ashford (toward the river) until the junction with Route 9. Sunnyside is at the Irvington-Tarrytown line, one mile south of the Tappan Zee Bridge on West Sunnyside Lane, just off Route 9. Philipsburg Manor is in North Tarrytown, on Route 9, two miles north of the Tappan Zee Bridge. Van Cortlandt Manor, in Croton-on-Hudson, is nine miles north of the Tappan Zee Bridge. Take Route 9, exit onto Croton Point Avenue, go one block east to South Riverside Avenue, then right one-quarter mile to the entrance.

There is no connection between the Sleepy Hollow Restorations and the Union Church of Pocantico Hills, but while you're visiting Philipsburg Manor, it would be a shame not to drive one mile uphill to the church. Here you'll find nine stained-glass panels executed by Marc Chagall (there are only two other sets of Chagall windows in the world) and a splendid rose window done by Henri Matisse, commissioned by the Rockefeller family (Pocantico Hills is the Rockefeller estate) in honor of their parents. You must call the church at 914/ME 1-2069 before you come. It is open to visitors (the windows are best viewed from inside the church) from 9 to 4 on weekdays, from 1 to 4 on Sunday.

Museum Village, in Orange County

A colorful picture of America's transformation from an agrarian to an industrialized economy is offered here. Around the village green are more than 30 buildings displaying thousands of 19th-century objects and tools. There are daily demonstrations of such crafts as pottery, broom-making, weaving, blacksmithing, and printing. Of major interest to children, it is open daily from May 1 through October 31. Admission is $3, children, $1.75. Free parking. The Village is four miles west of the New York State Thruway Exit 16 at Harriman.

FDR National Historic Site, Hyde Park

Another Roosevelt home—this one belonging to FDR—is located in this small town just north of Poughkeepsie. The house is an impressive one, standing on a promontory with a sweeping view of the Hudson. Inside, everything is just as FDR left it, which means the numerous rooms are filled with original furniture and mementos from the former president's eventful life. Particularly interesting is FDR's childhood bedroom, with everything carefully labeled and preserved by an adoring mother. Behind the house are the dignified graves of Franklin and his wife Eleanor, surrounded by the Rose Garden. After strolling through the house, you'll no doubt want to visit the FDR Library and Museum, filled with letters, state papers, and some of the many fabulous gifts he received during his years in Washington. Your ticket to the FDR house, by the way, entitles you to visit the adjacent Vanderbilt Mansion, a baronial country estate built in 1896 for F. W. Vanderbilt.

To reach Hyde Park, take the New York Thruway (north), get off at Exit 18 (New Paltz) and follow signs to Route 9 North and Mid-Hudson Bridge. After crossing the bridge, take Route 9 North for approximately eight miles.

The Roosevelt Home and Vanderbilt Mansion are open daily from 9 to 5, until 6 from Memorial Day through Labor Day. The Roosevelt Library-Museum is open 9 to 5 year round. Admission to all three is $1.50, free to children under 16 and adults over 62.

You can drive to West Point, too, (see ahead for details on getting there by boat) enjoying breathtaking views of the river from the famous Storm King Highway (Route 9W, north of Peekskill). The road snakes along the riverbank north of Peekskill (reached via the Saw Mill and Taconic Parkways north to Route 35, then west to the sign for Bear Mountain), climbs into the hills, then emerges midway on a cliff high above the shining Hudson. You'll cross the river on the Bear Mountain Bridge, then continue north along another cliff-hanging highway. If you stop at Bear Mountain, take the Perkins Memorial Drive to the top of the mountain, open from April to October during daylight hours.

If you don't have a car, consider taking the fascinating Gray Line tour that takes you to West Point by bus and back to New York by boat down the Hudson River. It's an all-day trip, including lunch at Hotel Thayer, and the price is $22. Phone 397-2600 for information.

West Point and Bear Mountain

Here's a chance to combine some sightseeing with a delightful cruise up the Hudson River. Although the old sidewheelers that once plied the river have all been retired, the **Circle Line** now runs a jaunty new, 3,000-passenger vessel, *The Dayliner,* up the Hudson, and the cruise itself is pure delight, offering striking views of Manhattan and the majestic Jersey Palisades before reaching the forested regions to the north. Quite a few of your fellow passengers will disembark at the first stop, Bear Mountain, an attractive swimming, picnic, and country area (you can rent a boat in the summer, ice-skate in the winter, swim in the pool, watch animals in the zoo). If you stay on board, another half hour's cruise, past craggy mountains topped by picturesque castles, will take you to the Military Academy at West Point. There's a Visitors Information Center at Thayer Gate (open April 15 to November 15), with free films and displays on cadet training. You can stroll around the campus, browse through the library or the famous military museum, or just absorb the atmosphere that nourished men like Patton, Eisenhower, MacArthur, and Pershing. (If you're planning your trip well in advance, write for the Parade Schedule to: Information Officer, U.S. Military Academy, West Point, N.Y.) No picnic grounds here, so plan to eat either on the boat or in the dining room of the lovely Hotel Thayer. If you wish to stay on the boat all day, after leaving West Point you can cruise on up to Poughkeepsie (no stop) where the vessel turns around, cruises back down the Hudson to pick up the Bear Mountain passengers, and returns you back to midtown New York by 7 p.m. Just one warning: You'll enjoy your trip much, much more during the less crowded week days; weekend boats are often packed.

The *Dayliner* sails every day at 10 from Memorial Day weekend through mid-September (usually excepting Mondays and Fridays in June, daily trips to Poughkeepsie starting July 1), from Pier 81, at the foot of West 41st Street. No reservations are necessary. The fare will probably be under $8.50 for adults, about half of that for children. For details, phone 279-5151.

ON TO CONNECTICUT: Now let's turn, briefly, to Connecticut, with its charming New England villages, exclusive suburbs, and great tracts of rolling woodlands. But before we reach it, let's stop short of the Connecticut border, in the northern, quite rural reaches of Westchester County, at North Salem, N.Y., where we find the—

Hammond Museum and Gardens

A 1½-hour drive from Manhattan brings you into a place that you might mistake for Japan. Here, surrounding the small and gracious Hammond Museum, are 3½ acres of Japanese gardens, an adaptation of the Stroll Garden which reached perfection in the Edo period of Japan. Wander past miniature waterfalls and stone bridges, watch the flashing carp and listen to the bird song—then emerge onto the Museum's flagstone terrace, "Beneath the Bough," where a delightful French buffet lunch or complete dinner is being served beneath the trees. (In poor weather, the restaurant moves indoors to become "Beside The Hearth.") Next, visit the intriguing humanities museum with its changing exhibits like "Fifty Years of New York—The News in Pictures" or "A Salute to American Industry." Finally, stop in at the tasteful and modestly priced gift shop featuring fine crafts by local artisans.

From May through November, lunch is served Wednesdays through Sundays, 12 to 2:30, $7.50; dinner Fridays and Saturdays 7 to 10, $12.50; reservations essential. Admission to the museum is $1.50, to the garden $1.50, and you must be a visitor at either to make use of the restaurant. For reservations and driving directions, phone 914/669-5135.

In another part of Connecticut, let's visit the—

American Shakespeare Festival

There are few places where one can watch Shakespeare as pleasantly as one can at the American Shakespeare Festival in Stratford, Conn. The theater's site is almost as pretty as the one in Stratford, England, and the theater is a splendidly modernized Elizabethan playhouse, standing on the scenic banks of the Housatonic River. Drive up early and you'll be able to enjoy the pleasant riverside surroundings—complete with little extras like strolling balladeers, a herbarium, picnic tables. The repertoire extends from Shakespeare to Shaw and sometimes beyond, but the emphasis is always on the Bard, and the company is growing more solid all the time. For dinner before the theater, the Mermaid Tavern in the Stratford Motor Inn is just right.

The Stratford season lasts from early July until mid-August, with ticket prices ranging from $3.50 to $10.50. For information and reservations, phone WO 6-3900 in New York or 203/375-4457 in Connecticut. You can reach Stratford via the speedy Connecticut Turnpike (exit 31) or take the more scenic Merritt Parkway to exit 51. Penn Central trains leave Grand Central for Stratford, too, and you can take a cab from the train station directly to the theater.

NEW JERSEY: It may seem incredible that, by driving roughly an hour from New York City, one can actually go on safari . . . in New Jersey. But with the opening of Great Adventure a little while back, it is now entirely feasible to drive your car through jungle-like acres and look out the windows (tightly closed, of course) as the great creatures of the wild—bears, buffaloes, caribou, rhinos, tigers, elephants, and even fierce lions —watch *us* in the people cages while they roam about unhindered.

Great Adventure

Billed as the largest family entertainment center in the Northeast, **Great Adventure** is located on 1,100 acres of forest and lakes in Jackson, New Jersey, 65 miles from New York City. Besides being the biggest safari park outside of Africa (2,000 wild animals on hundreds of acres, the largest group of Siberian tigers in the world, many rare and endangered species), Great Adventure also offers, in its themed Amusement Park, enough amusement, entertainment, rides, attractions, shopping, eating, and fantasy-type adventure to keep every member of the family enthralled for days. Major rides include the world's largest flume ride and ferris wheel, the brand-new Lightnin' Loops roller coaster (which speeds riders 45 miles an hour through two 58-foot high loops—both forwards and backwards!), antique cars and a 19th-century Dream Street Carousel. There's entertainment going on almost continuously: a full-fledged musical presentation, trick riders, circus and aerial acts, sky divers, performing tigers, and big name recording stars and bands, to mention just a few.

Restaurants include three cafeteria-style restaurants with everything from barbecued beef ribs to chicken, chile, and ice cream sundaes, plus dozens of foodstands. The shoppers may spend all their time just browsing through the International Bazaar, with its African artifacts, Mexican jewelry, rocks and fossils, crystal, wood, copper, glass, fanciful candles, plus a large section for Mexican and Western merchandise: charro hats, sombreros, blankets, pottery, belts and handcrafted leather items. And there are leather workers, wood carvers, glass blowers, and portrait artists to be observed.

Great Adventure is open daily from 10 to 10, spring through fall. Admission, which may be slightly higher by the time you read this, is $9.50 to the Themed Amusement Park only: $4.50 for the Safari only: and a combination admission to both, $11.50. The one-price policy includes admission to all rides (as many times as you want to take them), shows, attractions, and parking. For information call 201/928-2000.

To reach Great Adventure, take the New Jersey Turnpike to exit 7A (I-195); follow it east toward Freehold/Mt. Holly for 12 miles, and turn south on Route 537. Driving time should be about one hour and 20 minutes. Bus service is provided on a daily basis from the Port Authority Terminal in New York City by Gray Line (732-6751), Transport of New Jersey (732-6751), and Lincoln Transit (736-1640) for about $6.95, round trip.

Excursions Further Afield

With the city and its nearby attractions securely under your belt, we hope you'll still have time to tour the rural reaches of northern New York—"upstate" as everything north of the city line is referred to. "Upstate" has practically nothing in common with the city except the name New York. It is a land of genuine wilderness forests, romantic legend-filled mountains, splendid clear lakes, picturesque villages and small cities, and lots and lots of history. It is criss-crossed by highways of all description, ranging from Revolutionary carriage tracks, to the 550-mile super-expressway known as the New York State Thruway. It has the sort of open spaces many Easterners think don't exist this side of the Rockies, combined with old villages and isolated country houses that hark back to times centuries past. It's relaxed and homespun, in striking contrast to the electric lifestyle of the city. All in all, a very different place.

Our first stop is about 260 miles from New York City in the lovely Finger Lakes region of New York, in the town of—

CORNING: Although its own population is only about 17,000, Corning, N.Y., often plays host to more than 700,000 visitors a year. Known as the "Glass Center of the World," it is to glass what Detroit is to automobiles. But, happily, industrial blight seems to have bypassed this pretty city, situated in a little valley of the Chemung River. You won't find thick, hazy skies hanging over Corning or bleak, soot-stained boulevards, either. The town is pleasantly small in proportion and esthetically in tune with the surrounding countryside. New buildings are sprouting everywhere, part of an impressive rebuilding effort following the flooding caused by Hurricane Agnes in June, 1972.

Although the community has existed since 1796, Corning Glass opened its first glass works here in 1868. In 1903 the Steuben Glass Factory began producing some of the finest glass and crystal in the world, and it still does: many are displayed in the Steuben Glass Shop at 717 Fifth Avenue in Manhattan. But the Steuben factory is only a small part of the great Corning Glass complex—which makes anything and everything one could think of in glass. You tour the famous Glass Center on a do-it-yourself basis, wandering at will through exhibits guaranteed to intrigue even those normally indifferent to the industrial process. In the Museum, 16,000 glass objects, gathered from 35 countries, await you. In the Hall of Science and Industry you'll see glass that is as hard as diamonds, glass as soft as cotton, as strong as steel, or as fragile as an eggshell, glass that conducts electricity—even glass that goes into outer space in our manned spaceships. Visitors may also watch every step in the manufacture of Steuben crystal as they visit the factory.

The Corning Glass Center is open to visitors every day of the year (except Thanksgiving, Dec. 24 and 25, and New Year's

Day). Free admission and parking. Professional summer theater July and August.

HAMMONDSPORT: A remarkable pleasant little town, situated on the southern tip of Lake Keuka, Hammondsport has two claims to fame: not only is it New York's wine capital, it is also, thanks to a local son named Glenn Hammond Curtiss, the cradle of commercial aviation in America. But first, to the wine.

Nature has been generous in the Finger Lakes region, and their protected hillsides, rich soil, and relatively long growing season have combined to produce wine grapes of high quality (the area is in the same latitude as the champagne districts of Europe). This is where most New York State wines originate. No matter what time of year you visit here, it's fascinating to see the vineyards and tour the facilities of the largest wine companies. Free winery tours are offered by Gold Seal, Great Western, Hammondsport Wine, Taylor, and Bully Hill Vineyards (open May through October). Great Western (Pleasant Valley Wine Co.) conducts guided tours Monday to Friday, from 8:30 to 11 and from 1 to 3:30. Since summer crowds are large, they suggest you take a morning tour. At the end of most of the tours, you proceed to a hospitality room to taste hors d'oeuvres and sip your choices of wines and champagnes. The hostesses dispense vital information along with the grape, so this is a painless way to become an oenophile. All wineries are closed Sunday. The **Greyton H. Taylor Wine Museum,** the only wine museum in the United States, is worth a visit, and so is its Winemaker Shop, which provides instruction and supplies. Museum admission is 50¢ for adults, 25¢ for students. Open May 1 through October 31, Mondays through Saturdays, 9 to 4:30; Sundays 1 to 4:30.

Hammondsport's reputation in aviation circles is due to Glenn H. Curtiss, whose pioneering efforts in aviation engineering are commemorated at the Glenn H. Curtiss Museum of Local History. Curtiss, in case you forgot, was the first man to land a plane on the water (right here at Lake Keuka, 1910); he developed a flying boat (in 1912) and the famous "Jenny" (the World War I workhorse that trained most of the airmen of that era). Admission is $2 for adults, $1 students and senior citizens, 50¢ children seven to 12. Open May through October, Mondays through Saturdays from 9 to 5 and also on Sundays in July and August.

NIAGARA FALLS: There are two Niagara Falls, one in Canada and one in New York. Together they comprise what must surely be one of the most spectacular sights—in terms of sheer magnitude—to be seen anywhere in the world. But extravagant descriptions just can't convey the majesty of Niagara, an Indian name that aptly translates as "Thunderer of the Waters." Charles Dickens put it well enough when, on the brink of the falls, he remarked "how near to my Creator I was standing." And, happily, it's simple to cross back and forth between Canadian and American sides. U.S. citizens need identification in addition to a Social Security card; non-U.S. citizens require passports. Incidentally, those staying a minimum of 48 hours in Canada are allowed to bring back up to $100 worth of merchandise duty free. And American and Canadian dollars are used interchangeably everywhere up here.

For over a century, people have been fascinated with the falls, from the millions of viewers to the handful of showmen who were determined to go over it in barrels. A 19th-century Frenchman named Blondin went one better: he managed to cross the roaring gorge on a tightrope, then to follow that act by riding a bicycle over his tightrope and, for dessert, he cooked an omelet on a portable stove—while standing on that same tightrope! We can't guarantee that you'll see anything quite so spectacular on your trip but, for us, the falls are spectacle enough in themselves. When you take the famous *Maid of the Mist* boat trip, however, you're liable to feel a bit like Blondin himself as the boat heads out into the river, directly for the thundering base of Horseshoe Falls. The noise of the water soon drowns out everything else, and the passengers watch goggle-eyed as the boat pulls up to, almost into, the crushing column of fallen water. Actually, the ride is completely safe—they've been taking people on this cruise for more than 100 years with never an accident—and the boat starts making its turn away from the cataract while it is 150 feet from the base. But it's a thrill all the same. The dock is on the American side in Prospect Park; take the Observation Tower elevator to get down to the waterside.

The easiest way to get around the Niagara Reservation is to hop the Viewmobile, an open-sided train that stops at Green Island, the 61-acre park called Goat Island; the famous Cave of the Winds; and Terrapin Point, at the U.S. end of Horseshoe Falls. You can jump off the train whenever you like, explore at your leisure, and pick up the next train on the way.

The most exciting way to see Niagara is, of course, by helicopter; the choppers are now as permanent a fixture in the skies as the spray cloud. The standard route is over both the American and Horseshoe Falls, then over the Whirlpool and the big Robert Moses power plant—a breathtaking trip with incredible views. The Heussler Corporation, whose heliport is conveniently located in town, is one of several companies offering this service.

To catch some exciting entertainment in this area, you need go no further than seven miles, to Lewiston, New York, and the site of one of the area's biggest visitor attractions, **Artpark,** a New York State park that doubles as a center for the visual and performing arts, the first such of its kind. Artists-in-residence can be observed at work. The well-equipped theater seats 2,400 inside and 1,500 more on a rear seating lawn. Attractions include internationally famous dance, opera, and musical theater groups. Tickets are $4 evenings, $3 matinees inside, less on the lawn. Outdoor events are free. The season runs from mid-May to mid-September. Hours are noon to 6, or through evening performance time, Wednesdays through Sundays.

Niagara Falls has slews of tourist accommodations, from campsites to the Y.M.C.A. and from tourist homes to attractive hotels and motels. In the latter category, remember that rates are highest during the summer season and will go down drastically after Labor Day in most places. The **Red Coach Inn,** Buffalo Avenue at Main Street, has a choice location overlooking the rapids, and offers singles from $15, doubles from $20. During the summer season it opens its terrace for outdoor dining. **Howard Johnson's Motor Lodge,** 454 Main Street, has an indoor pool and sauna; singles run $20 to $40 and doubles are $25 to $40. Then there's the attractive **Holiday Inn,** 114 Buffalo Avenue, also with a pool, and singles from $33, doubles from $34. For more information on lodgings, write to the Niagara Falls Convention and Visitors Bureau, 300 Fourth Street, P.O. Box 786, Falls Street Station, Niagara Falls, NY 14303.

In New York City, you can visit the Canadian Government Office of Tourism, Room 1030, 1251 Avenue of the Americas, for information on accommodations in Niagara Falls, Ontario.

HOW TO SAVE MONEY
ON ALL YOUR TRAVELS

Saving money while traveling is never a simple matter—which is why, almost 16 years ago, the **$10-a-Day Travel Club** was formed. Actually, the idea came from readers of the Arthur Frommer Publications, who felt that such an organization could bring financial benefits, continuing travel information, and a sense of community to economy-minded travelers in all parts of the world. They were right. By combining the purchasing power of thousands of our readers, we've been able to obtain a wide range of exciting travel benefits—including, on occasion, substantial discounts to members from purveyors of tourist services throughout the world.

In keeping with the money-saving concept, the membership fee is low, and it is immediately exceeded by the value of your benefits. Upon receipt of $10 (U.S. residents), $12 (Canadian and Mexican residents), or $14 (other foreign residents) to cover one year's membership, we will send all new members by return mail (book rate):

(1) The latest edition of any *two* of the books listed on the following page.

(2) A copy of ARTHUR FROMMER'S GUIDE TO NEW YORK.

(3) A copy of SURPRISING AMSTERDAM AND HAPPY HOLLAND—a 224-page pocket-size guide by Ian Keown.

(4) A one-year subscription to the quarterly Club newspaper—THE WONDERFUL WORLD OF BUDGET TRAVEL (see below).

(5) A voucher entitling you to a $5 discount on any Arthur Frommer International, Inc. tour booked by you through any travel agent in the United States and Canada.

(6) Your personal membership card, which, once received, entitles you to purchase through the Club *all* Arthur Frommer Publications for a third to a half off their regular retail prices during the term of your membership.

These are the immediate and definite benefits which we can assure to members of the Club at this time. Even more exciting, however, are the further and more substantial benefits which it has been our continuing aim to achieve for members. These are announced in the Club's newspaper, THE WONDERFUL WORLD OF BUDGET TRAVEL, a full-size, eight-page newspaper that keeps members up-to-date on fast-breaking developments in low-cost travel in all parts of the world. The newspaper also carries such continuing features as "Travelers' Directory"— a list of members all over the world who are willing to provide hospitality to other members as they pass through their home cities; "Share-a-Trip" —requests from members for travel companions who can share costs; "Readers Ask...Readers Reply"—travel-related queries from members, to which other members reply with firsthand information. It also offers advance news of individual, group, and charter programs operated by Arthur Frommer International, Inc., plus in-depth articles on special destinations (most recently, Romania, Yugoslavia, and Costa Rica).

If you would like to join this hardy bunch of international travelers and participate in its exchange of information and hospitality, simply send $10 (U.S. residents), $12 (Canadian and Mexican residents), or $14 (other foreign residents) along with your name and address to: $10-a-Day Travel Club, Inc., 380 Madison Ave., New York, NY 10017. Remember to specify which *two* of the books in section one above you wish to receive in your initial package of members' benefits. Or tear out this page, check off any two books on the opposite side, and send it to us with your membership fee.